IMMANUEL KANT'S
PROLEGOMENA TO ANY FUTURE METAPHYSICS

in focus

How is knowledge possible? What kind of knowledge can be called metaphysical? What is the source of metaphysical knowledge?

Such are the questions addressed by Kant in his famous *Prolegomena to Any Future Metaphysics*. His ultimate argument, that there is no such thing as metaphysics, continues to fascinate and challenge contemporary philosophers.

This collection of seminal essays on the *Prolegomena* provides the student of philosophy with an invaluable overview of some issues and problems raised by Kant. The edition offers a substantive new introduction, the Carus translation of Kant's work, six papers never before published together and an extensive bibliography. Special attention is paid to the relationship between Kant and David Hume, whose philosophical investigations, according to Kant's famous quote, first interrupted Kant's "dogmatic slumber."

Beryl Logan is an Assistant Professor at Scarborough College, University of Toronto. She has published widely on David Hume and the philosophers of the early modern period.

ROUTLEDGE PHILOSOPHERS
IN FOCUS SERIES
Series editor: Stanley Tweyman
York University, Toronto

ARISTOTLE'S DE ANIMA IN FOCUS
Edited by Michael Durrant

GEORGE BERKELEY: *ALCIPHRON* IN FOCUS
Edited by David Berman

CIVIL DISOBEDIENCE IN FOCUS
Edited by Hugo Adam Bedau

RENE DESCARTES: *MEDITATIONS ON FIRST
PHILOSOPHY* IN FOCUS
Edited by Stanley Tweyman

GÖDEL'S *THEOREM* IN FOCUS
Edited by S. G. Shanker

DAVID HUME: *DIALOGUES CONCERNING NATURAL
RELIGION* IN FOCUS
Edited by Stanley Tweyman

WILLIAM JAMES: *PRAGMATISM* IN FOCUS
Edited by Doris Olin

JOHN LOCKE: *LETTER CONCERNING TOLERATION* IN
FOCUS
Edited by John Horton and Susan Mendus

J. S. MILL: *ON LIBERTY* IN FOCUS
Edited by John Gray and G. W. Smith

PLATO'S *MENO* IN FOCUS
Edited by Jane M. Day

IMMANUEL KANT'S
PROLEGOMENA TO ANY FUTURE METAPHYSICS

in focus

Edited by
Beryl Logan

London and New York

First published 1996
by Routledge
11 New Fetter Lane, London EC4P 4EE

Simultaneously published in the USA and Canada
by Routledge
29 West 35th Street, New York, NY 10001

Typeset in Bembo by Intype London Ltd
Printed and bound in Great Britain by
TJ Press (Padstow) Ltd, Padstow, Cornwall

British Library Cataloguing in Publication Data
A catalogue record for this book is available from the British Library

Library of Congress Cataloguing in Publication Data
Immanuel Kant's Prolegomena to any future metaphysics: in focus /
edited by Beryl Logan.
p.   cm. – (Routledge philosophers in focus series)
Includes bibliographical references (p.   ) and index.
1. Kant, Immanuel, 1724–1804. Prolegomena.   2. Knowledge, Theory
of.   3. Metaphysics.   I. Logan, Beryl, 1944–   . II. Kant,
Immanuel, 1724–1804. Prolegomena. English. III. Series.
B2787.Z7I48   1996
110–dc20   96–11897

ISBN 0–415–11575–2 (hbk)
ISBN 0–415–11576–0 (pbk)

CONTENTS

ACKNOWLEDGEMENTS

I am grateful to Open Court Publishing Co., La Salle, Illinois, for granting permission to use the text of the *Prolegomena to Any Future Metaphysics*, translated by Dr. Paul Carus. Permission to reprint was kindly granted by authors and publishers of the six reprinted papers: Lewis White Beck, "A Prussian Hume and a Scottish Kant," appeared in *Essays on Kant and Hume*, Yale University Press (1989); Manfred Kuehn, "Kant's Conception of Hume's Problem" in the *Journal of the History of Philosophy*, (21, 2, 1983); Patricia Kitcher, "Changing the Name of the Game: Kant's Cognitivism vs Hume's Psychologism" in *Philosophical Topics* (19, 1991); Theodore E. Uehling Jr., "Wahrnehmungsurteile And Erfahrungsurteile Reconsidered," in *Kant Studies* (1978); Daniel E. Anderson, "A Note on the Syntheticity of Mathematical Propositions in Kant's Prolegomena," in the *Southern Journal of Philosophy* (17, 1979); Jerry H. Gill, "Kant, Analogy and Natural Theology" in the *International Journal for Philosophy of Religion* (16, 1984), reprinted by permission of Kluwer Academic Publishers.

A debt of gratitude is owed to the general editor of the Philosophers In Focus series, Stanley Tweyman, for his ongoing support and encouragement, and for smoothing out the bumps in the road.

My efforts in this book were made possible by the dedication and cooperation of my husband, Shelly, and our children.

INTRODUCTION

In Preface (II) of the *Prolegomena* Kant states that "the suggestion of David Hume was the very thing, which, many years ago, first interrupted my dogmatic slumber and gave my investigations in the field of speculative philosophy quite a new direction" (p. 33). In the *Critique of Pure Reason* (CPR A769/B797) Kant refers to the "uncritical dogmatist" as one "who has not surveyed the sphere of his understanding, and therefore has not determined, in accordance with principles, the limits of his possible knowledge." The conclusions that Hume drew in his attack on "a single but important concept in metaphysics, viz., that of Cause and Effect" (p. 31) prompted Kant to undertake this survey in the *Prolegomena Concerning any Future Metaphysics* in order to determine the possibility and limits of metaphysical knowledge.

As a result of the importance that Kant places on Hume's arguments, I intend to adopt as my particular viewpoint in this Introduction what Kant perceives as problems in Hume's philosophy and his answers to those problems. Generally, this consists in responding to Humean skepticism by offering conditions under which objective validity is possible. Where appropriate, I will make reference to Hume's doctrines in order for the reader to be more familiar with some of the arguments to which Kant was responding in the *Prolegomena*. This will allow the reader not only to grasp the force and intent of Kant's own positions, but also to recognise the pivotal role played by one of Kant's precursors in the development of his critical philosophy. This focus is also reflected in the scholarly literature, as is evident in the Bibliography included in this volume.

The first issue dealt with is the nature of the causal connection, a dominant concern in the *Prolegomena*. Kant is seeking a way to provide objective validity for causal judgments, as Hume's position allows only subjective validity and results in skepticism. We then turn to Kant's arguments with respect to Hume's position on mathematics, which are closely allied to causality: because Hume considered all our judgments to be either matters of fact (synthetic propositions known a posteriori) or relations of ideas (analytic propositions known a priori), the causal relation was regarded by Hume to be the former and mathematics to be the latter. Kant claims that if Hume had only seen that mathematics consists of synthetic propositions known a priori, he would have realized that causality (as well as metaphysics) consists of the same, and been saved from his skepticism. Finally I address Kant's discussion of the limits and boundaries of reason which refers to arguments in Hume's *Dialogues Concerning Natural Religion*. Kant's intention is to save religious belief from the skepticism that he perceived in Hume's position. This section of the *Prolegomena* has received little attention in the Kant literature, but will be dealt with in some detail here.

HUME'S 'PROBLEMS'

The first three reprinted papers in this volume focus on what Kant thought was Hume's problem, and how he sought to solve it. In the Preface to the *Prolegomena*, Kant states that Hume's 'problem' lay in accounting for the origin of the causal concept. Hume is led to his position on causality by the restrictions of his empiricism and its theoretical constructs. As there is no impression of the concept of cause, there can be no idea of it. Hume questioned the stance of his predecessors that the concept of cause could be thought by reason a priori, independent of all experience. Kant was "awoken from his dogmatic slumber" by Hume's suggestion that the necessity in the causal principle arises solely from observation and experience, and his conclusion that the causal relation and its justification is a matter of fact. Kant goes beyond the empiricist picture of mental life as consisting only of impressions, ideas, and the associations between them to concern himself with "what types of faculties are necessary for cognition and how their existence might be established."[1]

From a Kantian perspective, Hume had several 'problems' which stem from his empiricism: this doctrine committed him to the view that the only objects of knowledge are the contents of consciousness – impressions and ideas – and the only judgments are those expressing matters of fact or relations of ideas. This led him, according to Kant to regard any a priori principles (such as the causal connection) to be fictitious and "custom-bred" (CPR A765/B793), resulting in

2

skepticism.[2] As there can be no empirical ground for the validity of causal inferences (as any empirical claim presupposes the principle in question), and the principle is not self-evident (as the concept of 'event' and 'cause' are separate ideas), the principle is natural and non-rational in character.[3] The resulting lack of rigorous grounding led Kant to seek "some criterion which is not subject to the defects of the rationalist and empirical methods of proof, and which is adequate to determine the validity or invalidity of general principles."[4]

Kant saw that a new conceptual context was necessary in order to justify philosophically the causal inferences. This context consists of the categories, of which causality is one: those principles, known a priori, yet synthetic, that determine or condition sense-impressions, providing a justification or objective validity that combats the perceived skepticism inherent in the traditional empiricist position. However, these concepts are also synthetic in nature: while they are logically independent of experience, and are applied to experience,[5] they are not tautological, nor are they logically necessary. This realisation represented an enlargement of the empiricists' epistemological context: it went beyond the traditional division of the types of human knowledge (which Hume endorsed) into relations of ideas (analytic a priori) and matters of fact (synthetic a posteriori) to include a third type of proposition: synthetic, yet known a priori. In order to avert the Humean skepticism that results from the traditional division of propositions, such propositions must be possible. In order for objectively valid causal inferences – and metaphysics – to be possible, such propositions must be possible.

To solve Hume's problems, Kant had to first ask and then answer the question "how are synthetic judgments possible a priori?" Given that we do make some judgments where the terms in the judgment are synthetically connected but whose validity seems to be established a priori, Kant must ask how such judgments are possible. The first five sections of the *Prolegomena* set this stage.

What is the source of metaphysical knowledge? (§1): Metaphysics is not empirical, but is knowledge of it a priori? The very concept of metaphysical knowledge, Kant claims, implies that such is its nature. It is knowledge that lies beyond experience.

What kind of knowledge can be called metaphysical? (§2): Here Kant draws the distinction between analytic a priori propositions[6] and synthetic a posteriori propositions. The former are logical in nature, and as their terms are connected through identity, e.g. all bodies are extended, they are dependent upon the principle of non-contradiction. Our knowledge is not expanded by knowing the truth of this proposition. On the other hand, we can only connect the terms in the proposition and determine the truth of 'some bodies have weight' by appeal to experience. My knowledge of the concept of body will be expanded by knowing the truth of this proposition. But it is Kant's insight to recognise that certain sciences consist of synthetic (not logically connected) judgments which have a priori certainty, and whose origin lies in pure understanding and reason. Judgments of experience and judgments of mathematics, while synthetic, are also a priori.[7] Hume's mistake with respect to mathematics was to regard mathematical knowledge to be analytic – given the traditional empiricist division, propositions known a priori could only be analytic in nature.

> [M]etaphysics is properly concerned with synthetical propositions a priori, and these alone constitute its end ... the generation of a priori cognition by concrete images as well as by concepts, in fine of synthetical propositions a priori in philosophical cognition, constitutes the essential subject of metaphysics. (p. 42)

Note to the analytic/synthetic division (§3): The dogmatic philosophers sought "the sources of metaphysical judgments in Metaphysics itself and not apart from it in the pure laws of reason generally" (p. 43). Rather than examining the workings of reason to know, first, what kinds of propositions are possible and then to seek where they may be applied, dogmatic philosophers look to the subject contents first, presupposing the analytic a priori/synthetic a posteriori distinction.

Is metaphysics possible at all? (§4): We do not have to ask whether synthetic a priori knowledge is possible, as mathematics and natural science "both contain propositions, which are thoroughly recognised, as apodeictically certain, partly by mere reason, partly by general consent arising from experience, and yet as independent of experience" (p. 45). In order for metaphysics ("knowledge of a highest being and of a future existence") to be possible as a science, it has to be shown that it too consists of such propositions.

The question to be asked then, is, *How is knowledge out of pure reason possible?* (§5). We begin with what we know: that mathematics and natural science consist of synthetic a priori propositions, show how these are possible within these sciences, and then apply our findings to metaphysics. The "main transcendental" questions that need to be answered are:

1 How is pure mathematics (first part: §§6–13)/pure natural science possible (second part: §§14–35)?
2 How is metaphysics possible in general?
3 How is metaphysics possible as a science?

These questions form the body of Kant's inquiry in the *Prolegomena*.

In §21 we find Kant's 'Logical Table of Judgments'. This table consists of the exhaustive[8] set of possible judgments, divided into four types: as to Quantity, as to Quality, as to Relation, and as to Modality. These judgments correspond to the 'Transcendental Table of the Concepts of the Understanding' which is also given in the CPR at A80/B106. Briefly, those concepts or judgments as to Quantity are concerned with how much of the subject term (S) the predicate term (P) refers to or pertains to (All S are P, Some S are P, No S are P). Judgments as to Quality are concerned with the reality of the terms in the judgment (T, F). Those as to Modality refer to mode of existence (S may be/may not be P, S is P, S must be P). Finally, those of Relation include claims as to inherence and subsistence (accidents and substances), community (interdependence), and causality.

The "complete solution to the Humean problem" occurs after Kant has shown that judgments of causality, as a species of synthetic a priori judgments, are possible, when the objects of experience are "subsumed under those pure concepts of the understanding." The solution occurs after Kant has "shown adequately that these concepts and the principles drawn from them stand a priori before all experience and have their undoubted objective rightness, though admittedly only in respect of experience." Knowledge has been enlarged, with apodeictic certainty.

HUME AND KANT ON CAUSALITY

As it was Hume's conclusions with respect to the subjective validity carried by causal inferences that roused Kant from his uncritical position and led him to examine the faculties of reason that make such judgments possible, a brief outline of Hume's position on causality is appropriate. An understanding of Hume's own position will allow the reader to see what Kant thought was lacking in this system – objective validity – and how he sought to remedy this lack.

5

Hume on causality as custom-bred

Hume argues that causality is the connection that the imagination is determined to make on the basis of repeated experience rather than it being a connection 'between objects'. He was satisfied that the only grounding possible for causal judgments was to be found in the natural propensity of the imagination to connect related objects. This psychological grounding and validity was sufficient to justify our causal claims, and, in fact, is all that is available to us in our empiricism.

The process, according to Hume, is as follows: I am presented with A and with B, and A occurs in time before B and they occur in close physical proximity. After repeatedly being presented with similar conjunctions of A and B, my imagination eventually comes to expect B whenever A is close at hand. So, on subsequent occasions, the appearance of A leads me to expect B, and I will likely be distressed if B does not appear and seek to determine why B did not appear (depending on the intensity and frequency of the conjunction). And the appearance of B leads me to attribute A as the cause of its appearance. The ground and validity of causal judgments is found in the natural and psychological 'necessity' in the imagination to connect related perceptions.

A person who is suddenly brought into this world would observe a continual succession of objects but could not reach the idea of cause and effect because the powers "by which all natural operations are performed, never appear to the senses."[9] By gradual experience, this person will come to infer the existence of the A (as the cause) whenever B (the effect) appears. This does not occur because this person has now acquired some insight into any powers, but because the person is determined, through the force of the associative principles of the imagination and repeated experience (custom), to draw the causal conclusion.

Hume's response to his predecessors consists of an attack on their claims of causal connections occurring 'in' the objects themselves, rather than in the observers of the objects.[10] The 'causal connection' is the result of the observer's imagination drawing associations between observed relata. Thus Hume, before Kant, made the first move in a Copernican revolution. He moved the observer to the centre of her experiential universe by making the observer the seat or source of the causal nexus. Given experience of a particular sort, that is the observer experiencing items in temporal and spatial proximity, and given the associative operations of the imagination, the observer will make causal associations and judgments.

Causality, then, is a principle drawn from custom and habit, the "great guide of life." Its necessity and validity are psychological, grounded in the associative faculty of the imagination.

Kant and causality as a synthetic a priori concept

The Humean observer is thus at the whim of her experience and her associative imagination. Her judgments, based on her perceptions, have subjective validity, as they refer to her experience as the thinking subject. The Kantian Copernican revolution, on the other hand, not only moves the observer to the centre, but makes the observer, the rational being, an active participant in the process, as she synthesizes her sense perceptions by means of the pure concepts of the understanding. Objective validity is conferred upon the judgments as they "agree with the object,"[11] and are not just expressions of her experience.

Kant sees Hume's problem with respect to causality to be the result of his "regarding, not the whole of his problem, but a part, which by itself can give us no information" (p. 68). By only accounting for the perceptual or experiential side of the causal connection, Hume leaves us with a dose of skepticism with respect to the validation of causal judgments, as their connection is synthetic and their only necessity is psychological. Kant's answer to Hume is that objective validity can only be given to an observed conjunction if the conjunction is conditioned or determined by a causal principle that is synthetic but is also a priori.

Kant gives the following example in a footnote on p. 68.

[W]hen the sun shines on the stone, it grows warm. This judgment, however often I and others may have perceived it, is a mere judgment of perception and contains no necessity; perceptions are only usually conjoined in this manner. [Hume stops here.] But if I say: the sun warms the stone, I add to the perception a concept of the understanding, viz., that of cause, which necessarily connects with the concept of sunshine that of heat, and the synthetic judgment becomes of necessity universally valid, viz., objective, and is converted from a perception into experience.

According to Hume's analysis of causality, as I repeatedly

encounter the sun shining and the stone gradually becoming warm, the association is gradually set up in my imagination between these two perceptions such that I will come to regard the sun as being the "cause" of the stone warming. It results from my experience and my imagination, and the more repetitious and intense my experience, the more immediate and forceful will be the association I establish between these two perceptions. This association is the core of Hume's analysis of causality, and it is all that the imagination needs (or has available) to make a judgment of causality: on the basis of my experience, I claim that the sun is the cause of the stone becoming warmer.

But for Kant succession is not sufficient: first observing the sun shining and then feeling the warmth in the stone or seeing a ship upstream and then downstream will not prompt us to regard the sun as being the cause of the stone being warm any more than it will prompt us to regard the ship upstream to be the cause of the ship downstream. The 'whole' problem of causality is not just accounting for or providing the psychological mechanism by which we make causal judgments, but it is providing the objective validity for these judgments. Hume mistook subjective necessity, the force of association based on custom or habit, for objective necessity. Without this objective component, "Hume . . . ran his ship ashore, for safety's sake, landing on skepticism, there to let it lie and rot" (p. 34). Kant's intent is to give the ship "a pilot who, by means of safe astronomical principles drawn from knowledge of the globe, and provided with a complete chart and compass may steer the ship safely, whither he listeth" (p. 34). The concept of causality is not derived from experience; rather, it is applied to experience. Only in its application would we ever think of calling the relationship between two perceptions a causal one. Simply observing succession and proximity in space, no matter how many times it occurred, would never lead us to see something called 'causality,' that without A occurring, B would not occur.

So we could argue for Kant, why does the person judge that one object has produced the other, i.e. has been the cause of the other, from his inference of the existence of one from the appearance of the other? First, perceptions are compared and conjoined in a consciousness of *my* state – subjective validity – but then a judgment with respect to consciousness in general – objective validity – must follow. Without viewing the succession, and making the inference, through or by means of the category of something called a causal relation, the production of B by A would never be inferred from either the appearance of A followed by B or from the inference of the existence of A from the appearance of B. In other words, there may be a psychological necessity in the process in the mind, but there is no objective validity in the judgment made. What is required, Kant argues, beyond coming to expect the stone to become warm whenever the sun shines, is the addition of a concept, that of *causality*, which confers objective validity on the judgment by referring it beyond our individual sensations to an object, and converts the judgment of perception (observed conjunction) to a judgment of experience (conditioned by the principle of causality). While perceptions of a particular sort or perceptions given to us in a particular way are not only necessary but limit the way or prescribe the conditions under which the category is applied (e.g. A and B must be observed successively), it is only by the use of the category of cause and effect that the general (or logical) form of the judgment 'All events have causes' can be applied to the perceptions.

In §20 Kant draws the distinction between judgments of perception and judgments of experience. This distinction, which Guyer calls "notorious,"[12] has been a topic of some discussion in the literature, and included in this volume is a paper by T. E. Uehling, "*Wahrnehmungsurteile* and *Erfahrungsurteile* Reconsidered." This paper focuses on sections 18, 19, and 20 of the *Prolegomena* which contain Kant's arguments relating to the categories, the a priori concepts "under which every perception must be first of all subsumed and then by their means changed into experience." Uehling points to a major, but interesting, conflict between the *Prolegomena* and the *CPR*. In the latter text, Kant seems to indicate that *all* judgments of perception do become judgments of experience when the categories are superadded. However, in the former text, Uehling says he "explicitly argues" that there are some judgments of perception that cannot become judgments of experience (such as aesthetic judgments which refer "merely to feeling" and not to any object). Those judgments of perception which can "stand under conditions" (be synthesized according to the categories) can become judgments of experience.

Young uses the judgments of perception/experience to clarify what Kant means by universal and objective validity. This is an important clarification because these are the features that mark judgments of experience. However, he argues that what Kant means by these terms is a point of interpretation. The nature of a judgment of perception is that it expresses how things are for me at this time. Its subjective validity derives from its reference to my sensations and the subjective necessity of their connection. "I do nothing but refer two of my sensations to one another" (p. 67). A judgment of experience, on the other hand, carries universal validity, by adding a third aspect to the connection. In making such judgments, we claim that a certain connection obtains generally, and that everyone under similar circumstances should make this connection. "The given intuition must be subsumed under a concept, which determines the form of judging in general relatively to the intuition, connects its empirical consciousness in consciousness generally, and thereby procures universal validity for empirical judgments" (p. 67). In other words, what is given to me as a sense of perception and which I connect in my consciousness in a judgment of perception ("I dropped the glass and it broke": the connection of two perceptions) is then conditioned by the understanding applying an *a priori concept*, for example, causality. Once connected with this concept, objective validity is conferred upon the judgment, so that anyone else experiencing a similar connection of perceptions will make the same judgment ("dropping a glass is the cause of it breaking": the two perceptions with the addition of the concept). In making such judgments we assert that a certain connection obtains universally, and hence that everyone should find this connection obtaining under similar circumstances.

In spite of the scholarly disputes raging around this distinction, some of which Uehling refers to, it is a useful one for our purposes: it helps to indicate the sense in which Kant thought Hume did not fully represent the whole problem of causality. By allowing only 'judgments of perception' (the observer's connection of her own experience) and finding necessity in the associative processes of the imagination, Hume took only the first step in accounting for causal judgments. For Hume, repeated observed succession is necessary and sufficient for the imagination to make a judgment of causality. With 'judgments of experience' (carrying the objective validity permitted by the addition of the third aspect, the a priori concept of *causality*), Kant took the final step. For Kant, observed succession is necessary, but it is not sufficient.

In Kant's system, causality is a synthetic proposition known a priori. It expands our knowledge, in that we are making connections in experience, but it is also a priori, in that it is applied *to* experience. The synthetic a priori nature of the causal claim can be shown by

10

the following distinction. The analytic a priori judgment in respect of causality would be "All effects are caused." If one analyzes the terms 'effects' and 'causes' one finds that what an effect *is* is something that is caused and the truth of the claim can be known before experience. The term 'effect' is found in, or is contained in, the term 'cause' so that it is not possible to conceive of an uncaused effect. However, the judgment "All events are caused" is a synthetic proposition known a priori. It is possible to imagine an uncaused event, as an event is an occurrence with no imputation of causality in it. But unless the causal connection is known a priori and applied *to* succession, no judgment of *causality* is possible. Only when the given intuition is subsumed under a concept which determines the form of judging in general with respect to the particular intuition will such judgments have an objective validity or justification.

According to Kant, Hume did not distinguish between two kinds of synthetic judgments: those by which we "pass beyond our concept of the object"[13] by experience (synthetic a posteriori), and those whereby we "pass a priori beyond our concept, and so to extend our knowledge."[14] Hume regarded the "self-increment of concepts" to be impossible, concluding that causality arose from "custom-bred habit" that carried a universality and necessity that were only suppositions. Hume's error was "in inferring from the contingency of our determination *in accordance with the law* [to] the contingency of the *law* itself" (CPR A766/B794) and in not carefully examining all the possible synthetic a priori propositions available to the understanding. If he had done so, he would have found that both causality and mathematics consisted of such propositions.

Kant thought that the causal judgments that we do in fact make could have objective validity only if the 'judgment of perception', the judgment of expectation and custom – "when the sun shines on the stone, it grows warm" – is converted into a 'judgment of experience' by "subsuming" the given perception under an a priori concept. By adding the concept of causality, reason judges that the observed succession, e.g. the sun shining and the stone becoming warmer, is an instance of causality. The resulting judgment has objective validity. Hume's problem lay in not seeing the 'whole' problem of causality. Kant's answer is that judgments of perception, while providing the content, lack the objective validity of a judgment of experience – "the sun warms the stone" – that is gained in applying an a priori concept to the observation.

11

KANT AND HUME ON MATHEMATICS AS SYNTHETIC A PRIORI PROPOSITIONS

The First Part of the Main Transcendental Question (§§6–14) is concerned with how pure mathematics is possible. An examination of mathematics, the propositions of which are synthetic, will reveal its a priori ground of knowledge. Mathematics is a science. It can only be possible as a science if its synthetic propositions can be known a priori. Kant claims that because Hume only utilized the synthetic a posteriori/analytic a priori distinction, he failed to notice that mathematics consisted of synthetic a priori propositions.

To show the synthetic a priori nature of mathematical judgments, we will use Kant's own example: 7+5=12. The analytic proposition a priori would be 7+5 = the sum of 7 and 5. In this case, the subject term is contained in, or thought in, the predicate term, and it would be contradictory to deny this proposition. However, 7+5=12 is synthetic because the sum, 12, is only equal to 7 added to 5 when one adds something to the equation 7+5, and what is added is counting:

> [C]alling in the aid of the fingers of my hand as intuition, I now add one by one to the number 7 the units which I previously took together to form the number 5, and with the aid of that figure [the hand] see the number 12 come into being. (CPR B16)

I cannot, by simply analyzing the terms '7' and '5', come up with the term '12' as I can with '7+5' equals 'the sum of 7 and 5.'

According to Kant, Hume rejected the synthetic nature of mathematics because he rejected its a priori nature, as he presupposed the exclusive disjunction of either analytic a priori or synthetic a posteriori. As mathematics was not known a posteriori, it was known a priori, and thus its propositions are analytic. Had he seen that mathematics consisted of synthetic a priori propositions, he could have, Kant claims, extended that category to include metaphysical propositions, and he could have saved them from their fate:

> If we take in our hand any volume; of divinity or school metaphysics, for instance; let us ask, *Does it contain any abstract reasoning concerning quantity or number* (analytic a priori reasoning)? No. *Does it contain any experimental reasoning concerning matter of fact and existence* (synthetic a posteriori

propositions)? No. Commit it then to the flames: For it can contain nothing but sophistry and illusion.[15]

Several authors have explored the suggestion that Hume supposed mathematics to consist of synthetic a priori propositions. However, they all generally recognise that the criterion of certainty for Kant is logical necessity while the hallmark of Hume's analysis is psychological necessity. Atkinson argues that

> [W]hilst Hume indubitably held mathematical propositions to be a priori and necessary, his apparent conception of a necessary proposition was wider than the current – or indeed Kant's – conception of an analytic one; that, whilst he did not explicitly pose the question, Analytic or Synthetic? – the terms are after all not his – he came closer in the Treatise to regarding mathematical propositions as synthetic necessary than analytic truths.[16]

Beck (in this volume) argues that Kant "thinks Hume was in error in failing to see the difference between a priori in the sense of 'going beyond possible experience' and a priori in the sense of 'underlying possible experience'."

Beck's claim leads us into an ongoing exegetical problem, one that is an important issue in Kant scholarship. It concerns the definitions of technical terms, and is the focus of Daniel E. Anderson's paper, "A Note on the Syntheticity of Mathematical Propositions in Kant's *Prolegomena*," included in this volume. *How* one uses technical terms such as 'analytic' and 'synthetic' is bound to bias one's outlook. Anderson is concerned with Ayer's attack (in *Language, Truth and Logic*) against Kant's means of distinguishing between analytic and synthetic judgments. Kant thinks he is adopting a logical distinction in mathematical propositions, whereas Ayer argues that in fact he is adopting a psychological one: holding that '7+5=12' is a synthetic proposition is based on the psychological criterion, not the logical one. Ayer's position seems to be, given *his* definition of syntheticity,[17] a return to the pre-Kantian view (held by Hume): if a given proposition is synthetic, it can only be known a posteriori. For Ayer this is analytically true, as what it is for a proposition to be synthetic is for that proposition to be known through experience. Ayer also presents his own definition of analyticity, "that [a proposition's] validity should follow simply from the definitions of the terms contained in it," to which Anderson replies that this is Ayer's own definition, and not Kant's.

Other scholars who have suggested that mathematics, for Hume, consists of synthetic truths known a priori urge caution with respect to drawing any similarities between these truths and Kant's synthetic a priori propositions. Coleman, for example, urges that Hume can only be rendered consistent if one adopts the position he held that mathematical propositions were synthetic a priori. However, she notes,

> The sense in which I am using "synthetic" a priori should not be confused with its Kantian meaning ... the sense in which he would maintain that there are synthetic a priori judgments must be understood only as indicating a necessary relation between empirical concepts which cannot be determined by the formal relation between these concepts, or by an analysis of these concepts.[18]

Newman also makes similar points. While,

> geometrical propositions are necessary truths but not analytic ... Hume makes no attempt to secure its necessary status with the Kantian formula ... although he maintains that where the propositions of geometry are concerned, "*the person who assents, not only conceives the ideas according to the propositions, but is necessarily determin'd to conceive them in that particular manner*" (p. 95) ... the only factor he makes appeal to as "determining" is the character of sensible space, the invariant nature of which seems to rest, in the *Treatise*, upon the constant character of physical space.[19]

KANT ON HUME'S *DIALOGUES CONCERNING NATURAL RELIGION*

Arguments concerning natural theology are raised in the Conclusion to the *Prolegomena*. Jerry H. Gill's paper, "Kant, Analogy and Natural Theology" (included in this volume) is one of the few scholarly treatments focusing directly on this section of the text.[20] It provides a clear overview of the arguments in sections 57 to 59. Gill focuses on Kant's use of the image of boundaries and limits, and is led to claim that

> [T]he results of one's approach to natural theology are going to be different depending on the sort of root metaphor one begins with. Kant's overall commitment to a *visual metaphor*

leads him to an interpretation of the bounds of reason whose inherent passivity and staticity renders the cognitive gulf between the human and the divine essentially unbridgeable.

This section of the Introduction will focus on Kant's answer to Hume's perceived skepticism with respect to the nature of the Deity, as he finds it in Hume's *Dialogues Concerning Natural Religion*. As with causality, Kant wants to provide an objective ground or validation that will avoid the skepticism that results when reason extends the limitations of items of possible experience to things in themselves. A German edition of the *Dialogues* was available in 1781, two years after the initial publication of the *Dialogues* in English. Kant's acquaintance with the text and appreciation of its arguments is evident not only in the *Prolegomena*, as we shall soon see. In his *Lectures on Philosophical Theology*,[21] he makes detailed reference to, and presents criticisms of, Hume's objections to what Kant calls the 'physiotheological proof': "which makes use of experience of the present world in general and infers from this to the existence of an author of the world and to the attributes which would belong to its author as such."[22]

Before introducing Hume's arguments into the discussion, I will look at some passages in §57, "On the Determination of the Bounds of Pure Reason," to show the context within which Kant refers to Hume's *Dialogues*. Kant begins this section of the *Prolegomena* by opposing two absurdities, or contradictions. The first concerns the limits of possible experience, and makes two claims. It would be contradictory to think that we can know anything more about an object "than belongs to the possible experience of it" (p. 109). That is, we can only have experience of objects through the forms of intuition of space and time, we can only know them as phenomena, as they appear to us as objects of sensory experience, and we cannot know more of them than is possible through such experience. Nor can we have knowledge of any object that is intuited[23] outside of space and time or how it can be — or whether or not it is — determined by its own nature in the way that intuited objects are determined by the a priori principles. This sets the limits of *our* knowledge, but something lies beyond the boundary of the limits of our knowledge, as determined objects are incomplete. "Bounds . . . always presuppose a space existing outside a certain definite place, and inclosing it; limits do not require this, but are mere negations,

which affect a quantity, in so far as it is not have absolutely complete"
(p. 111).

The second contradiction concerns what lies beyond the boundaries which enclose possible experience. It would be absurd first to
claim that there are no things in themselves beyond the boundary:

> The sensuous world is nothing but a chain of appearances
> connected according to universal laws; it has therefore no
> subsistence by itself; it is not the thing in itself, and conse-
> quently must point to that which contains the basis of this
> appearance, to beings which cannot be cognised merely as
> phenomena, but as things in themselves. (p. 112)

It would also be absurd to regard *our* way of knowing things as being
the *only* way of knowing. The objects of possible experience must
be intuited in space and time; as conditioned, they are limited to
being experienced in these ways. It would be presumptuous of us
to declare that the means by which empirical objects are known −
intuited in space and time conditioned by the principles of possible
experience − is the only way things in themselves *can* be known, so
that things in themselves are similarly conditioned. This is, of course,
a contradiction, because the things in themselves would no longer
be things in themselves, but would be objects of possible experience.

Thus, reason and the principles of possible experience, or a priori
concepts, the faculty and means by which the objects of experience
are conditioned or determined, must be and are only valid in their
application to experience. "A concept of this nature . . . does nothing
but determine for an intuition the general way in which it can be
used for judgments" (p. 112). So absurdity results if we regard the
limits of our principles and our experience and our reason to be
the limits of things in themselves as well; that is, valid and applicable
outside their empirical use. It also occurs if we regard things in
themselves as objects of reason (the role of reason being to apply
the "synthesis of representation" to its objects): only phenomena,
objects as they appear to us, are subject to union by reason and
governed by the a priori principles.

Neither our principles nor our reason are valid if they are applied
to anything other than the manifold of perceptions, or items of
possible experience.

> If certain concepts are not contained in us otherwise than as
> that by means of which experience is made possible from our

side, then, prior to all experience and yet with complete validity, they may be asserted of everything that can ever come before us. They are valid then, to be sure, not of things in general, but yet of everything which can ever be given to us through experience, since they contain the conditions by means of which these experiences are possible. Such propositions will therefore contain the conditions of the possibility not of things but of experience. However, things which cannot be given to us by any experience are nothing for us; therefore we can very well use such propositions as universal from a practical point of view, only not as principles of speculation concerning objects in general.[24]

The nature of the principles or conditions of possible experience is just that – they are valid only as they refer to those things that are capable of being experienced by us and not to all things in general. Given this nature, reason is limited in the application of these principles, limited to applying them only to items of possible experience. Without a "careful critique" (an examination of the objects and limits of reason), the conditioning principles "might become transcendent," and impose the limitations of experience (intuited in space and time, and conditioned) on what lies beyond possible experience.

We must guard against setting the limits of the principles and the reason that applies them as the limits of the possibility of things in themselves. The limits inherent in the principles and our reason (valid only as applied to possible experience) must not become transcendent – go beyond that to which they are by nature applicable – and be taken as the limits of things in themselves. This would lead us to the claim that the limitations on our mode of knowing and our objects of knowledge reflects upon the objects beyond the boundary. And Kant regards Hume's *Dialogues* as an example or illustration of this contradiction: "Our principles, which limit the use of reason to possible experience, might in this way become transcendent and the limits of our reason be set up as limits of the possibility of things in themselves (as Hume's *Dialogues* may illustrate)" (§57, p. 110).

It is now appropriate to introduce the *Dialogues* into our discussion to show what illustration Kant thought it provided, and what was Kant's answer to Hume's skepticism. In the *Dialogues*, Cleanthes presents the anthropomorphic "Argument from Design" that draws analogical inferences regarding the nature of the Deity from what is found in experience. He argues that the intelligence and benevolence of the Deity, the cause, can be inferred from what we find in the world, the effect, and that the qualities possessed by the Deity are similar to those possessed by humans, although on a much larger scale in proportion to the effects. This position assumes that reason can achieve results in natural theology by using the same methods that it would apply in any empirical investigation. Philo, arguing against this position, claims that the methods he is using are applicable *only* to empirical investigation, and not to objects that lie beyond the limits of human experience.

> So long as we confine our speculations to trade, or morals, or politics, or criticism, we make appeals, every moment to common sense and experience, which strengthen our philosophical conclusions and remove (at least in part) the suspicion, which we so justly entertain with regard to every reasoning, that is very subtle and refine. But in theological reasonings, we have not this advantage; while at the same time we are employed upon objects which, we must be sensible, are too large for our grasp. ... We are like foreigners in a strange country to whom everything must seem suspicious, and who are in danger every moment of transgressing against the laws and customs of the people with whom they live and converse. We know not how far we ought to trust our vulgar methods of reasoning in such a subject.[25]

The *Dialogues* may thus illustrate Kant's contradiction in the following way. Our principles declare that the range and limit of reason's application is to items of possible experience. But our principles cannot go beyond their own range and limit of validity (as applicable to items of possible experience) and declare that as reason cannot achieve any determination with respect to items beyond possible experience, i.e. God, such items are in fact undeterminable. That is, the only means by which objects – phenomenal or noumenal – may be known is by our sensible way of knowing. When the application of the empirical method falls short (in fact, it is inappropriately applied), Hume claims that this results in our inability to know anything at all of the nature of the Deity, leaving only one possible position in natural theology – that of skepticism. However, a critique of limits reason would "guard the boundaries of our reason with respect to its empirical use and set a limit to its pretensions" (p. 110), and reveal that phenomenal objects are correctly limited by our principles, but noumenal ones, i.e. God, are not.

In seeking to find a middle road between dogmatism ("which teaches us nothing") and skepticism ("which does not even promise us anything") (p. 44) in natural religion, Kant proposes a third way, one that would preserve theism by making use of a non-anthropomorphic argument. The series of arguments in sections 57, 58 and 59 leads to this conclusion.

Kant brings the contradictions from earlier paragraphs of §57 to bear on the concept of the highest being. Natural theology leads reason to the objective boundary of experience – on our side of the boundary is the world of phenomena, of appearances, of experience. At that boundary, reason connects experience with what lies beyond that boundary, in the world of things in themselves, which are not objects of experience but the grounds or conditions of experience.

> Natural theology is . . . a concept on the boundary of human reason, being constrained to look beyond this boundary to the Idea of a Supreme Being (and, for practical purposes to that of an intelligible world also), not in order to determine anything relatively to this pure creation of the understanding, which lies beyond the world of sense, but in order to guide the use of reason within it according to principles of the greatest possible (theoretical as well as practical) unity. For this purpose we make use of the reference of the world of sense to an independent reason, as the cause of all its connexions. Thereby we do not purely invest a being, but, as beyond the sensible world there must be something that can only be thought by the pure understanding, we determine that something in this particular way, although only of course according to analogy. (p. 118)

Hume is left on our side of the boundary, limited to experience alone, unable to make the connections with what would give perceptions an objective ground. He is thus left with the skepticism with respect to anything beyond perceptions.

Kant argues that, for Hume, theism and anthropomorphism are inseparable, such that if anthropomorphism falls so does theism. As Hume's arguments in the *Dialogues* devastate anthropomorphism, theism vanishes. This leaves only deism, "out of nothing can come, which is of no value, and cannot serve as any foundation to religion and morals." Deism, it seems for Kant, is a mere form of thinking, "by which form alone I can cognise nothing determinate and consequently no object" (p. 114). Deism consists of an empty concept, a concept that lacks the content provided by the sensible world. It is nothing for us.

According to the *Dialogues*, reason can achieve nothing that is useful for religion, as it is limited solely to the confines of sensible perceptions. According to Kant, though, while reason is limited to possible experience, or phenomena, its limits are only boundaries beyond which lie the things in themselves, or noumena. Kant thinks he can save theism by pushing possible experience to the boundary and making a 'connection' between possible experience and the Deity as a thing in itself. This connection will give content ('our' side) to the concept ('the other' side). He achieves this by proposing an analogical argument, but one that does not depend upon the similarities of objects being compared. It allows for what he calls "*symbolical* anthropomorphism," which "concerns only language and not the object itself." It is a way of talking about the Deity that reflects the relationship between the sensible world and the Deity without accurately describing the Deity. It is the point of connection between the worlds of phenomena and noumena.[26]

This symbolic anthropomorphism is an analogical argument that is relational rather than descriptive, i.e. it intends to establish similar relations between items, not to describe the items. It does not mean, as is commonly understood, "an imperfect similarity of two things, but a perfect similarity of two relations between quite dissimilar things" (p. 115).

A standard analogical argument infers a missing feature on the basis of the similarity of the items being compared. Car A has features a: standard transmission, b: V-6 engine, and c: it gets 20 miles per gallon of gasoline. If Car B has features a and b, then we can infer that it will also have feature c. The two cars being compared exhibit similar features (note that mere similarity is not sufficient – the similarities must be relevant to the comparison: colour of car or fabric type is not relevant to gas mileage but type of transmission and engine size is relevant) and on the basis of this similarity a conclusion may be drawn with respect to the missing feature. The two items being compared are placed in that comparison on the basis of their similarity, and the conclusion draws its strength from the degree (and relevance) of that similarity. There is a justification for placing these two items in the relationship and inferring the presence of the missing feature. Thus:

- Car A has features a and b, and it has feature c.
- Car B has features a and b, and we infer it has feature c.

In the *Dialogues*, Cleanthes' analogical argument states:

- Machines have features a (means to ends relations) and b (coherence of parts), and they have c (intelligent designers).
- The world has features a (means to ends relations) and b (coherence of parts), and we infer it has c (an intelligent designer).
- Because the world and machines are similar in that they both have features a (means to ends relations) and b (coherence of parts), and as we know that machines have features c (intelligent designer), we can infer that the world also has feature c (intelligent designer).

In a footnote, Kant gives an example of his analogical argument:

> I can obtain a notion of the relation of things which absolutely are unknown to me. For instance, as the promotion of the welfare of children (= a) is to the love of parents (= b), so the welfare of the human species (= c) is to that unknown [quantity which is] in God (= x), which we call love. (pp. 115–16)

In the next footnote, he gives his version of the causal argument which likens the world to works of human art:

> I may say, that the causality of Supreme Cause holds the same place with regard to the world that human reason does with regard to its works of art. Here the nature of the Supreme Cause itself remains unknown to me; I only compare its effects (the order of the world) which I know, and their conformity to reason, to the effects of human reason which I also know; and hence I term the former reason, without attributing to it on that account what I understand in man by this term, or attaching to it anything else known to me, as its property. (p. 117)

This is similar to the position of mysticism which Philo espouses throughout the *Dialogues*.

> [w]e ought never to image that we comprehend the attributes of this divine Being, or to suppose that his perfects have any analogy or likeness to the perfections of a human creature. Wisdom, thought, design knowledge – these we justly ascribe to him because these words are honourable among men, and

21

we have no other language or other conceptions by which we can express our adoration of him. But let us beware lest we think that our ideas anywise correspond to his perfects, or that his attributes have any resemblance to these qualities among men.[27]

Expressing the "Argument from Design" in Kant's terms, as the orderly and proper functioning of a machine is related to the intelligence of its designers, so in the same way the orderly and proper functioning of the world is related to some unknown quality or property of the Deity which in human beings we call intelligence. This is not to say that the faculty of reason or intelligence of the Deity has the "least similarity with any human inclination, but because we can posit its relation to the world as similar to that which things in the world have among themselves." Making this relational claim does not determine or condition the concept of the Deity as either *having* this feature or that property or, if it does have this property, that the Deity's intelligence is anything like human intelligence, but only "determine[s] it as regards the [sensible] world and therefore as regards ourselves." When *we* speak of the world as being intelligently ordered, we say much about ourselves in the world of phenomena when we *speak* of God being in a relation (one we can understand) to us like the relation of parent and child, but we say nothing *of* God. The 'predicates' that we attribute to God in this way are thus determined subjectively – for us and by us – and not objectively – this is what God is like.

> If I say that we are compelled to consider the world as if it were the work of a Supreme Understanding and Will, I really say nothing more, than that a watch, a ship, a regiment, bears the same relation to the watchmaker, the shipbuilder, the commanding officer, so the world of sense (or whatever constitutes the substratum of this complex of appearances) does to the unknown, which I do not hereby cognise as it is in itself, but as it is for me or in relation to the world, of which I am a part. (p. 115)

This, according to Kant, saves theism with its dependence upon anthropomorphism as it is not an anthropomorphic analogy. It makes no claim, as Cleanthes' argument does, that the nature or features of the Deity in any way resemble those of humans.

Kant claims that Hume's criticisms of Cleanthes' analogical argument presented in parts 2 and 4–8 in the *Dialogues* do not affect him. Not only do some arguments not affect Kant's claims, but this relational analogical argument provides an answer to one of the requirements for analogical arguments: that of similarity between items compared. A strong (or indeed any) analogical argument must compare similar items and any dissimilarity weakens the argument. Philo claims that the world (universe) and machines are too dissimilar to permit an analogical inference of any strength. Kant's "symbolic anthropomorphism" is immune to this criticism, as lack of similarity of *objects* is irrelevant; only similarity of relationship is relevant.

However, this argument is not immune from other criticisms. For instance, unless there is some kind of similarity established between the items in the relational analogy, i.e. the well-being of children and the well-being of the human race, and the world and its artefacts, there is no reason to suppose a similarity in relations, whether or not any claims are being made with respect to the similarity of parental love and divine love, or human reason and divine 'reason.' Cleanthes argues that the world resembles a machine and, since machines have intelligent designers, the world has an intelligent designer. The inference is based on the similarity between the world and machines.

To conclude, theism is defeated in the *Dialogues* when anthropomorphism, which is inseparable from it, is soundly defeated. Attacking anthropomorphism devastates theism. However, by providing predicates as "mere categories," as not being limited to any conditions of sensibility, via *symbolic* anthropomorphism which does not oblige one to attribute any particular properties to the Deity, theism can be preserved. Replacing *objective* anthropomorphism (which makes claims about the nature of the Deity) with *symbolic* anthropomorphism (which does not) counters the skepticism which Kant sees as being the result of Hume's arguments in the *Dialogues*: "the true mean between dogmatism, which Hume combats, and skepticism, which he would substitute for it – a mean which . . . can be exactly determined on principles" (p. 117).

Kant expands Hume's principle "not to carry the use of reason dogmatically outside the field of all possible experience," to "not to consider the field of experience as one which bounds itself in the eye of our reason" (p. 117). What reason can possibly determine is not necessarily how things are in themselves. However, the inability of reason to come to any determination with respect to the nature of the Deity does not mean we are left only with skepticism.

NOTES

1 Patricia Kitcher, "Changing the Name of the Game: Kant's Cognitivism Versus Hume's Psychologism," reprinted in this volume.

2 Kant writes that "Hume is perhaps the most ingenious of all the sceptics, and beyond all question is without rival in respect of the influence which the sceptical procedure can exercise in awakening reason to a thorough self-examination. It will therefore well repay us to make clear to ourselves, as far as may be relevant to our purpose, the course of the reasoning, and the errors, of so acute and estimable a man – a course of reasoning which at the start was certainly on the track of truth" (CPR A764/B792). In the *Enquiry* (according to Beck, Kant had read the *Enquiry* but not the *Treatise*) Hume writes of the value of skepticism in correcting dogmatism. In the *Dialogues Concerning Natural Religion*, skepticism becomes a tool used by Philo to move Cleanthes from his philosophical dogmatism.

3 See the Hume literature on the topic of "natural beliefs".

4 Norman Kemp Smith, *A Commentary to Kant's Critique of Pure Reason* (The Humanities Press, 1918), p. xxvii.

5 According to Hume, the concept of causality is *derived from* experience.

6 While synthetic statements enlarge our knowledge, analytic statements, which are apodictically certain, do not: the predicate cannot be denied of the subject without a contradiction (e.g. every body is extended) even though the terms may be empirical concepts (gold is a yellow metal). See *Prolegomena*, pp. 38ff.

7 "[T]he predicate is indeed attached to the concept necessarily ... not immediately ('note as thought in the concept itself') but by means of an intuition which must also be present."

8 "[T]hese functions specify the understanding completely, and yield an exhaustive inventory of its powers" (CPR A80/B106).

9 David Hume, *Enquiry Concerning Human Understanding*, ed. P. H. Nidditch (Hackett), p. 42.

10 An example of this shift may be found in Hume's discussion of the source of moral distinctions in the *Treatise*: "Take any action allow'd to be vicious: Wilful murder, for instance. Examine it in all lights, and see if you can find that matter of fact, or real existence, which you call *vice*. ... The vice entirely escapes you, as long as you consider the object. You can never find it, till you turn your reflexion into your own breast, and find a sentiment of disapprobation, which arises in you, towards this action. Here is a matter of fact; but 'tis the object of feeling, not of reason. It lies in yourself, not in the object. So that when you pronounce any action or character to be vicious, you mean nothing, but that from the constitution of your nature you have a feeling or sentiment of blame from the contemplation of it" (David Hume, *A Treatise of Human Nature*, T.469).

11 See T. E. Uehling, "*Wahrnehmungsurteile* and *Erfahrungsurteile* Reconsidered," in this volume.

12 Uehling quotes Kemp Smith, who says the distinction is "entirely worthless and can only serve to mislead the reader."

13 This is Kant's definition of a synthetic judgment (CPR A765/B793).

14 Kant continues: "This we attempt to do either through the pure understanding, in respect of that which is at least capable of being an *object of experience*, or through pure reason, in respect of such properties of things, or indeed even of the existence of such things, as can never be met with in experience" (ibid.).

15 Hume, *Enquiry Concerning Human Understanding*, p. 114.

16 R. F. Atkinson, "Hume on Mathematics," *Philosophical Quarterly* 10, 127–37, 1960.

17 Anderson quotes Ayer: "a proposition is analytic when its validity depends solely on the definitions of the symbols it contains, and synthetic when its validity is determined by the facts of experience" (*Language, Truth and Logic*, 1978, p. 78).

18 Dorothy P. Coleman, "Is Mathematics for Hume Synthetic a priori?" *Southwestern Journal of Philosophy*, 1979, p. 124). See also Donald Gotterbarn, "Kant, Hume, and Analyticity," *Kant-Studien*, 65, 1974, 274–83.

19 Rosemary Newman, "Hume on Space and Geometry", *Hume Studies*, 7, 1, 1981, 1–31.

20 See Manfred Kuehn, "Kant's Critique of Hume's Theory of Faith," in *Hume and Hume's Connexions*, ed. M. A. Stewart and J. P. Wright (Edinburgh University Press, 1994), pp. 239–55; von Dieter-Jurgen Lowisch, "Kant's *Kritik der Reinen Vernunft* und Hume's *Dialogues Concerning Natural Religion*", *Kant-Studien* (not available in English).

21 See *Lectures on Philosophical Theology*, trans. Allen W. Wood and Gertrude M. Clark (Cornell University Press, 1978). Kant also refers, approvingly, to Hume's *Natural History of Religion* in these lectures.

22 Ibid., pp. 31–2.

23 "[T]he business of the senses is to intuit" (p. 7).

24 Kant "Reflexionen," quoted in Paul Guyer, *Kant and the Claims of Knowledge*, p. 19.

25 David Hume, *Dialogues Concerning Natural Religion*, ed. S. Tweyman (Routledge In Focus Series, 1993), pp. 101–2.

26 In fact, Philo, in his mysticism, makes this very claim in Part 2 of the *Dialogues*. He says we can use words to describe the Deity, such as intelligent, wise, benevolent, but that we should not think that the words we use actually do refer to or accurately describe the characteristics or features of the Deity. "*Dogmatic* anthropomorphism," such as that employed by Cleanthes in the *Dialogues*, attributes to the highest being in itself those properties through which we think objects of experience. Cleanthes claims that the intelligence of the Deity is just like human intelligence, only far greater in magnitude to reflect the far greater complexity of the Deity's design as compared to that of human designers, and he attributes a mind just like human minds to the Deity because that is the only kind of mind he knows.

27 Hume, *Dialogues*, p. 108.

IMMANUEL KANT

PROLEGOMENA TO ANY FUTURE METAPHYSICS

originally published in 1783

Reprinted from Kant's *Prolegomena to Any Future Metaphysics*
Edited in English by Dr. Paul Carus
by permission of Open Court Publishing Company, LaSalle, Illinois

INTRODUCTION

These Prolegomena are destined for the use, not of pupils, but of future teachers, and even the latter should not expect that they will be serviceable for the systematic exposition of a ready-made science, but merely for the discovery of the science itself.

There are scholarly men, to whom the history of philosophy (both ancient and modern) is philosophy itself; for these the present Prolegomena are not written. They must wait till those who endeavor to draw from the fountain of reason itself have completed their work; it will then be the historian's turn to inform the world of what has been done. Unfortunately, nothing can be said, which in their opinion has not been said before, and truly the same prophecy applies to all future time; for since the human reason has for many centuries speculated upon innumerable objects in various ways, it is hardly to be expected that we should not be able to discover analogies for every new idea among the old sayings of past ages.

My object is to persuade all those who think Metaphysics worth studying, that it is absolutely necessary to pause a moment, and, neglecting all that has been done, to propose first the preliminary question, "Whether such a thing as metaphysics be at all possible?"

If it be a science, how comes it that it cannot, like other sciences, obtain universal and permanent recognition? If not, how can it maintain its pretensions, and keep the human mind in suspense with hopes, never ceasing, yet never fulfilled? Whether then we demonstrate our knowledge or our ignorance in this field, we must come once for all to a definite conclusion respecting the nature of this so-called science, which cannot possibly remain on its present footing. It seems almost ridiculous, while every other science is continually advancing, that in this, which pretends to be Wisdom incarnate, for whose oracle every one inquires, we should constantly move round the same spot, without gaining a single step. And so its followers having melted away, we do not find men confident of their ability to shine in other sciences venturing their reputation here, where everybody, however ignorant in other matters, may deliver a final verdict, as in this domain there is as yet no standard weight and measure to distinguish sound knowledge from shallow talk.

After all it is nothing extraordinary in the elaboration of a science, when men begin to wonder how far it has advanced, that the question should at last occur, whether and how such a science is possible? Human reason so delights in constructions, that it has several times built up a tower, and then razed it to examine the nature of the foundation. It is never too late to become wise; but if the change comes late there is always more difficulty in starting a reform.

The question whether a science be possible, presupposes a doubt as to its actuality. But such a doubt offends the men whose whole possessions consist of this supposed jewel; hence he who raises the doubt must expect opposition from all sides. Some, in the proud consciousness of their possessions, which are ancient, and therefore considered legitimate, will take their metaphysical compendia in their hands, and look down on him with contempt; others, who never see anything except it be identical with what they have seen before, will not understand him, and everything will remain for a time, as if nothing had happened to excite the concern, or the hope, for an impending change.

Nevertheless, I venture to predict that the independent reader of these Prolegomena will not only doubt his previous science, but ultimately be fully persuaded, that it cannot exist unless the demands here stated on which its possibility depends, be satisfied; and, as this has never been done, that there is, as yet, no such thing as Metaphysics. But as it can never cease to be in demand,[1] – since the interests of common sense are intimately interwoven with it, he must confess that a radical reform, or rather a new birth of the science after an original plan, are unavoidable, however men may struggle against it for a while.

Since the Essays of Locke and Leibnitz, or rather since the origin

---

[1]Says Horace:

"Rusticus expectat, dum defluat amnis, at ille
Labitur et labetur in omne volubilis aevum."

"A rustic fellow waiteth on the shore
For the river to flow away,
But the river flows, and flows on as before, And it flows forever and aye."

of metaphysics so far as we know its history, nothing has ever happened which was more decisive to its fate than the attack made upon it by David Hume. He threw no light on this species of knowledge, but he certainly struck a spark from which light might have been obtained, had it caught some inflammable substance and had its smouldering fire been carefully nursed and developed.

Hume started from a single but important concept in Metaphysics, viz., that of Cause and Effect (including its derivatives force and action, etc.). He challenges reason, which pretends to have given birth to this idea from herself, to answer him by what right she thinks anything to be so constituted, that if that thing be posited, something else also must necessarily be posited; for this is the meaning of the concept of cause. He demonstrated irrefutably that it was perfectly impossible for reason to think *a priori* and by means of concepts a combination involving necessity. We cannot at all see why, in consequence of the existence of one thing, another must necessarily exist, or how the concept of such a combination can arise *a priori*. Hence he inferred, that reason was altogether deluded with reference to this concept, which she erroneously considered as one of her children, whereas in reality it was nothing but a bastard of imagination, impregnated by experience, which subsumed certain representations under the Law of Association, and mistook the subjective necessity of habit for an objective necessity arising from insight. Hence he inferred that reason had no power to think such combinations, even generally, because her concepts would then be purely fictitious, and all her pretended *a priori* cognitions nothing but common experiences marked with a false stamp. In plain language there is not, and cannot be, any such thing as metaphysics at all.[1]

However hasty and mistaken Hume's conclusion may appear, it was at least founded upon investigation, and this investigation deserved the concentrated attention of the brighter spirits of his day as well as determined efforts on their part to discover, if possible, a happier solution of the problem in the sense proposed by him, all

[1]Nevertheless Hume called this very destructive science metaphysics and attached to it great value. Metaphysics and morals (he declares in the fourth part of his Essays) are the most important branches of science; mathematics and physics are not nearly so important. But the acute man merely regarded the negative use arising from the moderation of extravagant claims of speculative reason, and the complete settlement of the many endless and troublesome controversies that mislead mankind. He overlooked the positive injury which results, if reason be deprived of its most important prospects, which can alone supply to the will the highest aim for all its endeavor.

of which would have speedily resulted in a complete reform of the science.

But Hume suffered the usual misfortune of metaphysicians, of not being understood. It is positively painful to see how utterly his opponents, Reid, Oswald, Beattie, and lastly Priestley, missed the point of the problem; for while they were ever taking for granted that which he doubted, and demonstrating with zeal and often with impudence that which he never thought of doubting, they so misconstrued his valuable suggestion that everything remained in its old condition, as if nothing had happened.

The question was not whether the concept of cause was right, useful, and even indispensable for our knowledge of nature, for this Hume had never doubted; but whether that concept could be thought by reason *a priori*, and consequently whether it possessed an inner truth, independent of all experience, implying a wider application than merely to the objects of experience. This was Hume's problem. It was a question concerning the *origin*, not concerning the *indispensable need* of the concept. Were the former decided, the conditions of the use and the sphere of its valid application would have been determined as a matter of course.

But to satisfy the conditions of the problem, the opponents of the great thinker should have penetrated very deeply into the nature of reason, so far as it is concerned with pure thinking – a task which did not suit them. They found a more convenient method of being defiant without any insight, viz., the appeal to *common sense*. It is indeed a great gift of God, to possess right, or (as they now call it) plain common sense. But this common sense must be shown practically, by well-considered and reasonable thoughts and words, not by appealing to it as an oracle, when no rational justification can be advanced. To appeal to common sense, when insight and science fail, and no sooner – this is one of the subtle discoveries of modern times, by means of which the most superficial ranter can safely enter the lists with the most thorough thinker, and hold his own. But as long as a particle of insight remains, no one would think of having recourse to this subterfuge. For what is it but an appeal to the opinion of the multitude, of whose applause the philosopher is ashamed, while the popular charlatan glories and confides in it? I should think that Hume might fairly have laid as much claim to common sense as Beattie, and in addition to a critical reason (such as the latter did not possess), which keeps common sense in check and prevents it from speculating, or, if speculations are under discussion, restrains the desire to decide because it cannot satisfy itself concerning its own arguments. By this means alone can common sense remain sound. Chisels and hammers may suffice to work a piece of wood, but for steel-engraving we require an engraver's needle. Thus common sense and speculative understanding are each serviceable in their own way, the former in judgments which apply immediately to experience, the latter when we judge universally from mere concepts, as in metaphysics, where sound common sense, so called in spite of the inapplicability of the word, has no right to judge at all.

I openly confess, the suggestion of David Hume was the very thing, which many years ago first interrupted my dogmatic slumber, and gave my investigations in the field of speculative philosophy quite a new direction. I was far from following him in the conclusions at which he arrived by regarding, not the whole of his problem, but a part, which by itself can give us no information. If we start from a well-founded, but undeveloped, thought, which another has bequeathed to us, we may well hope by continued reflection to advance farther than the acute man, to whom we owe the first spark of light.

I therefore first tried whether Hume's objection could not be put into a general form, and soon found that the concept of the connexion of cause and effect was by no means the only idea by which the understanding thinks the connexion of things *a priori*, but rather that metaphysics consists altogether of such connexions. I sought to ascertain their number, and when I had satisfactorily succeeded in this by starting from a single principle, I proceeded to the deduction of these concepts, which I was now certain were not deduced from experience, as Hume had apprehended, but sprang from the pure understanding. This deduction (which seemed impossible to my acute predecessor, which had never even occurred to anyone else, though no one had hesitated to use the concepts without investigating the basis of their objective validity) was the most difficult task ever undertaken in the service of metaphysics; and the worst was that metaphysics, such as it then existed, could not assist me in the least, because this deduction alone can render metaphysics possible. But as soon as I had succeeded in solving Hume's problem not merely in a particular case, but with respect to the whole sphere of pure reason completely and from general principles, in its circumference as well as in its contents. This was required for metaphysics in order to construct its system according to a reliable method.

33

But I fear that the execution of Hume's problem in its widest extent (viz., my *Critique of Pure Reason*) will fare as the problem itself fared, when first proposed. It will be misjudged because it is misunderstood, and misunderstood because men choose to skim through the book, and not to think through it – a disagreeable task, because the work is dry, obscure, opposed to all ordinary notions, and moreover long-winded. I confess, however, I did not expect to hear from philosophers complaints of want of popularity, entertainment, and facility, when the existence of a highly prized and indispensable cognition is at stake, which cannot be established otherwise, than by the strictest rule of methodic precision. Popularity may follow, but is inadmissible at the beginning. Yet as regards a certain obscurity, arising partly from the diffuseness of the plan, owing to which the principal points of the investigation are easily lost sight of, the complaint is just, and I intend to remove it by the present Prolegomena.

The first-mentioned work, which discusses the pure faculty of reason in its whole compass and bounds, will remain the foundation, to which the Prolegomena, as a preliminary exercise, refer; for our critique must first be established as a complete and perfected science, before we can think of letting metaphysics appear on the scene, or even have the most distant hope of attaining it.

We have been long accustomed to seeing antiquated knowledge produced as new by taking it out of its former context, and reducing it to system in a new suit of any fancy pattern under new titles. Most readers will set out by expecting nothing else from the *Critique*; but these Prolegomena may persuade him that it is a perfectly new science, of which no one has ever even thought, the very idea of which was unknown, and for which nothing hitherto accomplished can be of the smallest use, except it be the suggestion of Hume's doubts. Yet even he did not suspect such a formal science but ran his ship ashore, for safety's sake, landing on scepticism, there to let it lie and rot; whereas my object is rather to give it a pilot, who, by means of safe astronomical principles drawn from a knowledge of the globe, and provided with a complete chart and compass, may steer the ship safely, whither he listeth.

If in a new science, which is wholly isolated and unique in its kind, we started with the prejudice that we can judge of things by means of our previously acquired knowledge, which is precisely what has first to be called in question, we should only fancy we saw everywhere what we had already known, the expressions, having a similar sound, only that all would appear utterly metamorphosed, senseless and unintelligible, because we should have as a foundation our own notions, made by long habit a second nature, instead of the author's. But the long-windedness of the work, so far as it depends on the subject, and not the exposition, its consequent unavoidable dryness and its scholastic precision are qualities which can only benefit the science, though they may discredit the book.

Few writers are gifted with the subtlety, and at the same time with the grace, of David Hume, or with the depth, as well as the elegance, of Moses Mendelssohn. Yet I flatter myself I might have made my own exposition popular, had my object been merely to sketch out a plan and leave its completion to others, instead of having my heart in the welfare of the science, to which I had devoted myself so long; in truth, it required no little constancy, and even self-denial, to postpone the sweets of an immediate success to the prospect of a slower, but more lasting, reputation.

Making plans is often the occupation of an opulent and boastful mind, which thus obtains the reputation of a creative genius, by demanding what it cannot itself supply; by censuring what it cannot improve; and by proposing what it knows not where to find. And yet something more should belong to a sound plan of a general critique of pure reason than mere conjectures, if this plan is to be other than the usual declamations of pious aspirations. But pure reason is a sphere so separate and self-contained, that we cannot touch a part without affecting all the rest. We can therefore do nothing without first determining the position of each part, and its relation to the rest; for, as our judgment cannot be corrected by anything without, the validity and use of every part depends upon the relation in which it stands to all the rest within the domain of reason.

So in the structure of an organized body, the end of each member can only be deduced from the full conception of the whole. It may, then, be said of such a critique that it is never trustworthy except it be perfectly complete, down to the smallest elements of pure reason. In the sphere of this faculty you can determine either everything or nothing.

But although a mere sketch, preceding the *Critique of Pure Reason*, would be unintelligible, unreliable, and useless, it is all the more useful as a sequel. For so we are able to grasp the whole, to examine in detail the chief points of importance in the science, and to improve in many respects our exposition, as compared with the first execution of the work.

After the completion of the work I offer here such a plan which is sketched out after an analytical method, while the work itself had to be executed in the synthetical style, in order that the science may present all its articulations, as the structure of a peculiar cognitive faculty, in their natural combination. But should any reader find this plan, which I publish as the Prolegomena to any future Metaphysics, still obscure, let him consider that not everyone is bound to study Metaphysics, that many minds will succeed very well, in the exact and even in deep sciences, more closely allied to practical experience[1] while they cannot succeed in investigations dealing exclusively with abstract concepts. In such cases men should apply their talents to other subjects. But he who undertakes to judge, or still more, to construct, a system of Metaphysics, must satisfy the demands here made, either by adopting my solution, or by thoroughly refuting it, and substituting another. To evade it is impossible.

In conclusion, let it be remembered that this much abused obscurity (frequently serving as a mere pretext under which people hide their own indolence or dullness) has its uses, since all who in other sciences observe a judicious silence, speak authoritatively in metaphysics and make bold decisions, because their ignorance is not here contrasted with the knowledge of others. Yet it does contrast with sound critical principles, which we may therefore commend in the words of Virgil:

"Ignavum, fucos, pecus a præsepibus arcent."
"Bees are defending their hives against drones, those indolent creatures."

---

[1]The term *Anschauung* here used means sense-perception. It is that which is given to the senses and apprehended immediately, as an object is seen by merely looking at it. The translation *intuition*, though etymologically correct, is misleading. In the present passage the term is not used in its technical significance but means "practical experience."-*Ed.*

PROLEGOMENA
Preamble on the Peculiarities of all Metaphysical Cognition

§ 1. Of the Sources of Metaphysics

If it becomes desirable to formulate any cognition as science, it will be necessary first to determine accurately those peculiar features which no other science has in common with it, constituting its characteristics; otherwise the boundaries of all sciences become confused, and none of them can be treated thoroughly according to its nature.

The characteristics of a science may consist of a simple difference of object or of the sources of cognition, or of the kind of cognition, or perhaps of all three conjointly. On this, therefore, depends the idea of a possible science and its territory.

First, as concerns the sources of metaphysical cognition, its very concept implies that they cannot be empirical. Its principles (including not only its maxims but its basic notions) must never be derived from experience. It must not be physical but metaphysical knowledge, viz., knowledge lying beyond experience. It can therefore have for its basis neither external experience, which is the source of physics proper, nor internal, which is the basis of empirical psychology. It is therefore *a priori* knowledge, coming from pure Understanding and pure Reason.

But so far Metaphysics would not be distinguishable from pure Mathematics; it must therefore be called pure philosophical cognition; and for the meaning of this term I refer to the *Critique of Pure Reason* (II. "Method of Transcendentalism," Chapter I, §i), where the distinction between these two employments of the reason is sufficiently explained. So far concerning the sources of metaphysical cognition.

§ 2. *Concerning the Kind of Cognition which can alone be called Metaphysical*

a. Of the Distinction between Analytical and Synthetical Judgments in general – The peculiarity of its sources demands that metaphysical cognition must consist of nothing but *a priori* judgments. But whatever be their origin, or their logical form, there is a distinction in judgments as to their content, according to which they are either merely explicative, adding nothing to the content of the cognition, or expansive, increasing the given cognition: the former may be called analytical, the latter synthetical, judgments.

Analytical judgments express nothing in the predicate but what has been already actually thought in the concept of the subject, though not so distinctly or with the same (full) consciousness. When I say: All bodies are extended, I have not amplified in the least my concept of body, but have only analysed it, as extension was really thought to belong to that concept before the judgment was made, though it was not expressed: this judgment is therefore analytical. On the contrary, this judgment, All bodies have weight, contains in its predicate something not actually thought in the general concept of the body; it amplifies my knowledge by adding something to my concept, and must therefore be called synthetical.

b. The Common Principle of all Analytical Judgments is the Law of Contradiction – All analytical judgments depend wholly on the law of Contradiction, and are in their nature *a priori* cognitions, whether the concepts that supply them with matter be empirical or not. For the predicate of an affirmative analytical judgment is already contained in the concept of the subject, of which it cannot be denied without contradiction. In the same way its opposite is necessarily denied of the subject in an analytical, but negative, judgment, by the same law of contradiction. Such is the nature of the judgments: all bodies are extended, and no bodies are unextended (i.e. simple).

For this very reason all analytical judgments are *a priori* even when the concepts are empirical, as, for example, gold is a yellow metal; for to know this I require no experience beyond my concept of gold as a yellow metal: it is, in fact, the very concept, and I need only analyse it, without looking beyond it elsewhere.

c. Synthetical Judgments require a different Principle from the Law of Contradiction – There are synthetical *a posteriori* judgments of empirical origin; but there are also others which are proved to be certain *a priori*, and which spring from pure Understanding and Reason. Yet they both agree in this, that they cannot possibly spring from the principle of analysis, viz., the law of contradiction, alone; they require a quite different principle, though, from whatever they may be deduced, they must be subject to the law of contradiction, which must never be violated, even though everything cannot be deduced from it. I shall first classify synthetical judgments.

1   *Empirical Judgments* are always synthetical. For it would be absurd to base an analytical judgment on experience, as our concept suffices for the purpose without requiring any testimony from experience. That body is extended, is a judgment established *a priori*, and not an empirical judgment. For before appealing to experience, we already have all the conditions of the judgment in the concept, from which we have but to elicit the predicate according to the law of contradiction, and thereby to become conscious of the necessity of the judgment, which experience could not even teach us.

2   *Mathematical Judgments* are all synthetical. This fact seems hitherto to have altogether escaped the observation of those who have analysed human reason; it even seems directly opposed to all their conjectures, though incontestably certain, and most important in its consequences. For as it was found that the conclusions of mathematicians all proceed according to the law of contradiction (as is demanded by all apodeictic certainty), men persuaded themselves that the fundamental principles were known from the same law. This was a great mistake, for a synthetical proposition can indeed be comprehended according to the law of contradiction, but only by presupposing another synthetical proposition from which it follows, but never in itself.

First of all, we must observe that all proper mathematical judgments are *a priori*, and not empirical, because they carry with them necessity, which cannot be obtained from experience. But if this be not conceded to me, very good; I shall confine my assertion to *pure Mathematics*, the very notion of which implies that it contains pure *a priori* and not empirical cognitions.

It might at first be thought that the proposition 7+5=12 is a mere analytical judgment, following from the concept of the sum of seven and five, according to the law of contradiction. But on closer examination it appears that the concept of the sum of 7+5 contains merely their union in a single number, without its being at all thought what the particular number is that unites them. The concept of twelve is by no means thought by merely thinking of the combination of seven and five; and analyse this possible sum as we may, we shall not discover twelve in the concept. We must go beyond these concepts, by calling to our aid some concrete image (*Anschauung*), i.e. either our five fingers, or five points (as Segner has it in his Arithmetic), and we must add successively the units of the five, given in some concrete image (*Anschauung*), to the concept of seven. Hence our concept is really amplified by the proposition 7+5=12, and we add to the first a second not thought in it. Arithmetical judgments are therefore synthetical, and the more plainly according as we take larger numbers; for in such cases it is clear that, however closely we analyse our concepts without calling visual images (*Anschauung*) to our aid, we can never find the sum by such mere dissection.

All principles of geometry are no less analytical. That a straight line is the shortest path between two points, is a synthetical proposition. For my concept of straight contains nothing of quantity, but only a quality. The attribute of shortness is therefore altogether additional, and cannot be obtained by any analysis of the concept. Here, too, visualisation (*Anschauung*) must come to aid us. It alone makes the synthesis possible.

Some other principles, assumed by geometers, are indeed actually analytical, and depend on the law of contradiction; but they only serve, as identical propositions, as a method of concatenation, and not as principles, e.g. $a=a$, the whole is equal to itself, or $a+b>a$, the whole is greater than its part. And yet even these, though they are recognised as valid from mere concepts, are only admitted in mathematics, because they can be represented in some visual form (*Anschauung*). What usually makes us believe that the predicate of such apodeictic judgments is already contained in our concept, and that the judgment is therefore analytical, is the duplicity of the expression, requesting us to think a certain predicate as of necessity implied in the thought of a given concept, which necessity attaches to the concept. But the question is not what we are requested to join in thought *to* the given concept, but what we actually think together with and in it, though obscurely; and so it appears that the predicate belongs to these concepts necessarily indeed, yet not directly but indirectly by an added visualisation (*Anschauung*).

**The essential and distinguishing feature of pure mathematical cognition among all other *a priori* cognitions is, that it cannot at all proceed from concepts, but only by means of the construction of concepts (see Critique II, Method of Transcendentalism, Chapter I, §1). As therefore in its judgments it must proceed beyond the concept to that which its corresponding visualization (*Anschauung*) contains, these judgments neither can, nor ought to, arise analytically, by dissecting the concept, but are all synthetical.

I cannot refrain from pointing out the disadvantage resulting to philosophy from the neglect of this easy and apparently insignificant observation. Hume being prompted (a task worthy of a philosopher) to cast his eye over the whole field of *a priori* cognitions in which human understanding claims such mighty possessions, heedlessly severed from it a whole, and indeed its most valuable, province, viz., pure mathematics; for he thought its nature, or, so to speak, the state-constitution of this empire, depended on totally different principles, namely, on the law of contradiction alone; and although he did not divide judgments in this manner formally and universally as I have done here, what he said was equivalent to this: that mathematics contains only analytical, but metaphysics synthetical, *a priori* judgments. In this, however, he was greatly mistaken, and the mistake had a decidedly injurious effect upon his whole conception. But for this, he would have extended his question concerning the origin of our synthetical judgments far beyond the metaphysical concept of causality, and included in it the possibility of mathematics *a priori* also, for this latter he must have assumed to be equally synthetical. And then he could not have based his metaphysical judgments on mere experience without subjecting the axioms of mathematics equally to experience, a thing which he was far too acute to do. The good company into which metaphysics would thus have been brought would have saved it from the danger of a contemptuous ill-treatment, for the thrust intended for it must have reached mathematics, which was not and could not have been Hume's intention. Thus that acute man would have been led into considerations which must needs be similar to those that now occupy us, but which would have gained inestimably by his inimitably elegant style.

Metaphysical judgments, properly so called, are all synthetical. We must distinguish judgments pertaining to metaphysics from metaphysical judgments properly so called. Many of the former are

**The portion of the text positioned between double asterisks has been placed in accordance with modern editions of the *Prolegomena*.

analytical, but they only afford the means for metaphysical judgments, which are the whole end of the science, and which are always synthetical. For if there be concepts pertaining to metaphysics (as, for example, that of substance) the judgments springing from simple analysis of them also pertain to metaphysics, as, for example, substance is that which only exists as subject; and by means of several such analytical judgments, we seek to approach the definition of the concept. But as the analysis of a pure concept of the understanding pertaining to metaphysics, does not proceed in any different manner from the dissection of any other, even empirical, concepts, not pertaining to metaphysics (such as: air is an elastic fluid, the elasticity of which is not destroyed by any known degree of cold), it follows that the concept indeed, but not the analytical judgment, is properly metaphysical. This science has something peculiar in the production of its *a priori* cognitions, which must therefore be distinguished from the features it has in common with other rational knowledge. Thus the judgment, that all the substance in things is permanent, is a synthetical and properly metaphysical judgment.

If the *a priori* principles, which constitute the materials of metaphysics have first been collected according to fixed principles, then their analysis will be of great value; it might be taught as a particular part (as a *philosophia definitiva*), containing nothing but analytical judgments pertaining to metaphysics, and could be treated separately from the synthetical which constitute metaphysics proper. For indeed these analyses are not elsewhere of much value, except in metaphysics, i.e. as regards the synthetical judgments, which are to be generated by these previously analysed concepts.

The conclusion drawn in this section then, is that metaphysics is properly concerned with synthetical propositions *a priori*, and these alone constitute its end, for which it indeed requires various dissections of its concepts, viz., of its analytical judgments, but wherein the procedure is not different from that in every other kind of knowledge, in which we merely seek to render our concepts distinct by analysis. But the generation of *a priori* cognition by concrete images as well as by concepts, in fine of synthetical propositions *a priori* in philosophical cognition, constitutes the essential subject of metaphysics.[1]

---

[1]The term "*apodeictic*" is borrowed by Kant from Aristotle who uses it in the sense of "certain beyond dispute." The word is derived from ἀποδείκνυμι (=*I show*) and is contrasted to dialectic propositions, i.e. such statements as admit of controversy.-*Ed.*

§ 3. A Remark on the General Division of Judgments into Analytical and Synthetical

This division is indispensable, as concerns the Critique of human understanding, and therefore deserves to be called classical, though otherwise it is of little use, but this is the reason why dogmatic philosophers, who always seek the sources of metaphysical judgments in Metaphysics itself, and not apart from it, in the pure laws of reason generally, altogether neglected this apparently obvious distinction. Thus the celebrated Wolf, and his acute follower Baumgarten, came to seek the proof of the principle of Sufficient Reason, which is clearly synthetical, in the principle of Contradiction. In Locke's Essay, however, I find an indication of my division. For in the fourth book (Chapter iii, § 9, seq.), having discussed the various connexions of representations in judgments, and their sources, one of which he makes "identity and contradiction" (analytical judgments), and another the coexistence of representations in a subject, he confesses (§ 10) that our *a priori* knowledge of the latter is very narrow, and almost nothing. But in his remarks on this species of cognition, there is so little of what is definite, and reduced to rules, that we cannot wonder if no one, not even Hume, was led to make investigations concerning this sort of judgment. For such general and yet definite principles are not easily learned from other men, who have had them obscurely in their minds. We must hit on them first by our own reflexion, then we find them elsewhere, where we could not possibly have found them at first, because the authors themselves did not know that such an idea lay at the basis of their observations. Men who never think independently have nevertheless the acuteness to discover everything, after it has been once shown them, in what was said long since, though no one ever saw it there before.

§ 4. The General Question of the Prolegomena — Is Metaphysics at all Possible?

Were a metaphysics, which could maintain its place as a science, really in existence; could we say, here is metaphysics, learn it, and it will convince you irresistibly and irrevocably of its truth: this question would be useless, and there would only remain that other question (which would rather be a test of our acuteness, than a proof of the existence of the thing itself), "How is the science possible, and how does reason come to attain it?" But human reason has not been so fortunate in this case. There is no single book to which you can point as you do to *Euclid*, and say: This is Metaphysics; here you may find the noblest objects of this science, the knowledge of a highest Being, and of a future existence, proved from principles of pure reason. We can be shown indeed many judgments, demonstrably certain, and never questioned; but these are all analytical, and rather concern the materials and the scaffolding for Metaphysics, than the extension of knowledge, which is our proper object in studying it (§ 2). Even supposing you produce synthetical judgments (such as the law of Sufficient Reason, which you have never proved, as you ought to, from pure reason *a priori*, though we gladly concede its truth), you lapse when they come to be employed for your principal object, into such doubtful assertions, that in all ages one Metaphysics has contradicted another, either in its assertions, or their proofs, and thus has itself destroyed its own claim to lasting assent. Nay, the very attempt to set up such a science are the main cause of the early appearance of scepticism, a mental attitude in which reason treats itself with such violence that it could never have arisen save from complete despair of ever satisfying our most important aspirations. For long before men began to inquire into nature methodically, they consulted abstract reason, which had to some extent been exercised by means of ordinary experience; for reason is ever present, while laws of nature must usually be discovered with labor. So Metaphysics floated to the surface, like foam, which dissolved the moment it was scooped off. But immediately there appeared a new supply on the surface, to be ever eagerly gathered up by some, while others, instead of seeking in the depths the cause of the phenomenon, thought they showed their wisdom by ridiculing the idle labor of their neighbors.**

Weary therefore as well of dogmatism, which teaches us nothing, as of scepticism, which does not even promise us anything, not even the quiet state of a contented ignorance; disquieted by the importance of knowledge so much needed; and lastly, rendered suspicious by long experience of all knowledge which we believe we possess, or which offers itself, under the title of pure reason: there remains but one critical question on the answer to which our future procedure depends, viz., *Is Metaphysics at all possible?* But this question must be answered not by skeptical objections to the asseverations of some actual system of metaphysics (for we do not as yet admit such a thing to exist), but from the conception, as yet only problematical, of a science of this sort.

In the *Critique of Pure Reason* I have treated this question synthetically, by making inquiries into pure reason itself, and endeavoring in this source to determine the elements as well as the laws of its pure use according to principles. The task is difficult, and requires a resolute reader to penetrate by degrees into a system, based on no data except reason itself, and which therefore seeks, without resting upon any fact, to unfold knowledge from its original germs. *Prolegomena*, however, are designed for preparatory exercises; they are intended rather to point out what we have to do in order if possible to actualise a science, than to propound it. They must therefore rest upon something already known as trustworthy, from which we can set out with confidence, and ascend to sources as yet unknown, the discovery of which will not only explain to us what we knew, but exhibit a sphere of many cognitions which all spring from the same sources. The method of *Prolegomena*, especially of those designed as a preparation for future metaphysics, is consequently analytical.

But it happens fortunately, that though we cannot assume metaphysics to be an actual science, we can say with confidence that certain pure *a priori* synthetical cognitions, pure Mathematics and pure Physics are actual and given; for both contain propositions, which are thoroughly recognised as apodeictically certain, partly by mere reason, partly by general consent arising from experience, and yet as independent of experience. We have therefore some at least uncontested synthetical knowledge *a priori*, and need not ask *whether* it be possible, for it is actual, but *how* it is possible, in order that we may deduce from the principle which makes the given cognitions possible the possibility of all the rest.

The General Problem: How is Cognition from Pure Reason Possible?

§ 5. We have above learned the significant distinction between analytical and synthetical judgments. The possibility of analytical propositions was easily comprehended, being entirely founded on the law of Contradiction. The possibility of synthetical *a posteriori* judgments, of those which are gathered from experience, also requires no particular explanation; for experience is nothing but a continual synthesis of perceptions. There remain therefore only synthetical propositions *a priori*, of which the possibility must be sought or investigated, because they must depend upon other principles than the law of contradiction.

But here we need not first establish the possibility of such propositions so as to ask whether they are possible. For there are enough of them which indeed are of undoubted certainty, and as our present method is analytical, we shall start from the fact, that such synthetical but purely rational cognition actually exists; but we must now inquire into the reason of this possibility, and ask, *how* such cognition is possible, in order that we may from the principles of its possibility be enabled to determine the conditions of its use, its sphere and its limits. The proper problem upon which all depends, when expressed with scholastic precision, is therefore:

How are Synthetic Propositions a priori possible?

For the sake of popularity I have above expressed this problem somewhat differently, as an inquiry into purely rational cognition, which I could do for once without detriment to the desired comprehension, because, as we have only to do here with metaphysics and its sources, the reader will, I hope, after the foregoing remarks, keep in mind that when we speak of purely rational cognition, we do not mean analytical, but synthetical cognition.[1]

Metaphysics stands or falls with the solution of this problem: its very existence depends upon it. Let anyone make metaphysical assertions with ever so much plausibility, let him overwhelm us with conclusions, if he has not previously proved able to answer this question satisfactorily, I have a right to say: this is all vain baseless philosophy and false wisdom. You speak through pure reason, and claim, as it were to create cognitions *a priori* by not only dissecting given concepts, but also by asserting connexions which do not rest upon the law of contradiction, and which you believe you conceive quite independently of all experience; how do you arrive at this, and how will you justify your pretensions? An appeal to the consent of the common sense of mankind cannot be allowed; for that is a witness whose authority depends merely upon rumor. Says Horace:

"Quodcunque ostendis mihi sic, incredulus odi."

[1] It is unavoidable that as knowledge advances, certain expressions which have become classical, after having been used since the infancy of science, will be found inadequate and unsuitable, and a newer and more appropriate application of the terms will give rise to confusion. (This is the case with the term "analytical.") The analytical method, so far as it is opposed to the synthetical, is very different from that which constitutes the essence of analytical propositions: it signifies only that we start from what is sought, as if it were given, and ascend to the only conditions under which it is possible. In this method we often use nothing but synthetical propositions, as in mathematical analysis, and it were better to term it the regressive method, in contradistinction to the synthetic or progressive. A principal part of Logic too is distinguished by the name of Analytics, which here signifies the logic of truth in contrast to Dialectics, without considering whether the cognitions belonging to it are analytical or synthetical.

"To all that which thou provest me thus, I refuse to give credence."

The answer to this question, though indispensable, is difficult; and though the principal reason that it was not made long ago is, that the possibility of the question never occurred to anybody, there is yet another reason, which is this that a satisfactory answer to this one question requires a much more persistent, profound, and painstaking reflexion, than the most diffuse work on Metaphysics, which on its first appearance promised immortality to its author. And every intelligent reader, when he carefully reflects what this problem requires, must at first be struck with its difficulty, and would regard it as insoluble and even impossible, did there not actually exist pure synthetical cognitions *a priori*. This actually happened to David Hume, though he did not conceive the question in its entire universality as is done here, and as must be done, should the answer be decisive for all Metaphysics. For how is it possible, says that acute man, that when a concept is given me, I can go beyond it and connect with it another, which is not contained in it, in such a manner as if the latter necessarily belonged to the former? Nothing but experience can furnish us with such connctions (thus he concluded from the difficulty which he took to be an impossibility), and all that vaunted necessity, or what is the same thing, all cognition assumed to be *a priori*, is nothing but a long habit of accepting something as true, and hence of mistaking subjective necessity for objective.

Should my reader complain of the difficulty and the trouble which I occasion him in the solution of this problem, he is at liberty to solve it himself in an easier way. Perhaps he will then feel under obligation to the person who has undertaken for him a labor of so profound research, and will rather be surprised at the facility with which, considering the nature of the subject, the solution has been attained. Yet it has cost years of work to solve the problem in its whole universality (using the term in the mathematical sense, viz., for that which is sufficient for all cases), and finally to exhibit it in the analytical form, as the reader finds it here.

All metaphysicians are therefore solemnly and legally suspended from their occupations till they shall have answered in a satisfactory manner the question, "How are synthetic cognitions *a priori* possible?" For the answer contains the only credentials which they must show when they have anything to offer in the name of pure reason.

But if they do not possess these credentials, they can expect nothing else of reasonable people, who have been deceived so often, than to be dismissed without further ado.

If they on the other hand desire to carry on their business, not as a science, but as an art of wholesome oratory suited to the common sense of man, they cannot in justice be prevented. They will then speak the modest language of a rational belief, they will grant that they are not allowed even to conjecture, far less to know, anything which lies beyond the bounds of all possible experience, but only to assume (not for speculative use, which they must abandon, but for practical purposes only) the existence of something that is possible and even indispensable for the guidance of the understanding and of the will in life. In this manner alone can they be called useful and wise men, and the more so as they renounce the title of metaphysicians; for the latter profess to be speculative philosophers, and since, when judgments *a priori* are under discussion, poor probabilities cannot be admitted (for what is declared to be known *a priori* is thereby announced as necessary), such men cannot be permitted to play with conjectures, but their assertions must be either science, or are worth nothing at all.

It may be said that the entire transcendental philosophy, which necessarily precedes all metaphysics, is nothing but the complete solution of the problem here propounded, in systematical order and completeness, and higherto we have never had any transcendental philosophy; for what goes by its name is properly a part of metaphysics, whereas the former science is intended first to constitute the possibility of the latter, and must therefore precede all metaphysics. And it is not surprising that when a whole science, deprived of all help from other sciences, and consequently in itself quite new, is required to answer a single question satisfactorily, we should find the answer troublesome and difficult, nay even shrouded in obscurity.

As we now proceed to this solution according to the analytical method, in which we assume that such cognitions from pure reasons actually exist, we can only appeal to two sciences of theoretical cognition (which alone is under consideration here), pure mathematics and pure natural science (physics). For these alone can exhibit to us objects in a definite and actualisable form (*in der Anschauung*), and consequently (if there should occur in them a cognition *a priori*) can show the truth or conformity of the cognition to the object *in concreto*, that is, its actuality, from which we could proceed to the reason of its possibility by the analytic method. This facilitates our work greatly for here universal considerations are not only applied to facts, but even start from them, while in a synthetic procedure they must strictly be derived *in abstracto* from concepts.

But, in order to rise from these actual and at the same time well-grounded pure cognitions *a priori* to such a possible cognition of the same as we are seeking, viz., to metaphysics as a science, we must comprehend that which occasions it, I mean the mere natural, though in spite of its truth not unsuspected, cognition *a priori* which lies at the bottom of that science, the elaboration of which without any critical investigation of its possibility is commonly called metaphysics. In a word, we must comprehend the natural conditions of such a science as a part of our inquiry, and thus the transcendental problem will be gradually answered by a division into four questions:

1 *How is pure mathematics possible?*
2 *How is pure natural science possible?*
3 *How is metaphysics in general possible?*
4 *How is metaphysics as a science possible?*

It may be seen that the solution of these problems, though chiefly designed to exhibit the essential matter of the Critique, has yet something peculiar, which for itself alone deserves attention. This is the search for the sources of given sciences in reason itself, so that its faculty of knowing something *a priori* may by its own deeds be investigated and measured. By this procedure these sciences gain, if not with regard to their contents, yet as to their proper use, and while they throw light on the higher question concerning their common origin, they give, at the same time, an occasion better to explain their own nature.

FIRST PART OF THE TRANSCENDENTAL PROBLEM

How is Pure Mathematics Possible?

§ 6. Here is a great and established branch of knowledge, encompassing even now a wonderfully large domain and promising an unlimited extension in the future. Yet it carries with it thoroughly apodeictical certainty, i.e. absolute necessity, which therefore rests upon no empirical grounds. Consequently it is a pure product of reason, and moreover is thoroughly synthetical. Here the question arises:

"*How then is it possible for human reason to produce a cognition of this nature entirely* a priori?"

Does not this faculty (which produces mathematics), as it neither is nor can be based upon experience, presuppose some ground of cognition *a priori*, which lies deeply hidden, but which might reveal itself by these its effects, if their first beginnings were but diligently ferreted out?

§ 7. But we find that all mathematical cognition has this peculiarity: it must first exhibit its concept in a visual form (*Anschauung*) and indeed *a priori*, therefore in a visual form which is not empirical, but pure. Without this mathematics cannot take a single step; hence its judgments are always visual, viz., "intuitive"; whereas philosophy must be satisfied with discursive judgments from mere concepts, and though it may illustrate its doctrines through a visual figure, can never derive them from it. This observation on the nature of mathematics gives us a clue to the first and highest condition of its possibility, which is, that some non-sensuous visualisation (called pure intuition, or *reine Anschauung*) must form its basis, in which all its concepts can be exhibited or constructed, *in concreto* and yet *a priori*. If we can find out this pure intuition and its possibility, we may thence easily explain how synthetical propositions *a priori* are

50

possible in pure mathematics, and consequently how this science itself is possible. Empirical intuition (viz., sense-perception) enables us without difficulty to enlarge the concept which we frame of an object of intuition (or sense-perception), by new predicates, which intuition (i.e. sense-perception) itself presents synthetically in experience. Pure intuition (viz., the visualization of forms in our imagination, from which every thing sensual, i.e. every thought of material qualities, is excluded) does so likewise, only with this difference, that in the latter case the synthetical judgment is *a priori* certain and apodeictical, in the former, only *a posteriori* and empirically certain; because this latter contains only that which occurs in contingent empirical intuition, but the former, that which must necessarily be discovered in pure intuition. Here intuition, being an intuition *a priori*, is *before all experience*, viz., before any perception of particular objects, inseparably conjoined with its concept.

§ 8. But with this step our perplexity seems rather to increase than to lessen. For the question now is, "How is it possible to intuite (in a visual form) anything *a priori?*" An intuition (viz., a visual sense-perception) is such a representation as immediately depends upon the presence of the object. Hence it seems impossible to intuite from the outset *a priori*, because intuition would in that event take place without either a former or a present object to refer to, and by consequence could not be intuition. Concepts indeed are such, that we can easily form some of them *a priori*, viz., such as contain nothing but the thought of an object in general; and we need not find ourselves in an immediate relation to the object. Take, for instance, the concepts of Quantity, of Cause, etc. But even these require, in order to make them understood, a certain concrete use – that is, an application to some sense-experience (*Anschauung*), by which an object of them is given us. But how can the intuition of the object (its visualization) precede the object itself?

§ 9. If our intuition (i.e. our sense-experience) were perforce of such a nature as to represent things as they are in themselves, there would not be any intuition *a priori*, but intuition would be always empirical. For I can only know what is contained in the object in itself when it is present and given to me. It is indeed even then incomprehensible how the visualising (*Anschauung*) of a present thing should make me know this thing as it is in itself, as its properties cannot migrate into my faculty of representation. But even granting this possibility, a visualising of that sort would not take place *a priori*, that is, before the object were presented to me; for without this latter fact no reason of a relation between my representation and the object can be imagined, unless it depend upon a direct inspiration.

Therefore in one way only can my intuition (*Anschauung*) anticipate the actuality of the object, and be a cognition *a priori*, viz.: if my intuition contains nothing but the form of sensibility, antedating in my subjectivity all the actual impressions through which I am affected by objects.

For that objects of sense can only be intuited according to this form of sensibility I can know *a priori*. Hence it follows: that propositions, which concern this form of sensuous intuition only, are possible and valid for objects of the senses; as also, conversely, that intuitions which are possible *a priori* can never concern any other things than objects of our senses.[1]

§ 10.   Accordingly, it is only the form of sensuous intuition by which we can intuite things *a priori*, but by which we can know objects only as they *appear* to us (to our senses), not as they are in themselves; and this assumption is absolutely necessary if synthetical propositions *a priori* be granted as possible, or if, in case they actually occur, their possibility is to be comprehended and determined beforehand.

Now, the intuitions which pure mathematics lays at the foundation of all its cognitions and judgments which appear at once apodeictic and necessary are Space and Time. For mathematics must first have all its concepts in intuition, and pure mathematics in pure intuition, that is, it must construct them. If it proceeded in any other way, it would be impossible to make any headway, for mathematics proceeds, not analytically by dissection of concepts, but synthetically, and if pure intuition be wanting, there is nothing in which the matter for synthetical judgments *a priori* can be given. Geometry is based upon the pure intuition of space. Arithmetic accomplishes its concept of number by the successive addition of units in time; and pure mechanics especially cannot attain its concepts of motion without employing the representation of time. Both representations, however, are only intuitions; for if we omit from the empirical intuitions of bodies and their alterations (motion) everything empirical, or belonging to sensation, space and time still remain, which are therefore pure intuitions that lie *a priori* at the basis of the empirical. Hence they can never be omitted, but at the same time, by their being pure intuitions *a priori*, they prove that they are mere forms of our

[1]This whole paragraph (§ 9) will be better understood when compared with Remark I, following this section, appearing in the present edition on page 55.-*Ed.*

sensibility, which must precede all empirical intuition, or perception of actual objects, and conformably to which objects can be known *a priori*, but only as they appear to us.

§ 11. The problem of the present section is therefore solved. Pure mathematics, as synthetical cognition *a priori*, is only possible by referring to no other objects than those of the senses. At the basis of their empirical intuition lies a pure intuition (of space and of time) which is *a priori*. This is possible, because the latter intuition is nothing but the mere form of sensibility, which precedes the actual appearance of the objects, in that it, in fact, makes them possible. Yet this faculty of intuiting *a priori* affects not the matter of the phenomenon (that is, the sense-element in it, for this constitutes that which is empirical), but its form, viz., space and time. Should any man venture to doubt that these are determinations adhering not to things in themselves, but to their relation to our sensibility, I should be glad to know how it can be possible to know the constitution of things *a priori*, viz., before we have any acquaintance with them and before they are presented to us. Such, however, is the case with space and time. But this is quite comprehensible as soon as both count for nothing more than formal conditions of our sensibility, while the objects count merely as phenomena; for then the form of the phenomenon, i.e. pure intuition, can by all means be represented as proceeding from ourselves, that is, *a priori*.

§ 12. In order to add something by way of illustration and confirmation, we need only watch the ordinary and necessary procedure of geometers. All proofs of the complete congruence of two given figures (where the one can in every respect be substituted for the other) come ultimately to this that they may be made to coincide; which is evidently nothing else than a synthetical proposition resting upon immediate intuition, and this intuition must be pure, or given *a priori*, otherwise the proposition could not rank as apodeictically certain, but would have empirical certainty only. In that case, it could only be said that it is always found to be so, and holds good only as far as our perception reaches. That everywhere space (which (in its entirety) is itself no longer the boundary of another space) has three dimensions, and that space cannot in any way have more, is based on the proposition that not more than three lines can intersect at right angles in one point; but this proposition cannot by any means be shown from concepts, but rests immediately on intuition, and indeed on pure and *a priori* intuition, because it is apodeictically certain. That we can require a line to be drawn to infinity (*in indefinitum*), or that a series of changes (for example, spaces traversed by motion) shall be infinitely continued, presupposes a representation of space and time, which can only attach to intuition, namely, so far as it in itself is bounded by nothing, for from concepts it could never be inferred. Consequently, the basis of mathematics actually are pure intuitions, which make its synthetical and apodeictically valid propositions possible. Hence our transcendental deduction of the notions of space and of time explains at the same time the possibility of pure mathematics. Without some such deduction its truth may be granted, but its existence could by no means be understood, and we must assume "that everything which can be given to our senses (to the external senses in space, to the internal one in time) is intuited by us as it appears to us, not as it is in itself."

§ 13. Those who cannot yet rid themselves of the notion that space and time are actual qualities inhering in things in themselves, may exercise their acumen on the following paradox. When they have in vain attempted its solution, and are free from prejudices at least for a few moments, they will suspect that the degradation of space and of time to mere forms of our sensuous intuition may perhaps be well founded.

If two things are quite equal in all respects as much as can be ascertained by all means possible, quantitatively and qualitatively, it must follow, that the one can in all cases and under all circumstances replace the other, and this substitution would not occasion the least perceptible difference. This in fact is true of plane figures in geometry; but some spherical figures exhibit, notwithstanding a complete internal agreement, such a contrast in their external relation, that the one figure cannot possibly be put in the place of the other. For instance, two spherical triangles on opposite hemispheres, which have an arc of the equator as their common base, may be quite equal, both as regards sides and angles, so that nothing is to be found in either, if it be described for itself alone and completed, that would not equally be applicable to both; and yet the one cannot be put in the place of the other (being situated upon the opposite hemisphere). Here then is an internal difference between the two triangles, which difference our understanding cannot describe as internal, and which only manifests itself by external relations in space.

But I shall adduce examples, taken from common life, that are more obvious still.

What can be more similar in every respect and in every part more alike to my hand and to my ear, than their images in a mirror? And yet I cannot put such a hand as is seen in the glass in the place of its archetype; for if this is a right hand, that in the glass is a left one, and the image or reflection of the right ear is a left one which never can serve as a substitute for the other. There are in this case no internal differences which our understanding could determine by thinking alone. Yet the differences are internal as the senses teach, for, notwithstanding their complete equality and similarity, the left hand cannot be enclosed in the same bounds as the right one (they are not congruent); the glove of one hand cannot be used for the other. What is the solution? These objects are not representations of things as they are in themselves, and as the pure understanding would cognise them, but sensuous intuitions, that is, appearances, the possibility of which rests upon the relation of certain things unknown in themselves to something else, viz., to our sensibility. Space is the form of the external intuition of this sensibility, and the internal determination of every space is only possible by the determination of its external relation to the whole space, of which it is a part (in other words, by its relation to the external sense). That is to say, the part is only possible through the whole, which is never the case with things in themselves, as objects of the mere understanding, but with appearances only. Hence the difference between similar and equal things, which are yet not congruent (for instance, two symmetric helices), cannot be made intelligible by any concept, but only by the relation to the right and the left hands which immediately refers to intuition.

REMARK I

Pure Mathematics, and especially pure geometry, can only have objective reality on condition that they refer to objects of sense. But in regard to the latter the principle holds good, that our sense-representation is not a representation of things in themselves, but of the way in which they appear to us. Hence it follows, that the propositions of geometry are not the results of a mere creation of our poetic imagination, and that therefore they cannot be referred with assurance to actual objects; but rather that they are necessarily valid of space, and consequently of all that may be found in space, because space is nothing else than the form of all external appearances, and it is this form alone in which objects of sense can be given. Sensibility, the form of which is the basis of geometry, is that upon which the possibility of external appearance depends. Therefore these appearances can never contain anything but what geometry prescribes to them.

It would be quite otherwise if the senses were so constituted as to represent objects as they are in themselves. For then it would not by any means follow from the conception of space, which with all its properties serves to the geometer as an *a priori* foundation, together with what is thence inferred, must be so in nature. The space of the geometer would be considered a mere fiction, and it would not be credited with objective validity, because we cannot see how things must of necessity agree with an image of them, which we make spontaneously and previous to our acquaintance with them. But if this image, or rather this formal intuition, is the essential property of our sensibility, by means of which alone objects are given to us, and if this sensibility represents not things in themselves, but their appearances: we shall easily comprehend, and at the same time indisputably prove, that all external objects of our world of sense must necessarily coincide in the most rigorous way with the propositions of geometry; because sensibility by means of its form of external intuition, viz., by space, the same with which the geometer is occupied, makes those objects at all possible as mere appearances.

It will always remain a remarkable phenomenon in the history of philosophy, that there was a time, when even mathematicians, who at the same time were philosophers, began to doubt, not of the accuracy of their geometrical propositions so far as they concerned space, but of their objective validity and the applicability of this concept itself, and of all its corollaries, to nature. They showed much concern whether a line in nature might not consist of physical points, and consequently that true space in the object might consist of simple (discrete) parts, while the space which the geometer has in his mind (being continuous) cannot be such. They did not recognise that this mental space renders possible the physical space, i.e. the extension of matter; that this pure space is not at all a quality of things in themselves, but a form of our sensuous faculty of representation; and that all objects in space are mere appearances, i.e. not things in themselves but representations of our sensuous intuition. But such is the case, for the space of the geometer is exactly the form of sensuous intuition which we find *a priori* in us, and contains the ground of the possibility of all external appearances (according to their form), and the latter must necessarily and most rigidly agree with the propositions of the geometer, which he draws not from any fictitious concept, but from the subjective basis of all external phenomena, which is sensibility itself. In this and no other way can geometry be made secure as to the undoubted objective reality of its propositions against all the intrigues of a shallow Metaphysics, which is surprised at them (the geometrical propositions), because it has not traced them to the sources of their concepts.

REMARK II

Whatever is given us as object, must be given us in intuition. All our intuition however takes place by means of the senses only; the understanding intuits nothing, but only reflects. And as we have just shown that the senses never and in no manner enable us to know things in themselves, but only their appearances, which are mere representations of the sensibility, we conclude that "all bodies, together with the space in which they are, must be considered nothing but mere representations in us, and exist nowhere but in our thoughts." You will say: Is not this manifest idealism?

Idealism consists in the assertion that there are none but thinking beings, all other things, which we think are perceived in intuition, being nothing but representations in the thinking beings, to which no object external to them corresponds in fact. Whereas I say that things as objects of our senses existing outside us are given, but we know nothing of what they may be in themselves, knowing only their appearances, i.e. the representations which they cause in us by affecting our senses. Consequently I grant by all means that there are bodies without us, that is, things which, though quite unknown to us as to what they are in themselves, we yet know by the representations which their influence on our sensibility procures us, and which we call bodies, a term signifying merely the appearance of the thing which is unknown to us, but not therefore less actual. Can this be termed idealism? It is the very contrary.

Long before Locke's time, but assuredly since him, it has been generally assumed and granted without detriment to the actual existence of external things, that many of their predicates may be said to belong not to the things in themselves, but to their appearances, and to have no proper existence outside our representation. Heat, color, and taste, for instance, are of this kind. Now, if I go farther, and for weighty reasons rank as mere appearances the remaining qualities of bodies also, which are called primary, such as extension, place, and in general space, with all that which belongs to it (impenetrability or materiality, space, etc.) – no one in the least can adduce the reason of its being inadmissible. As little as the man who admits colors not to be properties of the object in itself, but only as modifications of the sense of sight, should on that account be called an idealist, so little can my system be named idealistic, merely because I find that more, nay,

All the properties which constitute the intuition of a body belong merely to its appearance.

The existence of the thing that appears is thereby not destroyed, as in genuine idealism, but it is only shown, that we cannot possibly know it by the senses as it is in itself.

I should be glad to know what my assertions must be in order to avoid all idealism. Undoubtedly, I should say, that the representation of space is not only perfectly conformable to the relation which our sensibility has to objects – that I have said – but that it is quite similar to the object – an assertion in which I can find as little meaning as if I said that the sensation of red has a similarity to the property of vermilion, which in me excites this sensation.

REMARK III

Hence we may at once dismiss an easily foreseen but futile objection, "that by admitting the ideality of space and of time the whole sensible world would be turned into mere sham." At first all philosophical insight into the nature of sensuous cognition was spoiled, by making the sensibility merely a confused mode of representation, according to which we still know things as they are, but without being able to reduce everything in this our representation to a clear consciousness; whereas proof is offered by us that sensibility consists, not in this logical distinction of clearness and obscurity, but in the genetical one of the origin of cognition itself. For sensuous perception represents things not at all as they are, but only the mode in which they affect our senses, and consequently by sensuous perception appearances only and not things themselves are given to the understanding for reflexion. After this necessary corrective, an objection rises from an unpardonable and almost intentional misconception, as if my doctrine turned all the things of the world of sense into mere illusion.

When an appearance is given us, we are still quite free as to how we should judge the matter. The appearance depends upon the senses, but the judgment upon the understanding, and the only question is, whether in the determination of the object there is truth or not. But the difference between truth and dreaming is not ascertained by the nature of the representations, which are referred to objects (for they are the same in both cases), but by their connexion according to those rules, which determine the coherence of the representations in the concept of an object, and by ascertaining whether they can subsist together in experience or not. And it is not the fault of the appearances if our cognition takes illusion for truth, i.e. if the intuition, by which an object is given us, is considered a concept of the thing or of its existence also, which the understanding can only think. The senses represent to us the paths of the planets as now progressive, now retrogressive, and herein is neither falsehood nor truth, because as long as we hold this path to be nothing but appearance, we do not judge of the objective nature of their motion. But as a false judgment may easily arise when the understanding is not on its guard against this subjective mode of representation being considered objective, we say they appear to move backward; it is not the senses however which must be charged with the illusion, but the understanding, whose province alone it is to give an objective judgment on appearances.

Thus, even if we did not at all reflect on the origin of our representations, whenever we connect our intuitions of sense (whatever they may contain), in space and in time, according to the rules of the coherence of all cognition in experience, illusion or truth will arise according as we are negligent or careful. It is merely a question of the use of sensuous representations in the understanding, and not of their origin. In the same way, if I consider all the representations of the senses, together with their form, space and time, to be nothing but appearances, and space and time to be a mere form of the sensibility, which is not to be met with in objects out of it, and if I make use of these representations in reference to possible experience only, there is nothing in my regarding them as appearances that can lead astray or cause illusion. For all that they can correctly cohere according to rules of truth in experience. Thus all the propositions of geometry hold good of space as well as of all the objects of the senses, consequently of all possible experience, whether I consider space as a mere form of the sensibility, or as something cleaving to the things themselves. In the former case however I comprehend how I can know *a priori* these propositions concerning all the objects of external intuition. Otherwise, every-thing else as regards all possible experience remains just as if I had not departed from the vulgar view.

But if I venture to go beyond all possible experience with my notions of space and time, which I cannot refrain from doing if I proclaim them qualities inherent in things in themselves (for what should prevent me from letting them hold good of the same things, even though my senses might be different, and unsuited to them?), then a grave error may arise due to illusion, for thus I would proclaim to be universally valid what is merely a subjective condition of the intuition of things and sure only for all objects of sense, viz., for all possible experience; I would refer this condition to things in themselves, and do not limit it to the conditions of experience.

My doctrine of the ideality of space and of time, therefore, far from reducing the whole sensible world to mere illusion, is the only means of securing the application of one of the most important cognitions (that which mathematics propounds *a priori*) to actual objects, and of preventing its being regarded as mere illusion. For without this observation it would be quite impossible to make out whether the intuitions of space and time, which we borrow from no experience, and which yet lie in our representation *a priori*, are not mere phantasms of our brain, to which objects do not corre-spond, at least not adequately, and consequently, whether we have been able to show its unquestionable validity with regard to all the objects of the sensible world just because they are mere appearances.

Secondly, though these my principles make appearances of the representations of the senses, they are so far from turning the truth of experience into mere illusion, that they are rather the only means of preventing the transcendental illusion, by which metaphys-ics has hitherto been deceived, leading to the childish endeavor of catching at bubbles, because appearances, which are mere represen-tations, were taken for things in themselves. Here originated the remarkable event of the antimony of Reason which I shall mention by and by, and which is destroyed by the single observation, that appearance, as long as it is employed in experience, produces truth, but the moment it transgresses the bounds of experience, and conse-quently becomes transcendent, produces nothing but illusion.

Inasmuch, therefore, as I leave to things as we obtain them by the senses their actuality, and only limit our sensuous intuition of these things to this, that they represent in no respect, not even in the pure intuitions of space and of time, anything more than mere appearance of those things, but never their constitution in themselves, this is not a sweeping illusion invented for nature by me. My protestation too against all charges of idealism is so valid and clear as even to seem superfluous, were there not incompetent judges, who, while they would have an old name for every deviation from their perverse though common opinion, and never judge of the spirit of philosophic nomenclature, but cling to the letter only, are ready to put their own conceits in the place of well-defined notions, and thereby deform and distort them. I have myself given this my theory the name of transcendental idealism, but that cannot authorize anyone to confound it either with the empirical idealism of Descartes (indeed, his was only an insoluble problem, owing to which he thought everyone at liberty to deny the existence of the corporeal world, because it could never be proved satisfactorily), or with the mystical and visionary idealism of Berkeley, against which and other similar phantasms our Critique contains the proper antidote. My idealism concerns not the existence of things (the doubting of which, however, constitutes idealism in the ordinary sense), since it never came into my head to doubt it, but it concerns the sensuous representation of things, to which space and time especially belong. Of these (viz., space and time), consequently of all appearances in general, I have only shown, that they are neither things (but mere modes of representation), nor determinations belonging to things in themselves. But the word "transcendental," which with me means a reference of our cognition, i.e. not to things, but only to the cognitive faculty, was meant to obviate this misconception. Yet rather than give further occasion to it by this word, I now retract it, and desire this idealism of mine to be called critical. But if it be really an objectionable idealism to convert actual things (not appearances) into mere representations, by what name shall we call him who conversely changes mere representations to things? It may, I think, be called "dreaming idealism," in contradistinction to the former, which may be called "visionary," both of which are to be refuted by my transcendental, or, better, critical idealism.

SECOND PART OF THE TRANSCENDENTAL PROBLEM

How is the Science of Nature Possible?

§ 14.   Nature is the existence of things, so far as it is determined according to universal laws. Should nature signify the existence of things in themselves, we could never cognise it either *a priori* or *a posteriori*. Not *a priori*, for how can we know what belongs to things in themselves, since this never can be done by the dissection of our concepts (in analytical judgments)? We do not want to know what is contained in our concept of a thing (for the concept describes what belongs to its logical being), but what is in the actuality of the thing superadded to our concept, and by what the thing itself is determined in its existence outside the concept. Our understanding, and the conditions on which alone it can connect the determinations of things in their existence, do not prescribe any rule to things themselves; these do not conform to our understanding, but it must conform itself to them; they must therefore be first given us in order to gather these determinations from them, wherefore they would not be cognised *a priori*.

A cognition of the nature of things in themselves *a posteriori* would be equally impossible. For, if experience is to teach us laws, to which the existence of things is subject, these laws, if they regard things in themselves, must belong to them of necessity even outside our experience. But experience teaches us what exists and how it exists, but never that it must necessarily exist so and not otherwise. Experience therefore can never teach us the nature of things in themselves.

§ 15.   We nevertheless actually possess a pure science of nature in which are propounded, *a priori* and with all the necessity requisite to apodeictical propositions, laws to which nature is subject. I need only call to witness that propædeutic of natural science which, under the title of the universal Science of Nature, precedes all Physics (which is founded upon empirical principles). In it we have Mathematics applied to appearance, and also merely discursive principles (or those derived from concepts), which constitute the philosophical part of the pure cognition of nature. But there are several things in it, which are not quite pure and independent of empirical sources: such as the concept of *motion*, that of *impenetrability* (upon which the empirical concept of matter rests), that of *inertia*, and many others, which prevent its being called a perfectly pure science of nature. Besides, it only refers to objects of the external sense, and therefore does not give an example of a universal science of nature, in the strict sense, for such a science must reduce nature in general, whether it regards the object of the external or that of the internal sense (the object of Physics as well as Psychology), to universal laws. But among the principles of this universal physics there are a few which actually have the required universality; for instance, the propositions that "substance is permanent," and that "every event is determined by a cause according to constant laws," etc. These are actually universal laws of nature, which subsist completely *a priori*. There is then in fact a pure science of nature, and the question arises, *How is it possible?*

§ 16. The word "nature" assumes yet another meaning, which determines the object, whereas in the former sense it only denotes the conformity to law (*Gesetzmässigkeit*) of the determinations of the existence of things generally. If we consider it *materialiter* (i.e. in the matter that forms its objects) "nature is the complex of all the objects of experience." And with this only are we now concerned, for besides, things which can never be objects of experience, if they must be cognised as to their nature, would oblige us to have recourse to concepts whose meaning could never be given *in concreto* (by any example of possible experience). Consequently we must form for ourselves a list of concepts of their nature, the reality whereof (i.e. whether they actually refer to objects, or are mere creations of thought) could never be determined. The cognition of what cannot be an object of experience would be hyperphysical, and with things hyperphysical we are here not concerned, but only with cognition of nature, the actuality of which can be confirmed by experience, though it (the cognition of nature) is possible *a priori* and precedes all experience.

§ 17. The formal (aspect) of nature in this narrower sense is therefore the conformity to law of all the objects of experience, and so far as it is cognised *a priori*, their necessary conformity. But it has just been shown that the laws of nature can never be cognised *a priori* in objects so far as they are considered not in reference to possible experience, but as things in themselves. And our inquiry here extends not to things in themselves (the properties of which we pass by), but to things as objects of possible experience, and the complex of these is what we properly designate as nature. And now I ask, when the possibility of a cognition of nature *a priori* is in question, whether it is better to arrange the problem thus: How can we cognise *a priori* that things as objects of experience necessarily conform to law? Or thus: How is it possible to cognise *a priori* the necessary conformity to law of experience itself as regards all its objects generally?

Closely considered, the solution of the problem, represented in either way, amounts, with regard to the pure cognition of nature (which is the point of the question at issue), entirely to the same thing. For the subjective laws, under which alone an empirical cognition of things is possible, hold good of these things, as objects of possible experience (not as things in themselves, which are not considered here). Either of the following statements means quite the same:

A judgment of observation can never rank as experience, without the law, that "whenever an event is observed, it is always referred to some antecedent, which it follows according to a universal rule."

"Everything, of which experience teaches that it happens, must have a cause."

It is, however, more commendable to choose the first formula. For we can *a priori* and previous to all given objects have a cognition of those conditions, on which alone experience is possible, but never of the laws to which things may in themselves be subject, without reference to possible experience. We cannot therefore study the nature of things *a priori* otherwise than by investigating the conditions and the universal (though subjective) laws, under which alone such a cognition as experience (as to mere form) is possible, and we determine accordingly the possibility of things, as objects of experience. For if I should choose the second formula, and seek the conditions *a priori*, on which nature as an object of experience is possible, I might easily fall into error, and fancy that I was speaking of nature as a thing in itself, and then move round in endless circles, in a vain search for laws concerning things of which nothing is given me.

Accordingly we shall here be concerned with experience only, and the universal conditions of its possibility which are given *a priori*. Thence we shall determine nature as the whole object of all possible experience. I think it will be understood that I here do not mean the rules of the observation of a nature that is already given, for these already presuppose experience. I do not mean how (through experience) we can study the laws of nature; for these would not then be laws *a priori*, and would yield us no pure science of nature; but (I mean to ask) how the conditions *a priori* of the possibility of experience are at the same time the sources from which all the universal laws of nature must be derived.

§ 18.   In the first place we must state that, while all judgments of experience (*Erfahrungsurtheile*) are empirical (i.e. have their ground in immediate sense-perception), vice versa, all empirical judgments (*empirische Urtheile*) are not judgments of experience, but, besides the empirical, and in general besides what is given to the sensuous intuition, particular concepts must yet be superadded – concepts which have their origin quite *a priori* in the pure understanding, and under which every perception must be first of all subsumed and then by their means changed into experience.[1]

Empirical judgments, so far as they have objective validity, are *judgments of experience*; but those which are only subjectively valid, I name mere *judgments of perception*. The latter require no pure concept of the understanding, but only the logical connexion of perception in a thinking subject. But the former always require, besides the representation of the sensuous intuition, particular *concepts originally begotten in the understanding*, which produce the objective validity of the judgment of experience.

All our judgments are at first merely judgments of perception; they hold good only for us (i.e. for our subject), and we do not till afterwards give them a new reference (to an object), and desire that they shall always hold good for us and in the same way for everybody else; for when a judgment agrees with an object, all judgments concerning the same object must likewise agree among themselves, and thus the objective validity of the judgment of experience signifies nothing else than its necessary universality of application. And conversely when we have reason to consider a judgment necessarily universal (which never depends upon perception, but upon the

---

[1]Empirical judgments (*empirische Urtheile*) are either mere statements of fact, viz., records of a perception, or statements of a natural law, implying a causal connexion between two facts. The former Kant calls "judgments of perception" (*Wahrnehmungsurtheile*), the latter "judgments of experience" (*Erfahrungsurtheile*).-*Ed*.

pure concept of the understanding, under which the perception is subsumed), we must consider it objective also, that is, that it expresses not merely a reference of our perception to a subject, but a quality of the object. For there would be no reason for the judgments of other men necessarily agreeing with mine, if it were not the unity of the object to which they all refer, and with which they accord; hence they must all agree with one another.

§ 19. Therefore objective validity and necessary universality (for everybody) are equivalent terms, and though we do not know the object in itself, yet when we consider a judgment as universal, and also necessary, we understand it to have objective validity. By this judgment we cognise the object (though it remains unknown as it is in itself) by the universal and necessary connexion of the given perceptions. As this is the case with all objects of sense, judgments of experience take their objective validity not from the immediate cognition of the object (which is impossible), but from the condition of universal validity in empirical judgments, which, as already said, never rests upon empirical, or, in short, sensuous conditions, but upon a pure concept of the understanding. The object always remains unknown in itself; but when by the concept of the understanding the connexion of the representations of the object, which are given to our sensibility, is determined as universally valid, the object is determined by this relation, and it is the judgment that is objective.

To illustrate the matter: When we say, "the room is warm, sugar sweet, and wormwood bitter,"[1] – we have only subjectively valid judgments. I do not at all expect that I or any other person shall always find it as I now do; each of these sentences only expresses a relation of two sensations to the same subject, to myself, and that only in my present state of perception; consequently they are not valid of the object. Such are judgments of perception. Judgments of experience are of quite a different nature. What experience teaches me under certain circumstances, it must always teach me and everybody; and its validity is not limited to the subject nor to its state at

---

[1] I freely grant that these examples do not represent such judgments of perception as ever could become judgments of experience, even though a concept of the understanding were superadded, because they refer merely to feeling, which everybody knows to be merely subjective, and which of course can never be attributed to the object, and consequently never become objective. I only wished to give here an example of a judgment that is merely subjectively valid, containing no ground for universal validity, and thereby for a relation to the object. An example of the judgments of perception, which become judgments of experience by superadded concepts of the understanding, will be given in the next note.

a particular time. Hence I pronounce all such judgments as being objectively valid. For instance, when I say the air is elastic, this judgment is as yet a judgment of perception only – I do nothing but refer two of my sensations to one another. But, if I would have it called a judgment of experience, I require this connexion to stand under a condition, which makes it universally valid. I desire therefore that I and everybody else should always connect necessarily the same perceptions under the same circumstances.

§ 20.   We must consequently analyse experience in order to see what is contained in this product of the senses and of the understanding, and how the judgment of experience itself is possible. The foundation is the intuition of which I become conscious, i.e. perception (*perceptio*), which pertains merely to the senses. But in the next place, there are acts of judging (which belong only to the understanding). But this judging may be twofold – first, I may merely compare perceptions and connect them in a particular state of my consciousness; or, secondly, I may connect them in consciousness generally. The former judgment is merely a judgment of perception, and of subjective validity only: it is merely a connexion of perceptions in my mental state, without reference to the object. Hence it is not, as is commonly imagined, enough for experience to compare perceptions and to connect them in consciousness through judgment; there arises no universality and necessity, for which alone judgments can become objectively valid and be called experience.

Quite another judgment therefore is required before perception can become experience. The given intuition must be subsumed under a concept, which determines the form of judging in general relatively to the intuition, connects its empirical consciousness in consciousness generally, and thereby procures universal validity for empirical judgments. A concept of this nature is a pure *a priori* concept of the Understanding, which does nothing but determine for an intuition the general way in which it can be used for judgments. Let the concept be that of cause, then it determines the intuition which is subsumed under it, e.g. that of air, relative to judgments in general, viz., the concept of air serves with regard to its expansion in the relation of antecedent to consequent in a hypothetical judgment. The concept of cause accordingly is a pure concept of the understanding, which is totally disparate from all possible perception, and only serves to determine the representation subsumed under it, relatively to judgments in general, and so to make a universally valid judgment possible.

Before, therefore, a judgment of perception can become a judgment of experience, it is requisite that the perception should be subsumed under some such concept of the understanding; for instance, air ranks under the concept of causes, which determines our judgment about it in regard to its expansion as hypothetical.[1] Thereby the expansion of the air is represented not as merely belonging to the perception of the air in my present state or in several states of mine, or in the state of perception of others, but as belonging to its necessarily. The judgment, "the air is elastic," becomes universally valid, and a judgment of experience, only by certain judgments preceding it, which subsume the intuition of air under the concept of cause and effect: and they thereby determine the perceptions not merely as regards one another in me, but relatively to the form of judging in general, which is here hypothetical, and in this way they render the empirical judgment universally valid.

If all our synthetical judgments are analysed so far as they are objectively valid, it will be found that they never consist of mere intuitions connected only (as is commonly believed) by comparison into a judgment; but that they would be impossible were not a pure concept of the understanding superadded to the concepts abstracted from intuition, under which concept these latter are subsumed, and in this manner only combined into an objectively valid judgment. Even the judgments of pure mathematics in their simplest axioms are not exempt from this condition. The principle, "a straight line is the shortest between two points," presupposes that the line is subsumed under the concept of quantity, which certainly is no mere intuition, but has its seat in the understanding alone, and serves to determine the intuition (of the line) with regard to the judgments which may be made about it, relatively to their quantity, that is, to plurality (as *judicia plurativa*).[2] For under them it is understood that

---

[1] As an easier example, we may take the following: "When the sun shines on the stone, it grows warm." This judgment, however often I and others may have perceived it, is a mere judgment of perception, and contains no necessity; perceptions are only usually conjoined in this manner. But if I say, "The sun warms the stone," I add to the perception a concept of the understanding, viz., that of cause, which connects with the concept of sunshine that of heat as a necessary consequence, and the synthetical judgment becomes of necessity universally valid, viz., objective, and its converted from a perception into experience.

[2] This name seems preferable to the term *particularia*, which is used for these judgments in logic. For the latter implies the idea that they are not universal. But when I start from unity (in single judgments) and so proceed to universality, I must not (even indirectly and negatively) imply any reference to universality. I think plurality merely without universality, and not the exception from universality. This is necessary, if logical considerations shall form the basis of the pure concepts of the understanding. However, there is no need of making changes in logic.

in a given intuition there is contained a plurality of homogenous parts.

§ 21. To prove, then, the possibility of experience so far as it rests upon pure concepts of the understanding *a priori*, we must first represent what belongs to judgments in general and the various functions of the understanding, in a complete table. For the pure concepts of the understanding must run parallel to these functions, as such concepts are nothing more than concepts of intuitions in general, so far as these are determined by one or other of these functions of judging, in themselves, that is, necessarily and universally. Hereby also the *a priori* principles of the possibility of all

Logical Table of Judgments

1	2
As to Quantity	*As to Quality*
Universal	Affirmative
Particular	Negative
Singular	Infinite
3	**4**
As to Relation	*As to Modality*
Categorical	Problematical
Hypothetical	Assertorical
Disjunctive	Apodeictical

Transcendental Table of the Pure Concepts of the Understanding

1	2
As to Quantity	*As to Quality*
Unity (the Measure)	Reality
Plurality (the Quantity)	Negation
Totality (the Whole)	Limitation
3	**4**
As to Relation	*As to Modality*
Substance	Possibility
Cause	Existence
Community	Necessity

Pure Physiological Table of the Universal Principles of the Science of Nature

1	2
Axioms of Intuition	Anticipations of Perception
3	**4**
Analogies of Experience	Postulates of Empirical Thinking generally

experience, as of an objectively valid empirical cognition, will be precisely determined. For they are nothing but propositions by which all perception is (under certain universal conditions of intuition) subsumed under those pure concepts of the understanding.

§ 21*a*. In order to comprise the whole matter in one idea, it is first necessary to remind the reader that we are discussing not the origin of experience, but of that which lies in experience. The former pertains to empirical psychology, and would even then never be adequately explained without the latter, which belongs to the Critique of cognition, and particularly of the understanding.

Experience consists of intuitions, which belong to the sensibility, and of judgments, which are entirely a work of the understanding. But the judgments, which the understanding forms alone from sensuous intuitions, are far from being judgments of experience. For in the one case the judgment connects only the perceptions as they are given in the sensuous intuition, while in the other the judgments must express what experience in general, and not what the mere perception (which possesses only subjective validity) contains. The judgment of experience must therefore add to the sensuous intuition and its logical connexion in a judgment (after it has been rendered universal by comparison) something that determines the synthetical judgment as necessary and therefore as universally valid. This can be nothing else than that concept which represents the intuition as determined in itself with regard to one form of judgment rather than another, viz., a concept of that synthetical unity of intuitions which can only be represented by a given logical function of judgments.

§ 22. The sum of the matter is this: the business of the senses is to intuit – that of the understanding is to think. But thinking is uniting representations in one consciousness. This union originates either merely relative to the subject, and is accidental and subjective, or is absolute, and is necessary or objective. The union of representations in one consciousness is judgment. Thinking therefore is the same as judging, or referring representations to judgments in general. Hence judgments are either merely subjective, when representations are referred to a consciousness in one subject only, and united in it, or objective, when they are united in a consciousness generally, that is, necessarily. The logical functions of all judgments are but various modes of uniting representations in consciousness. But if they serve for concepts, they are concepts of their necessary union in a consciousness, and so principles of objectively valid judgments. This union in a consciousness is either analytical, by identity, or synthetical, by the combination and addition of various representations one to another. Experience consists in the synthetical connexion of phenomena (perceptions) in consciousness, so far as this connexion is necessary. Hence the pure concepts of the understanding are those under which all perceptions must be subsumed ere they can serve for judgments of experience, in which the synthetical unity of the perceptions is represented as necessary and universally valid.[1]

§ 23. Judgments, when considered merely as the condition of the union of given representations in a consciousness, are rules. These rules, so far as they represent the union as necessary, are rules *a priori*, and so far as they cannot be deduced from higher rules, are fundamental principles. But in regard to the possibility of all experience, merely in relation to the form of thinking in it, no conditions of judgments of experience are higher than those which bring the phenomena, according to the various form of their intuition, under pure concepts of the understanding, and render the empirical judgment objectively valid. These concepts are therefore the *a priori* principles of possible experience.

The principles of possible experience are then at the same time universal laws of nature, which can be cognised *a priori*. And thus the problem in our second question, "How is the pure Science of Nature possible?" is solved. For the system which is required for the form of a science is to be met with in perfection here, because, beyond the above-mentioned formal conditions of all judgments in general offered in logic, no others are possible, and these constitute a logical system. The concepts grounded thereupon, which contain the *a priori* conditions of all synthetical and necessary judgments, accordingly constitute a transcendental system. Finally the principles, by means of which all phenomena are subsumed under these

---

[1]But how does this proposition, "that judgments of experience contain necessity in the synthesis of perceptions," agree with my statement so often before inculcated, that "experience as cognition *a posteriori* can afford contingent judgments only?" When I say that experience teaches me something, I mean only the perception that lies in experience – for example, that heat always follows the shining of the sun on a stone; consequently the proposition of experience is always so far accidental. That this heat necessarily follows the shining of the sun is contained indeed in the judgment of experience (by means of the concept of cause), yet is a fact not learned by experience; for conversely, experience is first of all generated by this addition of the concept of the understanding (of cause) to perception. How perception attains this addition may be seen by referring in the *Critique* itself to the section on the Transcendental faculty of Judgment (viz., in the first edition, *Von dem Schematismus der reinen Verstandsbegriffe*).

concepts, constitute a physical[1] system, that is, a system of nature, which precedes all empirical cognition of nature, makes it even possible, and hence may in strictness be denominated the universal and pure science of nature.

§ 24. The first one[2] of the physiological principles subsumes all phenomena, as intuitions in space and time, under the concept of Quantity, and is so far a principle of the application of Mathematics to experience. The second one subsumes the empirical element, viz., sensation, which denotes the real in intuitions, not indeed directly under the concept of quantity, because sensation is not an intuition that contains either space or time, though it places the respective object into both. But still there is between reality (sense-representation) and the zero, or total void of intuition in time, a difference which has a quantity. For between every given degree of light and of darkness, between every degree of heat and of absolute cold, between every degree of weight and of absolute lightness, between every degree of occupied space and of totally void space, diminishing degrees can be conceived, in the same manner as between consciousness and total unconsciousness (the darkness of a psychological blank) ever diminishing degrees obtain. Hence there is no perception that can prove an absolute absence of it; for instance, no psychological darkness that cannot be considered as a kind of consciousness, which is only outbalanced by a stronger consciousness. This occurs in all cases of sensation, and so the understanding can anticipate even sensations, which constitute the peculiar quality of empirical representations (appearances), by means of the principle: "that they all have (consequently that what is real in all phenomena has) a degree." Here is the second application of mathematics (*mathesis intensorum*) to the science of nature.

§ 25. Anent the relation of appearances merely with a view to their existence, the determination is not mathematical but dynamical, and can never be objectively valid, consequently never fit for experience, if it does not come under *a priori* principles by which the cognition of experience relative to appearances becomes even possible. Hence appearances must be subsumed under the concept of

---

[1]Kant uses the term physiological in its etymological meaning as "pertaining to the science of physics," i.e. nature in general, not as we use the term now as "pertaining to the functions of the living body." Accordingly it has been translated "physical."-*Ed.*

[2]The three following paragraphs will hardly be understood unless reference be made to what the *Critique* itself says on the subject of the Principles; they will, however, be of service in giving a general view of the Principles, and in fixing the attention on the main points.

Substance, which is the foundation of all determination of existence, as a concept of the thing itself; or secondly – so far as a succession is found among phenomena, that is, an event – under the concept of an Effect with reference to Cause; or lastly – so far as coexistence is to be known objectively, that is, by a judgment of experience – under the concept of Community (action and reaction).[1] Thus *a priori* principles form the basis of objectively valid, though empirical judgments, that is, of the possibility of experience so far as it must connect objects as existing in nature. These principles are the proper laws of nature, which may be termed dynamical.

Finally the cognition of the agreement and connexion not only of appearances among themselves in experience, but of their relation to experience in general, belongs to the judgments of experience. This relation contains either their agreement with the formal conditions, which the understanding cognises, or their coherence with the materials of the senses and of perception, or combines both into one concept. Consequently it contains Possibility, Actuality, and Necessity according to universal laws of nature; and this constitutes the physical doctrine of method, or the distinction of truth and of hypotheses, and the bounds of the certainty of the latter.

§ 26. The third table of Principles drawn from the nature of the understanding itself after the critical method, shows an inherent perfection, which raises it far above every other table which has hitherto though in vain been tried or may yet be tried by analysing the objects themselves dogmatically. It exhibits all synthetical *a priori* principles completely and according to one principle, viz., the faculty of judging in general, constituting the essence of experience as regards the understanding, so that we can be certain that there are no more such principles, which affords a satisfaction such as can never be attained by the dogmatical method. Yet this is not all: there is a still greater merit in it.

We must carefully bear in mind the proof which shows the possibility of this cognition *a priori*, and at the same time limits all such principles to a condition which must never be lost sight of, if we desire it not to be misunderstood, and extended in use beyond the original sense which the understanding attaches to it. This limit is that they contain nothing but the conditions of possible experience in general so far as it is subjected to laws *a priori*. Consequently I do not say that things *in themselves* possess a quantity, that their

---

[1]Kant uses here the equivocal term *Wechselwirkung.* – Ed.

actuality possesses a degree, their existence a connexion of accidents in a substance, etc. This nobody can prove, because such a synthetical connexion from mere concepts, without any reference to sensuous intuition on the one side, or connexion of it in a possible experience on the other, is absolutely impossible. The essential limitation of the concepts in these principles then is: That all things stand necessarily *a priori* under the aforementioned conditions, as objects of experience only.

Hence there follows secondly a specifically peculiar mode of proof of these principles: they are not directly referred to appearances and to their relations, but to the possibility of experience, of which appearances constitute the matter only, not the form. Thus they are referred to objectively and universally valid synthetical propositions, in which we distinguish judgments of experience from those of perception. This takes place because appearances, as mere intuitions, occupying a part of space and time, come under the concept of Quantity, which unites their multiplicity *a priori* according to rules synthetically. Again, so far as the perception contains, besides intuition, sensibility, and between the latter and nothing (i.e. the total disappearance of sensibility), there is an ever-decreasing transition, it is apparent that that which is in appearances must have a degree, so far as it (viz., the perception) does not itself occupy any part of space or of time.[1] Still the transition to actuality from empty time or empty space is only possible in time; consequently though sensibility, as the quality of empirical intuition, can never be cognised *a priori*, by its specific difference from other sensibilities, yet it can, in a possible experience in general, as a quantity of perception be intensely distinguished from every other similar perception. Hence the application of mathematics to nature, as regards the sensuous intuition by which nature is given to us, becomes possible and is thus determined.

Above all, the reader must pay attention to the mode of proof of the principles which occur under the title of Analogies of experience.

[1]Heat and light are in a small space just as large as to degree as in a large one; in like manner the internal representations, pain, consciousness in general, whether they last a short or a long time, need not vary as to the degree. Hence the quantity is here in a point and in a moment just as great as in any space or time however great. Degrees are therefore capable of increase, but not in intuition, rather in mere sensation (or the quantity of the degree of an intuition). Hence they can only be estimated quantitatively by the relation of 1 to 0, viz., by their capability of decreasing by infinite intermediate degrees to disappearance, or of increasing from naught through infinite gradations to a determinate sensation in a certain time. *Quantitas qualitatis est gradus* (i.e. the degrees of quality must be measured by equality).

For these do not refer to the genesis of intuitions, as do the principles of applied mathematics, but to the connexion of their existence in experience; and this can be nothing but the determination of their existence in time according to necessary laws, under which alone the connexion is objectively valid, and thus becomes experience. The proof therefore does not turn on the synthetical unity in the connexion of things in themselves, but merely of perceptions, and of these not in regard to their matter, but to the determination of time and of the relation of their existence in it, according to universal laws. If the empirical determination in relative time is indeed objectively valid (i.e. experience), these universal laws contain the necessary determination of existence in time generally (viz., according to a rule of the understanding *a priori*).

In these *Prolegomena* I cannot further descant on the subject, but my reader (who has probably been long accustomed to consider experience a mere empirical synthesis of perceptions, and hence not considered that it goes much beyond them, as it imparts to empirical judgments universal validity, and for that purpose requires a pure and *a priori* unity of the understanding) is recommended to pay special attention to this distinction of experience from a mere aggregate of perceptions, and to judge the mode of proof from this point of view.

§ 27.   Now we are prepared to remove Hume's doubt. He justly maintains that we cannot comprehend by reason the possibility of Causality, that is, of the reference of the existence of one thing to the existence of another, which is necessitated by the former. I add that we comprehend just as little the concept of Subsistence, that is, the necessity that at the foundation of the existence of things there lies a subject which cannot itself be a predicate of any other thing; nay, we cannot even form a notion of the possibility of such a thing (though we can point out examples of its use in experience). The very same incomprehensibility affects the Community of things, as we cannot comprehend how from the state of one thing an inference to the state of quite another thing beyond it, and *vice versa*, can be drawn, and how substances which have each their own separate existence should depend upon one another necessarily. But I am very far from holding these concepts to be derived merely from experience, and the necessity represented in them, to be imaginary and a mere illusion produced in us by long habit. On the contrary, I have amply shown that they and the theorems derived from them are firmly established *a priori*, or before all experience, and have their undoubted objective value, though only with regard to experience.

§ 28.   Though I have no notion of such a connexion of things in themselves, that they can either exist as substances, or act as causes, or stand in community with others (as parts of a real whole), and I can just as little conceive such properties in appearances as such (because those concepts contain nothing that lies in the appearances, but only what the understanding alone must think): we have yet a notion of such a connexion of representations in our understanding, and in judgments generally; consisting in this that representations appear in one sort of judgments as subject in relation to predicates, in another as reason in relation to consequences, and in a third as parts, which constitute together a total possible cognition. Besides, we cognise *a priori* that without considering the representation of an object as determined in some of these respects, we can have no valid cognition of the object, and, if we should occupy ourselves about the object in itself, there is no possible attribute, by which I could know that it is determined under any of these aspects, that is, under the concept either of substance, or of cause, or (in relation to other substances) of community, for I have no notion of the possibility of such a connexion of existence. But the question is not how things in themselves, but how the empirical cognition of things is determined, as regards the above aspects of judgments in general, that is, how things, as objects of experience, can and shall be subsumed under these concepts of the understanding. And then it is clear, that I completely comprehend not only the possibility, but also the necessity of subsuming all phenomena under these concepts, that is, of using them for principles of the possibility of experience.

§ 29.   When making an experiment with Hume's problematical concept (his *crux metaphysicorum*), the concept of cause, we have, in the first place, given *a priori*, by means of logic, the form of a conditional judgment in general, i.e. we have one given cognition as antecedent and another as consequence. But it is possible that in perception we may meet with a rule of relation, which runs thus: that a certain phenomenon is constantly followed by another (though not conversely), and this is a case for me to use the hypothetical judgment, and, for instance, to say, if the sun shines long enough upon a body, it grows warm. Here there is indeed as yet no necessity of connexion, or concept of cause. But I proceed and say, that if this proposition, which is merely a subjective connexion of perceptions, is to be a judgment of experience, it must be considered as necessary and universally valid. Such a proposition would be, "the sun is byt its light the cause of heat." The empirical rule is now considered as a law, and as valid not merely of appearances but valid of them for the purposes of a possible experience which requires universal and therefore necessarily valid rules. I therefore easily comprehend the concept of cause, as a concept necessarily belonging to the mere form of experience, and its possibility as a synthetical union of perceptions in consciousness generally; but I do not at all comprehend the possibility of a thing generally as a cause, because the concept of cause denotes a condition not at all belonging to things, but to experience. It is nothing in fact but an objectively valid cognition of appearances and of their succession, so far as the antecedent can be conjoined with the consequent according to the rule of hypothetical judgments.

§ 30.   Hence if the pure concepts of the understanding do not refer to objects of experience but to things in themselves (*noumena*), they have no signification whatever. They serve, as it were, only to decipher appearances, that we may be able to read them as experience. The principles which arise from their reference to the sensible world only serve our understanding for empirical use. Beyond this they are arbitrary combinations, without objective reality, and we can neither cognise their possibility *a priori*, nor verify their reference to objects, let alone make it intelligible by any example; because examples can only be borrowed from some possible experience, consequently the objects of these concepts can be found nowhere but in a possible experience.

This complete (though to its originator unexpected) solution of Hume's problem rescues for the pure concepts of the understanding their *a priori* origin, and for the universal laws of nature their validity, as laws of the understanding, yet in such a way as to limit their use to experience, because their possibility depends solely on the reference of the understanding to experience, but with a completely reversed mode of connexion which never occurred to Hume, not by deriving them from experience, but by deriving experience from them.

This is therefore the result of all our foregoing inquiries: "All synthetical principles *a priori* are nothing more than principles of possible experience, and can never be referred to things in themselves, but to appearances as objects of experience. And hence pure mathematics as well as a pure science of nature can never be referred to anything more than mere appearances, and can only represent either that which makes experience generally possible, or else that which, as it is derived from these principles, must always be capable of being represented in some possible experience."

§ 31.   And thus we have at last something definite, upon which to depend in all metaphysical enterprises, which have hitherto, boldly enough but always at random, attempted everything without discrimination. That the aim of their exertions should be so near struck neither the dogmatical thinkers nor those who, confident in their supposed sound common sense, started with concepts and principles of pure reason (which were legitimate and natural, but destined for mere empirical use) in quest of fields of knowledge, to which they neither knew nor could know any determinate bounds, because they had never reflected nor were able to reflect on the nature or even on the possibility of such a pure understanding.

Many a naturalist of pure reason (by which I mean the man who believes he can decide in matters of metaphysics without any science) may pretend that he long ago by the prophetic spirit of his sound sense, not only suspected, but knew and comprehended, what is here propounded with so much ado, or, if he likes, with prolix and pedantic pomp: "That with all our reason we can never reach beyond the field of experience." But when he is questioned about his rational principles individually, he must grant that there are many of them which he has not taken from experience, and which are therefore independent of it and valid *a priori*. How then and on what grounds will he restrain both himself and the dogmatist, who makes use of these concepts and principles beyond all possible experience, because they are recognised to be independent of it? And even he, this adept in sound sense, in spite of all his assumed and cheaply acquired wisdom, is not exempt from wandering inadvertently beyond objects of experience into the field of chimeras. He is often deeply enough involved in them, though in announcing everything as mere probability, rational conjecture, or analogy, he gives by his popular language a color to his groundless pretensions.

§ 32.   Since the oldest days of philosophy inquirers into pure reason have conceived, besides the things of sense, or appearances (phenomena), which make up the sensible world, certain creations of the understanding (*verstandeswesen*), called noumena, which should constitute an intelligible world. And as appearance and illusion were by those men identified (a thing which we may well excuse in an undeveloped epoch), actuality was only conceded to the creations of thought.

And we indeed, rightly considering objects of sense as mere appearances, confess thereby that they are based upon a thing in itself, though we know not this thing in its internal constitution, but only know its appearances, viz., the way in which our senses are affected by this unknown something. The understanding therefore, by assuming appearances, grants the existence of things in themselves also, and so far we may say, that the representation of such things as form the basis of phenomena, consequently of mere creations of the understanding, is not only admissible, but unavoidable.

Our critical deduction by no means excludes things of that sort (noumena), but rather limits the principles of the Aesthetic (the science of the sensibility) to this, that they shall not extend to all things, as everything would then be turned into mere appearance, but that they shall only hold good of objects of possible experience. Hereby then objects of the understanding are granted, but with the inculcation of this rule which admits of no exception: "that we neither know nor can know anything at all definite of these pure objects of the understanding, because our pure concepts of the understanding as well as our pure intuitions extend to nothing but objects of possible experience, consequently to mere things of sense, and as soon as we leave this sphere these concepts retain no meaning whatever."

§ 33.   There is indeed something seductive in our pure concepts of the understanding, which tempts us to a transcendent use – a use which transcends all possible experience. Not only are our concepts of substance, of power, of action, of reality, and others, quite independent of experience, containing nothing of sense appearance, and so apparently applicable to things in themselves (noumena), but what strengthens this conjecture, they contain a necessity of determination in themselves, which experience never attains. The concept of cause implies a rule, according to which one state follows another necessarily; but experience can only show us that one state of things often, or at most, commonly, follows another, and therefore affords neither strict universality nor necessity.

Hence the Categories seem to have a deeper meaning and import than can be exhausted by their empirical use, and so the understanding inadvertently adds for itself to the house of experience a much more extensive wing, which it fills with nothing but creatures of thought, without ever observing that it has transgressed with its otherwise lawful concepts the bounds of their use.

§ 34. Two important, and even indispensable though very dry, investigations had therefore become indispensable in the *Critique of Pure Reason* – viz., the two chapters "Vom Schematismus der reinen Verstandsbegriffe," and "Vom Grunde der Unterscheidung aller Verstandesbegriffe überhaupt in Phänomena und Noumena." In the former it is shown that the senses furnish not the pure concepts of the understanding *in concreto*, but only the schedule for their use, and that the object conformable to it occurs only in experience (as the product of the understanding from materials of the sensibility). In the latter it is shown that, although our pure concepts of the understanding and our principles are independent of experience, and despite the apparently greater sphere of their use, still nothing whatever can be thought by them beyond the field of experience, because they can do nothing but merely determine the logical form of the judgment relatively to given intuitions. But as there is no intuition at all beyond the field of the sensibility, these pure concepts, as they cannot possibly be exhibited *in concreto*, are void of all meaning; consequently all these noumena, together with their complex, the intelligible world,[1] are nothing but a representation of a problem, of which the object in itself is possible, but the solution, from the nature of our understanding, totally impossible. For our understanding is not a faculty of intuition, but of the connexion of given intuitions in experience. Experience must therefore contain all the objects for our concepts; but beyond it no concepts have any significance, as there is no intuition that might offer them a foundation.

§ 35. The imagination may perhaps be forgiven for occasional vagaries, and for not keeping carefully within the limits of experience, since it gains life and vigor by such flights, and since it is always easier to moderate its boldness than to stimulate its languor. But the understanding which ought to *think* can never be forgiven for indulging in vagaries; for we depend upon it alone for assistance to set bounds, when necessary, to the vagaries of the imagination.

---

[1] We speak of the "intelligible world" not (as the usual expression is) "intellectual world." For cognitions are intellectual through the understanding, and refer to our world of sense also; but objects, so far as they can be represented merely by the understanding, and to which none of our sensible intuitions can refer, are termed "intelligible." But as some possible intuition must correspond to every object, we would have to assume an understanding that intuits things immediately; but of such we have not the least notion, nor have we of the *things of the understanding* (*verstandeswesen*), to which it should be applied.

But the understanding begins its aberrations very innocently and modestly. It first elucidates the elementary cognitions, which inhere in it prior to all experience, but yet must always have their application in experience. It gradually drops these limits, and what is there to prevent it, as it has quite freely derived its principles from itself? And then it proceeds first to newly imagined powers in nature, then to beings outside nature; in short to a world, for whose construction the materials cannot be wanting, because fertile fiction furnishes them abundantly, and though not confirmed, is never refuted, by experience. This is the reason that young thinkers are so partial to metaphysics of the truly dogmatical kind, and often sacrifice to it their time and their talents which might be otherwise better employed.

But there is no use in trying to moderate these fruitless endeavors of pure reason by all manner of cautions as to the difficulties of solving questions so occult, by complaints of the limits of our reason, and by degrading our assertions into mere conjectures. For if their impossibility is not distinctly shown, and reason's cognition of its own essence does not become a true science, in which the field of its right use is distinguished, so to say, with mathematical certainty from that of its worthless and idle use, these fruitless efforts will never be abandoned for good.

§ 36. *How is Nature itself possible?*

This question – the highest point that transcendental philosophy can ever reach, and to which, as its boundary and completion, it must proceed – properly contains two questions.

First: How is nature at all possible in the material sense, by intuition, considered as the totality of appearances; how are space, time, and that which fills both – the object of sensation, in general possible? The answer is: By means of the constitution of our sensibility, according to which it is specifically affected by objects, which are in themselves unknown to it, and totally distinct from those phenomena. This answer is given in the *Critique* itself in the transcendental aesthetic, and in these *Prolegomena* by the solution of the first general problem.

Secondly: How is nature possible in the formal sense, as the totality of the rules, under which all phenomena must come, in order to be thought as connected in experience? The answer must be this: It is only possible by means of the constitution of our

Understanding, according to which all the above representations of the sensibility are necessarily referred to a consciousness, and by which the peculiar way in which we think (viz., by rules), and hence experience also, are possible, but must be clearly distinguished from an insight into the objects in themselves. This answer is given in the *Critique* itself in the transcendental Logic, and in these *Prolegomena*, in the course of the solution of the second main problem.

But how this peculiar property of our sensibility itself is possible, or that of our understanding and of the apperception which is necessarily its basis and that of all thinking, cannot be further analysed or answered, because it is of them that we are in need for all our answers and for all our thinking about objects.

There are many laws of nature which we can only know by means of experience; but conformity to law in the connexion of appearances, i.e. in nature in general, we cannot discover by any experience, because experience itself requires laws which are *a priori* at the basis of its possibility.

The possibility of experience in general is therefore at the same time the universal law of nature, and the principles of the experience are the very laws of nature. For we do not know nature but as the totality of appearances, i.e. of representations in us, and hence we can only derive the laws of its connexion from the principles of their connexion in us, that is, from the conditions of their necessary union in consciousness, which constitutes the possibility of experience.

Even the main proposition expounded throughout this section – that universal laws of nature can be distinctly cognised *a priori* – leads naturally to the proposition: that the highest legislation of nature must lie in ourselves, i.e. in our understanding, and that we must not seek the universal laws of nature in nature by means of experience, but conversely must seek nature, as to its universal conformity to law, in the conditions of the possibility of experience, which lie in our sensibility and in our understanding. For how were it otherwise possible to know *a priori* these laws, as they are not rules of analytical cognition, but truly synthetical extensions of it?

Such a necessary agreement of the principles of possible experience with the laws of the possibility of nature, can only proceed from one of two reasons: either these laws are drawn from nature by means of experience, or conversely nature is derived from the laws of the possibility of experience in general, and is quite the same as the mere universal conformity to law of the latter. The former is self-contradictory, for the universal laws of nature can and must be cognised *a priori* (that is, independent of all experience), and be the foundation of all empirical use of the understanding; the latter alternative therefore alone remains.[1]

But we must distinguish the empirical laws of nature, which always presuppose particular perceptions, from the pure or universal laws of nature, which, without being based on particular perceptions, contain merely the conditions of their necessary union in experience. In relation to the latter, nature and possible experience are quite the same, and as the conformity to law here depends upon the necessary connexion of appearances in experience (without which we cannot cognise any object whatever in the sensible world), consequently upon the original laws of the understanding, it seems at first strange, but is not the less certain, to say:

The understanding does not derive its laws (a priori) from, but prescribes them to, nature.

§ 37. We shall illustrate this seemingly bold proposition by an example, which will show that laws, which we discover in objects of sensuous intuition (especially when these laws are cognised as necessary), are commonly held by us to be such as have been placed there by the understanding, in spite of their being similar in all points to the laws of nature, which we ascribe to experience.

§ 38. If we consider the properties of the circle, by which this figure combines so many arbitrary determinations of space in itself, at once in a universal rule, we cannot avoid attributing a constitution (*eine Natur*) to this geometrical thing. Two right lines, for example, which intersect one another and the circle, howsoever they may be drawn, are always divided so that the rectangle constructed with the segments of the one is equal to that constructed with the segments of the other. The question now is: Does this law lie in the circle or in the understanding, that is, Does this figure, independently of the understanding, contain in itself the ground of the law, or does the understanding, having constructed according to its concepts (according to the quality of the radii) the figure itself, introduce into it this law of the chords cutting one another in geometrical proportion? When we follow the proofs of this law, we soon perceive

---

[1]Crusius alone thought of a compromise: that a Spirit, who can neither err nor deceive, implanted these laws in us originally. But since false principles often intrude themselves, as indeed the very system of this man shows in not a few examples, we are involved in difficulties as to the use of such a principle in the absence of sure criteria to distinguish the genuine origin from the spurious, as we never can know certainly what the Spirit of truth or the father of lies may have instilled into us.

that it can only be derived from the condition on which the understanding founds the construction of this figure, and which is that of the equality of the radii. But, if we enlarge this concept, to pursue further the unity of various properties of geometrical figures under common laws, and consider the circle as a conic section, which of course is subject to the same fundamental conditions of construction as other conic sections, we shall find that all the chords which intersect within the ellipse, parabola, and hyperbola, always intersect so that the rectangles of their segments are not indeed equal, but always bear a constant ratio to one another. If we proceed still farther, to the fundamental laws of physical astronomy, we find a physical law of reciprocal attraction diffused over all material nature, the rule of which is: "that it decreases inversely as the square of the distance from each attracting point, i.e. as the spherical surfaces increase, over which this force spreads," which law seems to be necessarily inherent in the very nature of things, and hence is usually propounded as cognizable *a priori*. Simple as the sources of this law are, merely resting upon the relation of spherical surfaces of different radii, its consequences are so valuable with regard to the variety of their agreement and its regularity that not only are all possible orbits of the celestial bodies conic sections, but such a relation of these orbits to each other results, that no other law of attraction, than that of the inverse square of the distance, can be imagined as fit for a cosmical system.

Here accordingly is a nature that rests upon laws which the understanding cognises *a priori*, and chiefly from the universal principles of the determination of space. Now I ask:

Do the laws of nature lie in space, and does the understanding learn them by merely endeavoring to find out the enormous wealth of meaning that lies in space; or do they inhere in the understanding and in the way in which it determines space according to the conditions of the synthetical unity in which its concepts are all centred?

Space is something so uniform and as to all particular properties so indeterminate, that we should certainly not seek a store of laws of nature in it. Whereas that which determines space to assume the form of a circle or the figures of a cone and a sphere, is the understanding, so far as it contains the ground of the unity of their constructions.

The mere universal form of intuition, called space, must therefore be the substratum of all intuitions determinable to particular objects, and in it of course the condition of the possibility and of the variety of these intuitions lies. But the unity of the objects is entirely determined by the understanding, and on conditions which lie in its own nature; and thus the understanding is the origin of the universal order of nature, in that it comprehends all appearances under its own laws, and thereby first constructs, *a priori*, experience (as to its form), by means of which whatever is to be cognised only by experience, is necessarily subjected to its laws. For we are not now concerned with the nature of things in themselves, which is independent of the conditions both of our sensibility and our understanding, but with nature, as an object of possible experience, and in this case the understanding, whilst it makes experience possible, thereby insists that the sensuous world is either not an object of experience at all, or must be nature (viz., an existence of things, determined according to universal laws[1]).

APPENDIX TO THE PURE SCIENCE OF NATURE

§ 39. *Of the System of the Categories*

There can be nothing more desirable to a philosopher than to be able to derive the scattered multiplicity of the concepts or the principles, which had occurred to him in concrete use, from a principle *a priori*, and to unite everything in this way in one cognition. He formerly only believed that those things, which remained after a certain abstraction, and seemed by comparison among one another to constitute a particular kind of cognition, were completely collected; but this was only an aggregate. Now he knows that just so many, neither more nor less, can constitute the mode of cognition, and perceives the necessity of his division, which constitutes comprehension; and now only he has attained a *System*.

To search in our daily cognition for the concepts, which do not rest upon particular experience, and yet occur in all cognition of experience, where they as it were constitute the mere form of connexion, presupposes neither greater reflexion nor deeper insight, than to detect in a language the rules of the actual use of words generally, and thus to collect elements for a grammar. In fact both researches are very nearly related, even though we are not able to give a reason why each language has just this and no other formal

[1]The definition of nature is given in the beginning of the Second Part of the "Transcendental problem," in § 14.

constitution, and still less why an exact number of such formal determinations in general are found in it.

Aristotle collected ten pure elementary concepts under the name of Categories.[1] To these, which are also called predicaments, he found himself obliged afterwards to add five post-predicaments,[2] some of which however (*prius, simul,* and *motus*) are contained in the former; but this random collection must be considered (and commended) as a mere hint for future inquirers, not as a regularly developed idea, and hence it has, in the present more advanced state of philosophy, been rejected as quite useless.

After long reflexion on the pure elements of human knowledge (those which contain nothing empirical), I at last succeeded in distinguishing with certainty and in separating the pure elementary notions of the Sensibility (space and time) from those of the Understanding. Thus the seventh, eighth, and ninth Categories had to be excluded from the old list. And the others were of no service to me; because there was no principle (in them), on which the understanding could be investigated, measured in its completion, and all the functions, whence its pure concepts arise, determined exhaustively and with precision.

But in order to discover such a principle, I looked about for an act of the understanding which comprises all the rest, and is distinguished only by various modifications or phases, in reducing the multiplicity of representation to the unity of thinking in general: I found this act of the understanding to consist in judging. Here then the labors of the logicians were ready at hand, though not yet quite free from defects, and with this help I was enabled to exhibit a complete table of the pure functions of the understanding, which are however undetermined in regard to any object. I finally referred these functions of judging to objects in general, or rather to the condition of determining judgments as objectively valid, and so there arose the pure concepts of the understanding, concerning which I could make certain that these, and this exact number only, constitute our whole cognition of things from pure understanding. I was justified in calling them by their old name, *Categories,* while I reserved for myself the liberty of adding, under the title of "Predicables," a complete list of all the concepts deducible from them, by combinations whether among themselves or with the pure form of the

[1] 1. *Substantia.* 2. *Qualitas.* 3. *Quantitas.* 4. *Relatio.* 5. *Actio.* 6. *Passio.* 7. *Quando.* 8. *Ubi.* 9. *Situs.* 10. *Habitus.*

[2] *Oppositum. Prius. Simul. Motus. Habere.*

appearance, i.e. space or time, or with its matter, so far as it is not yet empirically determined (viz., the object of sensation in general), as soon as a system of transcendental philosophy should be completed with the construction of which I am engaged in the *Critique of Pure Reason* itself.

Now the essential point in this system of Categories, which distinguishes it from the old rhapsodical collection without any principle, and for which alone it deserves to be considered as philosophy, consists in this: that by means of it the true significance of the pure concepts of the understanding and the condition of their use could be precisely determined. For here it became obvious that they are themselves nothing but logical functions, and as such do not produce the least concept of an object, but require some sensuous intuition as a basis. They therefore only serve to determine empirical judgments, which are otherwise undetermined and indifferent as regards all functions of judging, relatively to these functions, thereby procuring them universal validity, and by means of them making judgments of experience in general possible.

Such an insight into the nature of the categories, which limits them at the same time to the mere use of experience, never occurred either to their first author, or to any of his successors; but without this insight (which immediately depends upon their derivation or deduction), they are quite useless and only a miserable list of names, without explanation or rule for their use. Had the ancients ever conceived such a notion, doubtless the whole study of the pure rational knowledge, which under the name of metaphysics has for centuries spoiled many a sound mind, would have reached us in quite another shape, and would have enlightened the human understanding, instead of actually exhausting it in obscure and vain speculations, thereby rendering it unfit for true science.

This system of categories makes all treatment of every object of pure reason itself systematic, and affords a direction or clue how and through what points of inquiry every metaphysical consideration must proceed in order to be complete; for its exhausts all the possible movements (*momenta*) of the understanding, among which every concept must be classed. In like manner the table of Principles has been formulated, the completeness of which we can only vouch for by the system of the categories. Even in the division of the concepts,[1] which must go beyond the physical application of the understanding,

[1]See the two tables in the chapters *Von den Paralogismen der reinen Vernunft* and the first division of the Antinomy of Pure Reason, *System der kosmologisten Ideen.*

it is always the very same clue, which, as it must always be determined *a priori* by the same fixed points of the human understanding, always forms a closed circle. There is no doubt that the object of a pure conception either of the understanding or of reason, so far as it is to be estimated philosophically and on *a priori* principles, can in this way be completely cognised. I could not therefore omit to make use of this clue with regard to one of the most abstract ontological divisions, viz., the various distinctions of "the notions of something and of nothing," and to construct accordingly (*Critique*, p. 207) a regular and necessary table of their divisions.[1]

And this system, like every other true one founded on a universal principle, shows its inestimable value in this, that it excludes all foreign concepts, which might otherwise intrude among the pure concepts of the understanding, and determines the place of every cognition. Those concepts, which under the name of "concepts of reflexion" have been likewise arranged in a table according to the clue of the categories, intrude, without having any privilege or title to be among the pure concepts of the understanding in Ontology. They are concepts of connexion, and thereby of the objects themselves, whereas the former are only concepts of a mere comparison of concepts already given, hence of quite another nature and use. By my systematic division[2] they are saved from this confusion. But the value of my special table of the categories will be still more obvious, when we separate the table of the transcendental concepts of Reason from the concepts of the understanding. The latter being of quite another nature and origin, they must have quite another form than the former. This so necessary separation has never

---

[1] On the table of the categories many neat observations may be made, for instance: (1) that the third arises from the first and the second joined in one concept; (2) that in those of Quantity and of Quality there is merely a progress from unity to totality or from something to nothing (for this purpose the categories of Quality must stand thus: reality, limitation, total negation), without *correlata* or *opposita*, whereas those of Relation and of Modality have them; (3) that, as in *Logic* categorical judgments are the basis of all others, so the category of Substance is the basis of all concepts of actual things; (4) that as Modality in the judgment is not a particular predicate, so by the modal concepts a determination is not superadded to things, etc., etc. Such observations are of great use. If we besides enumerate all the predicables, which we can find pretty completely in any good ontology (for example, Baumgarten's), and arrange them in classes under the categories, in which operation we must not neglect to add as complete a dissection of all these concepts as possible, there will then arise a merely analytical part of metaphysics, which does not contain a single synthetical proposition, which might precede the second (the synthetical), and would by its precision and completeness be not only useful, but, in virtue of its system, be even to some extent elegant.

[2] See *Critique of Pure Reason, Von der Amphibolie der Reflexbegriffe.*

yet been made in any system of metaphysics for, as a rule, these rational concepts all mixed up with the categories, like children of one family, which confusion was unavoidable in the absence of a definite system of categories.

THIRD PART OF THE MAIN TRANSCENDENTAL PROBLEM

How is Metaphysics in General Possible?

§ 40.   Pure mathematics and pure science of nature had no occasion for such a deduction, as we have made of both, for their own safety and certainty. For the former rests upon its own evidence; and the latter (though sprung from pure sources of the understanding) upon experience and its thorough confirmation. Physics cannot altogether refuse and dispense with the testimony of the latter; because with all its certainty, it can never, as philosophy, rival mathematics. Both sciences therefore stood in need of this inquiry, not for themselves, but for the sake of another science, metaphysics.

Metaphysics has to do not only with concepts of nature, which always find their application in experience, but also with pure rational concepts, which never can be given in any possible experience. Consequently the objective reality of these concepts (viz., that they are not mere chimeras), and the truth or falsity of metaphysical assertions, cannot be discovered or confirmed by any experience. This part of metaphysics however is precisely what constitutes its essential end, to which the rest is only a means, and thus this science is in need of such a deduction for its own sake. The third question now proposed relates therefore as it were to the root and essential difference of metaphysics, i.e. the occupation of Reason with itself, and the supposed knowledge of objects arising immediately from this incubation of its own concepts, without requiring, or indeed being able to reach that knowledge through, experience.[1]

[1]If we can say that a science is actual at least in the idea of all men, as soon as it appears that the problems which lead to it are proposed to everybody by the nature of human reason, and that therefore many (though faulty) endeavors are unavoidably made in its behalf, then we are bound to say that metaphysics is subjectively (and indeed necessarily) actual, and therefore we justly ask, how is it (objectively) possible?

90

Without solving this problem, reason never is justified. The empirical use to which reason limits the pure understanding does not fully satisfy the proper destination of the latter. Every single experience is only a part of the whole sphere of its domain, but the absolute totality of all possible experience is itself not experience. Yet it is a necessary (concrete) problem for reason, the mere representation of which requires concepts quite different from the categories, whose use is only immanent, or refers to experience, so far as it can be given. Whereas the concepts of reason aim at the completeness, i.e. the collective unity of all possible experience, and thereby transcend every given experience. Thus they become *transcendent*.

As the understanding stands in need of categories for experience, reason contains in itself the source of ideas, by which I mean necessary concepts, whose object cannot be given in any experience. The latter are inherent in the nature of reason, as the former are in that of the understanding. While the former carry with them an illusion likely to mislead, the illusion of the latter is inevitable, though it certainly can be kept from misleading us.

Since all illusion consists in holding the subjective ground of our judgments to be objective, a self-knowledge of pure reason in its transcendent (exaggerated) use is the sole preservative from the aberrations into which reason falls when it mistakes its destination, and refers that to the object transcendently, which only regards its own subject and its guidance in all immanent use.

§ 41.   The distinction of ideas, that is, of pure concepts of reason, from categories, or pure concepts of the understanding, as cognitions of a quite distinct species, origin and use, is so important a point in founding a science which is to contain the system of all these *a priori* cognitions, that without this distinction metaphysics is absolutely impossible, or is at best a random, bungling attempt to build a castle in the air without a knowledge of the materials or of their fitness for any purpose. Had the *Critique of Pure Reason*, done nothing but first point out this distinction, it had thereby contributed more to clear up our conception of, and to guide our inquiry in, the field of metaphysics than all the vain efforts which have hitherto been made to satisfy the transcendent problems of pure reason, without ever surmising that we were in quite another field than that of the understanding, and hence classing concepts of the understanding and those of reason together, as if they were of the same kind.

§ 42.   All pure cognitions of the understanding have this feature, that their concepts present themselves in experience, and their principles can be confirmed by it; whereas the transcendent cognitions of reason cannot, either as ideas, appear in experience, or as propositions ever be confirmed or refuted by it. Hence whatever errors may slip in unawares can only be discovered by pure reason itself – a discovery of much difficulty, because this very reason naturally becomes dialectical by means of its ideas, and this unavoidable illusion cannot be limited by any objective and dogmatical researches into things, but by a subjective investigation of reason itself as a source of ideas.

§ 43. In the *Critique of Pure Reason* it was always my greatest care to endeavor not only carefully to distinguish the several species of cognition, but to derive concepts belonging to each one of them from their common source. I did this in order that by knowing whence they originated, I might determine their use with safety, and also have the unanticipated but invaluable advantage of knowing the completeness of my enumeration, classification and specification of concepts *a priori*, and therefore according to principles. Without this, metaphysics is mere rhapsody, in which no one knows whether he has enough, or whether and where something is still wanting. We can indeed have this advantage only in pure philosophy, but of this philosophy it constitutes the very essence.

As I had found the origin of the categories in the four logical functions of all the judgments of the understanding, it was quite natural to seek the origin of the ideas in the three functions of the syllogisms of reason. For as soon as these pure concepts of reason (the transcendental ideas) are given, they could hardly, except they be held innate, be found anywhere else, than in the same activity of reason, which, so far as it regards mere form, constitutes the logical element of the syllogisms of reason; but, so far as it represents judgments of the understanding with respect to the one or to the other form *a priori*, constitutes transcendental concepts of pure reason.

The formal distinction of syllogisms renders their division into categorical, hypothetical, and disjunctive necessary. The concepts of reason founded on them contained therefore, first, the idea of the complete subject (the substantial); secondly, the idea of the complete series of conditions; thirdly, the determination of all concepts in the idea of a complete complex of that which is possible.[1] The first idea

---

[1]In disjunctive judgments we consider all possibility as divided in respect to a particular concept. By the ontological principle of the universal determination of a thing in general, I understand the principle that either the one or the other of all possible contradictory

is psychological, the second cosmological, the third theological, and, as all three give occasion to Dialectics, yet each in its own way, the division of the whole Dialects of pure reason into its Paralogism, its Antinomy, and its Ideal, was arranged accordingly. Through this deduction we may feel assured that all the claims of pure reason are completely represented, and that none can be wanting; because the faculty of reason itself, whence they all take their origin, is thereby completely surveyed.

§ 44. In these general considerations it is also remarkable that the ideas of reason are unlike the categories, of no service to the use of our understanding in experience, but quite dispensable, and become even an impediment to the maxims of a rational cognition of nature. Yet in another aspect still to be determined they are necessary. Whether the soul is or is not a simple substance is of no consequence to us in the explanation of its phenomena. For we cannot render the notion of a simple being intelligible by any possible experience that is sensuous or concrete. The notion is therefore quite void as regards all hoped-for insight into the cause of phenomena, and cannot at all serve as a principle of the explanation of that which internal or external experience supplies. So the cosmological ideas of the beginning of the world or of its eternity (*a parte ante*) cannot be of any greater service to us for the explanation of any event in the world itself. And finally we must, according to a right maxim of the philosophy of nature, refrain from all explanations of the design of nature, drawn from the will of a Supreme Being; because this would not be natural philosophy, but an acknowledgment that we have come to the end of it. The use of these ideas, therefore, is quite different from that of those categories by which (and by the principles built upon which) experience itself first becomes possible. But our laborious analytics of the understanding would be superfluous if we had nothing else in view than the mere cognition of nature as it can be given in experience; for reason does its work, both in mathematics and in the science of nature, quite safely and well without any of this subtle deduction. Therefore our Critique of the Understanding combines with the ideas of pure

predicates must be assigned to any object. This is at the same time the principle of all disjunctive judgments, constituting the foundation of our conception of possibility, and in it the possibility of every object in general is considered as determined. This may serve as a slight explanation of the above proposition: that the activity of reason in disjunctive syllogisms is formally the same as that by which it fashions the idea of a universal conception of all reality, containing in itself that which is positive in all contradictory predicates.

reason for a purpose which lies beyond the empirical use of the understanding; but this we have above declared to be in this aspect totally inadmissible, and without any object or meaning. Yet there must be a harmony between that of the nature of reason and that of the understanding, and the former must contribute to the perfection of the latter, and cannot possibly upset it.

The solution of this question is as follows: pure reason does not in its ideas point to particular objects, which lie beyond the field of experience, but only requires completeness of the use of the understanding in the system of experience. But this completeness can be a completeness of principles only, not of intuitions (i.e. concrete atsights or *Anschauungen*) and of objects. In order however to represent the ideas definitely, reason conceives them after the fashion of the cognition of an object. The cognition is, as far as these rules are concerned, completely determined, but the object is only an idea invented for the purpose of bringing the cognition of the understanding as near as possible to the completeness represented by that idea.

Prefatory Remarks to the Dialectics of Pure Reason

§ 45. We have above shown in §§ 33 and 34 that the purity of the categories from all admixture of sensuous determinations may mislead reason into extending their use, quite beyond all experience, to things in themselves; though as these categories themselves find no intuition which can give them meaning or sense *in concreto*, they, as mere logical functions, can represent a thing in general, but not give by themselves alone a determinate concept of anything. Such hyperbolical objects are distinguished by the appellation of *Noümena*, or pure beings of the understanding (or better, beings of thought), such as, for example, "substance," but conceived without permanence in time, or "cause," but not acting in time, etc. Here predicates, that only serve to make the conformity-to-law of experience possible, are applied to these concepts, and yet they are deprived of all the conditions of intuition, on which alone experience is possible, and so these concepts lose all significance.

There is no danger, however, of the understanding spontaneously making an excursion so very wantonly beyond its own bounds into the field of the mere creatures of thought, without being impelled by foreign laws. But when reason, which cannot be fully satisfied with any empirical use of the rules of the understanding, as being always conditioned, requires a completion of this chain of conditions, then the understanding is forced out of its sphere. And then it partly represents objects of experience in a series so extended that no experience can grasp, partly even (with a view to complete the series) it seeks entirely beyond it noumena, to which it can attach that chain, and so, having at last escaped from the conditions of experience, make its attitude as it were final. These are then the transcendental ideas, which, though according to the true but hidden ends of the natural determination of our reason, they may aim not at extravagant concepts, but at an unbounded extension of their empirical use, yet seduce the understanding by an unavoidable illusion to a transcendent use, which, though deceitful, cannot be restrained within the bounds of experience by any resolution, but only by scientific instruction and with much difficulty.

I *The Psychological Idea*[1]

§ 46. People have long since observed that in all substances the proper subject, that which remains after all the accidents (as predicates) are abstracted, consequently that which forms the substance of things remains unknown, and various complaints have been made concerning these limits to our knowledge. But it will be well to consider that the human understanding is not to be blamed for its inability to know the substance of things, that is, to determine it by itself, but rather for requiring to cognise it which is a mere idea definitely as though it were a given object. Pure reason requires us to seek for every predicate of a thing its proper subject, and for this subject, which is itself necessarily nothing but a predicate, its subject, and so on indefinitely (or as far as we can reach). But hence it follows that we must not hold anything, at which we can arrive, to be an ultimate subject, and that substance itself never can be thought by our understanding, however deep we may penetrate, even if all nature were unveiled to us. For the specific nature of our understanding consists in thinking everything discursively, that is, representing it by concepts, and so by mere predicates, to which therefore the absolute subject must always be wanting. Hence all the real properties, by which we cognise bodies, are mere accidents, not excepting impenetrability, which we can only represent to ourselves as the effect of a power of which the subject is unknown to us.

[1]See *Critique of Pure Reason, Von den Paralogismen der reinen Vernunft.*

Now we appear to have this substance in the consciousness of ourselves (in the thinking subject), and indeed in an immediate intuition; for all the predicates of an internal sense refer to the *ego*, as a subject, and I cannot conceive myself as the predicate of any other subject. Hence completeness in the reference of the given concepts as predicates to a subject – not merely an idea, but an object – that is, the absolute subject itself, seems to be given in experience. But this expectation is disappointed. For the ego is not a concept,[1] but only the indication of the object of the internal sense, so far as we cognise it by no further predicate. Consequently it cannot be in itself a predicate of any other thing; but just as little can it be a determinate concept of an absolute subject, but is, as in all other cases, only the reference of the internal phenomena to their unknown subject. Yet this idea (which serves very well, as a regulative principle, totally to destroy all materialistic explanations of the internal phenomena of the soul) occasions by a very natural misunderstanding a very specious argument, which, from this supposed cognition of the substance of our thinking being, infers its nature, so far as the knowledge of it falls quite without the complex of experience.

§ 47. But though we may call this thinking self (the soul) substance, as being the ultimate subject of thinking which cannot be further represented as the predicate of another thing; it remains quite empty and without significance, if permanence – the quality which renders the concept of substances in experience fruitful – cannot be proved of it.

But permanence can never be proved of the concept of a substance, as a thing in itself, but for the purposes of experience only. This is sufficiently shown by the first Analogy of Experience,[2] and whoever will not yield to this proof may try for himself whether he can succeed in proving, from the concept of a subject which does not exist itself as the predicate of another thing, that its existence is thoroughly permanent, and that it cannot either in itself or by any natural cause originate or be annihilated. These synthetical *a priori* propositions can never be proved in themselves, but only in reference to things as objects of possible experience.

[1] Were the representation of the apperception (the Ego) a concept, by which anything could be thought, it could be used as a predicate of other things or contain predicates in itself. But it nothing more than the feeling of an existence without the least definite conception and is only the representation of that to which all thinking stands in relation (*relatione accidentis*).

[2] Cf. *Critique, Von den Analogien der Erfahrung.*

§ 48.   If therefore from the concept of the soul as a substance, we would infer its permanence, this can hold good as regards possible experience only, not (of the soul) as a thing in itself and beyond all possible experience. But life is the subjective condition of all our possible experience, consequently we can only infer the permanence of the soul in life; for the death of man is the end of all experience which concerns the soul as an object of experience, except the contrary be proved, which is the very question in hand. The permanence of the soul can therefore only be proved (and no one cares for that) during the life of man, but not, as we desire to do, after death; and for this general reason, that the concept of substance, so far as it is to be considered necessarily combined with the concept of permanence, can be so combined only according to the principles of possible experience, and therefore for the purposes of experience only.[1]

§ 49.   That there is something real without us which not only corresponds, but must correspond, to our external perceptions, can likewise be proved to be not a connexion of things in themselves, but for the sake of experience. This means that there is something empirical, i.e. some phenomenon in space without us, that admits of a satisfactory proof, for we have nothing to do with other objects than those which belong to possible experience; because objects which cannot be given us in any experience, do not exist for us. Empirically without me is that which appears in space, and space, together with all the phenomena which it contains, belongs to the representations, whose connexion according to laws of experience proves their objective truth, just as the connexion of the phenomena

[1]It is indeed very remarkable how carelessly metaphysicians have always passed over the principle of the permanence of substances without ever attempting a proof of it; doubtless because they found themselves abandoned by all proofs as soon as they began to deal with the concept of substance. Common sense, which felt distinctly that without this presupposition no union of perceptions in experience is possible, supplied the want by a postulate. From experience itself it never could derive such a principle, partly because substances cannot be so traced in all their alterations and dissolutions, that the matter can always be found undiminished, partly because the principle contains *necessity*, which is always the sign of an *a priori* principle. People then boldly applied this postulate to the concept of soul as a *substance*, and concluded a necessary continuance of the soul after the death of man (especially as the simplicity of this substance, which is inferred from the indivisibility of consciousness, secured it from destruction by dissolution). Had they found the genuine source of this principle – a discovery which requires a deeper researches than they were ever inclined to make – they would have seen that the law of the permanence of substances has place for the purposes of experience only, and hence can hold good of things so far as they are to be cognised and conjoined with others in experience, but never independently of all possible experience, and consequently cannot hold good of the soul after death.

of the internal sense proves the actuality of my soul (as an object of the internal sense). By means of external experience I am conscious of the actuality of bodies, as external phenomena in space, in the same manner as by means of the internal experience I am conscious of the existence of my soul in time, but this soul is only cognised as an object of the internal sense by phenomena that constitute an internal state, and of which the essence in itself, which forms the basis of these phenomena, is unknown. Cartesian idealism therefore does nothing but distinguish external experience from dreaming; and the conformity to law (as a criterion of its truth) of the former, from the irregularity and the false illusion of the latter. In both it presupposes space and time as conditions of the existence of objects, and it only inquires whether the objects of the external senses, which we when awake put in space, are as actually to be found in it, as the object of the internal sense, the soul, is in time; that is, whether experience carries with it sure criteria to distinguish it from imagination. This doubt, however, may easily be disposed of, and we always do so in common life by investigating the connexion of phenomena in both space and time according to universal laws of experience, and we cannot doubt, when the representation of external things throughout agrees therewith, that they constitute truthful experience. Material idealism, in which phenomena are considered as such only according to their connexion in experience, may accordingly be very easily refuted; and it is just as sure an experience, that bodies exist without us (in space), as that I myself exist according to the representation of the internal sense (in time): for the notion without us only signifies existence in space. However, as the Ego in the proposition "I am" means not only the object of internal intuition (in time), but the subject of consciousness, just as body means not only external intuition (in space), but the thing-in-itself, which is the basis of this phenomenon; (as this is the case) the question, whether bodies (as phenomena of the external sense) exist as bodies apart from my thoughts, may without any hesitation be denied in nature. But the question, whether I myself as a phenomenon of the internal sense (the soul according to empirical psychology) exist apart from my faculty of representation in time, is an exactly similar inquiry, and must likewise be answered in the negative. And in this manner everything, when it is reduced to its true meaning, is decided and certain. The formal (which I have also called transcendental) actually abolishes the material, or Cartesian, idealism. For if space be nothing but a form of my sensibility, it is as a representation in me just as actual as I myself am, and nothing but the empirical truth of the representations in it remains for consideration. But, if this is not the case, if space and the phenomena in it are something existing without us, then all the criteria of experience beyond our perception can never prove the actuality of these objects without us.

II The Cosmological Idea[1]

§ 50. This product of pure reason in its transcendent use is its most remarkable curiosity. It serves as a very powerful agent to rouse philosophy from its dogmatic slumber, and to stimulate it to the arduous task of undertaking a *Critique of Reason* itself.

I term this idea cosmological, because it always takes its object only from the sensible world, and does not use any other than those whose object is given to sense; consequently it remains in this respect in its native home, it does not become transcendent, and is therefore so far not mere idea; whereas, to conceive the soul as a simple substance already means to conceive such an object (the simple) as cannot be presented to the senses. Yet the cosmological idea extends the connexion of the conditioned with its condition (whether the connexion is mathematical or dynamical) so far, that experience never can keep up with it. It is therefore with regard to this point always an idea, whose object never can be adequately given in any experience.

§ 51. In the first place, the use of a system of categories becomes here so obvious and unmistakable, that even if there were not several other proofs of it, this alone would sufficiently prove it indispensable in the system of pure reason. There are only four such transcendent ideas, as there are so many classes of categories; in each of which, however, they refer only to the absolute completeness of the series of the conditions for a given conditioned. In analogy to these cosmological ideas there are only four kinds of dialectical assertions of pure reason, which, as they are dialectical, thereby prove that to each of them, on equally specious principles of pure reason, a contradictory assertion stands opposed. As all the metaphysical art of the most subtle distinction cannot prevent this opposition, it compels the philosopher to recur to the first sources of pure reason itself. This antinomy, not arbitrarily invented, but founded in the

[1]Cf. *Critique, Die Antinomie der reinen Vernunft.*

nature of human reason, and hence unavoidable and never ceasing, contains the following four theses together with their antitheses:

I
Thesis
The World has, as to Time and Space, a Beginning (limit).
Antithesis
The World is, as to Time and Space, infinite.

2
Thesis
Everything in the World consists of (elements that are) simple.
Antithesis
There is nothing simple, but everything is composite.

3
Thesis
There are in the World Causes through Freedom.
Antithesis
There is no Liberty, but all is Nature.

4
Thesis
In the Series of the World-Causes there is some necessary Being.
Antithesis
There is Nothing necessary in the World, but in this Series All is incidental.

§ 52(*a*)   Here is the most singular phenomenon of human reason, no other instance of which can be shown in any other use. If we, as is commonly done, represent to ourselves the appearances of the sensible world as things in themselves if we assume the principles of their combination as principles universally valid of things in themselves and not merely of experience, as is usually, nay without our *Critique*, unavoidably done, there arises an unexpected conflict, which never can be removed in the common dogmatical way; because the thesis, as well as the antithesis, can be shown by equally clear, evident, and irresistible proofs – for I pledge myself as to the correctness of all these proofs – and reason therefore perceives that it is divided with itself, a state at which the skeptic rejoices, but which must make the critical philosopher pause and feel ill at ease.

§ 52(*b*)   We may blunder in various ways in metaphysics without any fear of being detected in falsehood. For we never can be refuted by experience if we but avoid self-contradiction, which in synthetical, though purely fictitious propositions, may be done whenever the concepts, which we connect, are mere ideas, that cannot be given (in their whole content) in experience. For how can we make out by experience, whether the world is from eternity or had a beginning, whether matter is infinitely divisible or consists of simple parts? Such a concept cannot be given in any experience, be it ever so extensive, and consequently the falsehood either of the positive or the negative proposition cannot be discovered by this touch-stone.

The only possible way in which reason could have revealed unintentionally its secret Dialectics, falsely announced as Dogmatics, would be when it were made to ground an assertion upon a universally admitted principle, and to deduce the exact contrary with the greatest accuracy of inference from another which is equally granted. This is actually here the case with regard to four natural ideas of reason, whence four assertions on the one side, and as many counter-assertions on the other arise, each consistently following from universally-acknowledged principles. Thus they reveal by the use of these principles the dialectical illusion of pure reason which would otherwise forever remain concealed.

This is therefore a decisive experiment, which must necessarily expose any error lying hidden in the assumptions of reason.[1] Contradictory propositions cannot both be false, except the concept, which is the subject of both, is self-contradictory; for example, the propositions, "a square circle is round, and a square circle is not round," are both false. For, as to the former it is false, that the circle is round, because it is quadrangular; and it is likewise false that it is not round, that is, angular, because it is a circle. For the logical criterion of the impossibility of a concept consists in this, that if we presuppose it, two contradictory propositions both become false; consequently, as no middle between them is conceivable, nothing at all is thought by that concept.

§ 52(c)   The first two antinomies, which I call mathematical, because they are concerned with the addition or division of the homogeneous, are founded on such a self-contradictory concept;

---

[1] I therefore would be pleased to have the critical reader devote to this antinomy of pure reason his chief attention, because nature itself seems to have established it with a view to stagger reason in its daring pretentions, and to force it to self-examination. For every proof, which I have given, as well of the thesis as of the antithesis, I undertake to be responsible, and thereby to show the certainty of the inevitable antinomy of reason. When the reader is brought by this curious phenomenon to fall back upon the proof of the presumption upon which it rests, he will feel himself obliged to investigate the ultimate foundation of all the cognition of pure reason with me more thoroughly.

and hence I explain how it happens, that both the Thesis and Antithesis of the two are false.

When I speak of objects in time and in space, it is not of things in themselves, of which I know nothing, but of things in appearance, that is, of experience, as the particular way of cognising objects which is afforded to man. I must not say of what I think in time or in space, that in itself, and independent of these my thoughts, it exists in space and in time; for in that case I should contradict myself; because space and time, together with the appearances in them, are nothing existing in themselves and outside of my representations, but are themselves only modes of representation, and it is palpably contradictory to say that a mere mode of representation exists without our representation. Objects of the senses therefore exist only in experience; whereas to give them a self-subsisting existence apart from experience or before it is merely to represent to ourselves that experience actually exists apart from experience or before it.

Now if I inquire after the quantity of the world, as to space and time, it is equally impossible, as regards all my notions, to declare it infinite or to declare it finite. For neither assertion can be contained in experience, because experience either of an infinite space, or of an infinite time elapsed, or again, of the boundary of the world by a void space, or by an antecedent void time, is impossible; these are mere ideas. This quantity of the world, which is determined in either way, should therefore exist in the world itself apart from all experience. This contradicts the notion of a world of sense, which is merely a complex of the appearances whose existence and connexion occur only in our representations, that is, in experience, since this latter is not an object in itself, but a mere mode of representation. Hence it follows that as the concept of an absolutely existing world of sense is self-contradictory, the solution of the problem concerning its quantity, whether attempted affirmatively or negatively, is always false.

The same holds good of the second antinomy, which relates to the division of phenomena. For these are mere representations, and the parts exist merely in their representation, consequently in the division, or in a possible experience where they are given, and the division reaches only as far as this latter reaches. To assume that an appearance, e.g. that of body, contains in itself before all experience all the parts, which any possible experience can ever reach, is to impute to a mere appearance, which can exist only in experience, an existence previous to experience. In other words, it would mean that mere representations exist before they can be found in our faculty of representation. Such an assertion is self-contradictory, as also every solution of our misunderstood problem, whether we maintain that bodies in themselves consist of an infinite number of parts, or of a finite number of simple parts.

§ 53. In the first (the mathematical) class of antinomies the falsehood of the assumption consists in representing in one concept something self-contradictory as if it were compatible (i.e. an appearance as an object in itself). But, as to the second (the dynamical) class of antinomies, the falsehood of the representation consists in representing as contradictory what is compatible; so that, as in the former case, the opposed assertions are both false, in this case, on the other hand, where they are opposed to one another by mere misunderstanding, they may both be true.

Any mathematical connexion necessarily presupposes homogeneity of what is connected (in the concept of magnitude), while the dynamical one by no means requires the same. When we have to deal with extended magnitudes, all the parts must be homogeneous with one another and with the whole; whereas, in the connexion of cause and effect, homogeneity may indeed likewise be found, but is not necessary; for the concept of causality (by means of which something is posited through something else quite different from it), at all events, does not require it.

If the objects of the world of sense are taken for things in themselves, and the above laws of nature for the laws of things in themselves, the contradiction would be unavoidable. So also, if the subject of freedom were, like other objects, represented as mere appearance, the contradiction would be just as unavoidable, for the same predicate would at once be affirmed and denied of the same kind of object in the same sense. But if natural necessity is referred merely to appearances, and freedom merely to things in themselves, no contradiction arises, if we at once assume, or admit both kinds of causality, however difficult or impossible it may be to make the latter kind conceivable.

As appearance every effect is an event, or something that happens in time; it must, according to the universal law of nature, be preceded by a determination of the causality of its cause (a state), which follows according to a constant law. But this determination of the cause as causality must likewise be something that takes place or happens; the cause must have begun to act, otherwise no succession between it and the effect could be conceived. Otherwise the effect, as well as the causality of the cause, would have always existed. Therefore the determination of the cause to act must also have originated among appearances, and must consequently, as well as its effect, be an event, which must again have its cause, and so on; hence natural necessity must be the condition, on which effective causes are determined. Whereas if freedom is to be a property of certain causes of appearances, it must, as regards these, which are events, be a faculty of starting them spontaneously, that is, without the causality of the cause itself, and hence without requiring any other ground to determine its start. But then the cause, as to its causality, must not rank under time-determinations of its state, that is, it cannot be an appearance, and must be considered a thing in itself, while its effects would be only appearances.[1] If without contradiction we can think of the beings of understanding (Verstandeswesen) as exercising such an influence on appearances, then natural necessity will attach to all connexions of cause and effect in the sensuous world, though on the other hand, freedom can be granted to such cause, as it is itself not an appearance (but the foundation of appearance). Nature therefore and freedom can without contradiction be attributed to the very same thing, but in different relations – on one side as a phenomenon, on the other as a thing in itself.

We have in us a faculty, which not only stands in connexion with its subjective determining grounds that are the natural causes of its actions, and is so far the faculty of a being that itself belongs to appearances, but is also referred to objective grounds, that are only ideas, so far as they can determine this faculty, a connexion which is expressed by the word *ought*. This faculty is called *reason*, and, so far as we consider a being (man) entirely according to this objectively determinable reason, he cannot be considered as a being of sense, but this property is that of a thing in itself, of which we cannot comprehend the possibility – I mean how the *ought* (which however has never yet taken place) should determine its activity, and can become

---

[1] The idea of freedom occurs only in the relation of the intellectual, as cause, to the appearance, as effect. Hence we cannot attribute freedom to matter in regard to the incessant action by which it fills its space, though this action takes place from an internal principle. We can likewise find no notion of freedom suitable to purely rational beings, for instance, to God, so far as his action is immanent. For his action, though independent of external determining causes, is determined in his eternal reason, that is, in the divine *nature*. It is only, if *something is to start* by an action, and so the effect occurs in the sequence of time, or in the world of sense (e.g. the beginning of the world), that we can put the question, whether the causality of the cause must in its turn have been started, or whether the cause can originate an effect without its causality itself beginning. In the former case the concept of this causality is a concept of natural necessity, in the latter, that of freedom. From this the reader will see that, as I explained freedom to be the faculty of starting an event spontaneously, I have exactly hit the notion which is the problem of metaphysics.

the cause of actions, whose effect is an appearance in the sensible world. Yet the causality of reason would be freedom with regard to the effects in the sensuous world, so far as we can consider objective grounds, which are themselves ideas, as their determinants. For its action in that case would not depend upon subjective conditions, consequently not upon those of time, and of course not upon the law of nature, which serves to determine them, because grounds of reason give to actions the rule universally, according to principles, without the influence of the circumstances of either time or place.

What I adduce here is merely meant as an example to make the thing intelligible, and does not necessarily belong to our problem, which must be decided from mere concepts, independently of the properties which we meet in the actual world.

Now I may say without contradiction: that all the actions of rational beings, so far as they are appearances (occurring in any experience), are subject to the necessity of nature; but the same actions, as regards merely the rational subject and its faculty of acting according to mere reason, are free. For what is required for the necessity of nature? Nothing more than the determinability of every event in the world of sense according to constant laws, that is, a reference to cause in the appearance; in this process the thing in itself at its foundation and its causality remain unknown. But I say that the law of nature remains, whether the rational being is the cause of the effects in the sensuous world from reason, that is, through freedom, or whether it does not determine them on grounds of reason. For, if the former is the case, the action is performed according to maxims, the effect of which as appearance is always conformable to constant laws; if the latter is the case, and the action not performed on principles of reason, it is subjected to the empirical laws of the sensibility, and in both cases the effects are connected according to constant laws; more than this we do not require or know concerning natural necessity. But in the former case reason is the cause of these laws of nature, and therefore free; in the latter the effects follow according to mere natural laws of sensibility, because reason does not influence it; but reason itself is not determined on that account by the sensibility, and is therefore free in this case too. Freedom is therefore no hindrance to natural law in appearance, neither does this law abrogate the freedom of the practical use of reason, which is connected with things in themselves, as determining grounds.

Thus practical freedom, viz., the freedom in which reason possesses causality according to objectively determining grounds, is rescued and yet natural necessity is not in the least curtailed with regard to the very same effects, as appearances. The same remarks will serve to explain what we had to say concerning transcendental freedom and its compatibility with natural necessity (in the same subject, but not taken in the same reference). For, as to this, every beginning of the action of a being from objective causes regarded as determining grounds, is always a first start, though the same action is in the series of appearances only a subordinate start, which must be preceded by a state of the cause, which determines it, and is itself determined in the same manner by another immediately preceding. Thus we are able, in rational beings, or in beings generally, so far as their causality is determined in them as things in themselves, to imagine a faculty of beginning from itself a series of states, without falling into contradiction with the laws of nature. For the relation of the action to objective grounds of reason is not a time-relation; in this case that which determines the causality does not precede in time the action, because such determining grounds represent not a reference to objects of sense, e.g. to causes in the appearances, but to determining causes, as things in themselves, which do not rank under conditions of time. And in this way the action, with regard to the causality of reason, can be considered as a first start in respect to the series of appearances, and yet also as a merely subordinate beginning. We may therefore without contradiction consider it in the former aspect as free, but in the latter (in so far as it is merely appearance) as subject to natural necessity.

As to the fourth Antinomy, it is solved in the same way as the conflict of reason with itself in the third. For, provided the cause *in* the appearance is distinguished from the cause *of* the appearance (so far as it can be thought as a thing in itself), both propositions are perfectly reconcilable: the one, that there is nowhere in the sensuous world a cause (according to similar laws of causality), whose existence is absolutely necessary; the other, that this world is nevertheless connected with a Necessary Being as its cause (but of another kind and according to another law). The incompatibility of these propositions entirely rests upon the mistake of extending what is valid merely of appearances to things in themselves, and in general confusing both in one concept.

§ 54. This then is the proposition and this the solution of the whole antinomy, in which reason finds itself involved in the application of its principles to the sensible world. The former alone (the mere proposition) would be a considerable service in the cause of our knowledge of human reason, even though the solution might fail to fully satisfy the reader, who has here to combat a natural illusion, which has been but recently exposed to him, and which he had hitherto always regarded as genuine. For one result at least is unavoidable. As it is quite impossible to prevent this conflict of reason with itself – so long as the objects of the sensible world are taken for things in themselves, and not for mere appearances, which they are in fact – the reader is thereby compelled to examine over again the deduction of all our *a priori* cognition and the proof which I have given of my deduction in order to come to a decision on the question. This is all I require at present; for when in this occupation he shall have thought himself deep enough into the nature of pure reason, those concepts by which alone the solution of the conflict of reason is possible will become sufficiently familiar to him. Without this preparation I cannot expect an unreserved assent even from the most attentive reader.

III. *The Theological Idea*[1]

§ 55. The third transcendental Idea, which affords matter for the most important, but, if pursued only speculatively, transcendent and thereby dialectical use of reason, is the ideal of pure reason. Reason in this case does not, as with the psychological and the cosmological Ideas, begin from experience, and err by exaggerating its grounds, in striving to attain, if possible, the absolute completeness of their series. It rather totally breaks with experience, and from mere concepts of what constitutes the absolute completeness of a thing in general, consequently by means of the idea of a most perfect primal Being, it proceeds to determine the possibility and therefore the actuality of all other things. And so the mere presupposition of a Being, who is conceived not in the series of experience, yet for the purposes of experience – for the sake of comprehending its connexion, order, and unity – i.e. the idea (the notion of it), is more easily distinguished from the concept of the understanding here, than in the former cases. Hence we can easily expose the dialectical illusion which arises from our making the subjective conditions of our thinking objective conditions of objects themselves, and a hypothesis necessary for the satisfaction of our reason, a dogma. As the observations of the *Critique* on the pretensions of transcendental

---

[1] Cf. *Critique*, the chapter on "Transcendental Ideals."

theology are intelligible, clear, and decisive, I have nothing more to add on the subject.

General Remark on the Transcendental Ideas

§ 56.   The objects, which are given us by experience, are in many respects incomprehensible, and many questions, to which the law of nature leads us, when carried beyond a certain point (though quite conformably to the laws of nature), admit of no answer; as, for example, the question: why do substances attract one another? But if we entirely quit nature, or in pursuing its combinations, exceed all possible experience, and so enter the realm of mere ideas, we cannot then say that the object is incomprehensible, and that the nature of things proposes to us insoluble problems. For we are not then concerned with nature or in general with given objects, but with concepts, which have their origin merely in our reason, and with mere creations of thought; and all the problems that arise from our notions of them must be solved, because of course reason can and must give a full account of its own procedure.[1] As the psychological, cosmological, and theological Ideas are nothing but pure concepts of reason, which cannot be given in any experience, the questions which reason asks us about them are put to us not by the objects, but by mere maxims of our reason for the sake of its own satisfaction. They must all be capable of satisfactory answers, which is done by showing that they are principles which bring our use of the understanding into thorough agreement, completeness, and synthetical unity, and that they so far hold good of experience only, but of experience as a whole.

Although an absolute whole of experience is impossible, the idea of a whole of cognition according to principles must impart to our knowledge a peculiar kind of unity, that of a system, without which it is nothing but piecework, and cannot be used for proving the existence of a highest purpose (which can only be the general system

[1]Herr Platner in his Aphorisms acutely says (§§ 728, 729), "If reason be a criterion, no concept, which is incomprehensible to human reason, can be possible. Incomprehensibility has place in what is actual only. Here incomprehensibility arises from the insufficiency of the acquired ideas." It sounds paradoxical, but is otherwise not strange to say, that in nature there is much incomprehensible (e.g. the faculty of generation) but if we mount still higher, and even go beyond nature, everything again becomes comprehensible; for we then quit entirely the objects, which can be given us, and occupy ourselves merely about ideas, in which occupation we can easily comprehend the law that reason prescribes by them to the understanding for its use in experience, because the law is the reason's own production.

of all purposes), I do not here refer only to the practical, but also to the highest purpose of the speculative use of reason.

The transcendental Ideas therefore express the peculiar application of reason as a principle of systematic unity in the use of the understanding. Yet if we assume this unity of the mode of cognition to be attached to the object of cognition, if we regard that which is merely regulative to be constitutive, and if we persuade ourselves that we can by means of these Ideas enlarge our cognition transcendently, or far beyond all possible experience, while it only serves to render experience within itself as nearly complete as possible, i.e. to limit its progress by nothing that cannot belong to experience: we suffer from a mere misunderstanding in our estimate of the proper application of our reason and of its principles, and from a Dialectic, which both confuses the empirical use of reason, and also sets reason at variance with itself.

CONCLUSION

On the Determination of the Bounds of Pure Reason

§ 57. Having adduced the clearest arguments, it would be absurd for us to hope that we can know more of any object than belongs to the possible experience of it, or lay claim to the least atom of knowledge about anything not assumed to be an object of possible experience, which would determine it according to the constitution it has in itself. For how could we determine anything in this way, since time, space, and the categories, and still more all the concepts formed by empirical experience or perception in the sensible world (*Anschauung*), have and can have no other use than to make experience possible. And if this condition is omitted from the pure concepts of the understanding, they do not determine any object, and have no meaning whatever.

But it would be on the other hand a still greater absurdity if we conceded no things in themselves, or set up our experience for the only possible mode of knowing things, our way of beholding (*Anschauung*) them in space and in time for the only possible way, and our discursive understanding for the archetype of every possible understanding; in fact if we wished to have the principles of the possibility of experience considered universal conditions of things in themselves.

Our principles, which limit the use of reason to possible

experience, might in this way become transcendent, and the limits of our reason be set up as limits of the possibility of things in themselves (as Hume's dialogues may illustrate), if a careful critique did not guard the bounds of our reason with respect to its empirical use, and set a limit to its pretensions. Scepticism originally arose from metaphysics and its licentious dialectics. At first it might, merely to favor the empirical use of reason, announce everything that transcends this use as worthless and deceitful; but by and by, when it was perceived that the very same principles that are used in experience, insensibly, and apparently with the same right, led still further than experience extends, then men began to doubt even the propositions of experience. But here there is no danger; for common sense will doubtless always assert its rights. A certain confusion, however, arose in science which cannot determine how far reason is to be trusted, and why only so far and no further, and this confusion can only be cleared up and all future relapses obviated by a formal determination, on principle, of the boundary of the use of our reason.

We cannot indeed, beyond all possible experience, form a definite notion of what things in themselves may be. Yet we are not at liberty to abstain entirely from inquiring into them; for experience never satisfies reason fully, but in answering questions, refers us further and further back, and leaves us dissatisfied with regard to their complete solution. This anyone may gather from the Dialectics of pure reason, which therefore has its good subjective grounds. Having acquired, as regards the nature of our soul, a clear conception of the subject, and having come to the conviction that its manifestations cannot be explained materialistically, who can refrain from asking what the soul really is, and, if no concept of experience suffices for the purpose, from accounting for it by a concept of reason (that of a simple immaterial being), though we cannot by any means prove its objective reality? Who can satisfy himself with mere empirical knowledge in all the cosmological questions of the duration and of the quantity of the world, of freedom or of natural necessity, since every answer given on principles of experience begets a fresh question, which likewise requires its answer and thereby clearly shows the insufficiency of all physical modes of explanation to satisfy reason? Finally, who does not see in the thoroughgoing contingency and dependence of all his thoughts and assumptions on mere principles of experience, the impossibility of stopping there? And who does not feel himself compelled, notwithstanding all interdictions against losing himself in transcendent ideas, to seek rest and contentment beyond all the concepts which he can vindicate by experience, in the concept of a Being, the possibility of which we cannot conceive, but at the same time cannot be refuted, because it relates to a mere being of the understanding, and without it reason must needs remain forever dissatisfied?

Bounds (in extended beings) always presuppose a space existing outside a certain definite place, and enclosing it; limits do not require this, but are mere negations, which affect a quantity, so far as it is not absolutely complete. But our reason, as it were, sees in its surroundings a space for the cognition of things in themselves, though we can never have definite notions of them, and are limited to appearances only.

As long as the cognition of reason is homogeneous, definite bounds to it are inconceivable. In mathematics and in natural philosophy human reason admits of limits, but not of bounds, viz., that something indeed lies without it, at which it can never arrive, but not that it will at any point find completion in its internal progress. The enlarging of our views in mathematics, and the possibility of new discoveries, are infinite; and the same is the case with the discovery of new properties of nature, of new powers and laws, by continued experience and its rational combination. But limits cannot be mistaken here, for mathematics refers to appearances only, and what cannot be an object of sensuous contemplation, such as the concepts of metaphysics and of morals, lies entirely without its sphere, and it can never lead to them; neither does it require them. It is therefore not a continual progress and an approximation towards these sciences, and there is not, as it were, any point or line of contact. Natural science will never reveal to us the internal constitution of things, which though not appearance, yet can serve as the ultimate ground of explaining appearance. Nor does that science require this for its physical explanations. Nay even if such grounds should be offered from other sources (for instance, the influence of immaterial beings), they must be rejected and not used in the progress of its explanations. For these explanations must only be grounded upon that which as an object of sense can belong to experience, and be brought into connexion with our actual perceptions and empirical laws.

But metaphysics leads us towards bounds in the dialectical attempts of pure reason (not undertaken arbitrarily or wantonly, but stimulated thereto by the nature of reason itself). And the transcendental Ideas, as they do not admit of evasion, and are never capable of realisation, serve to point out to us actually not only the bounds of the pure use of reason, but also the way to determine them. Such is the end and the use of this natural predisposition of our reason, which has brought forth metaphysics as its favorite child, whose generation, like every other in the world, is not to be ascribed to blind chance, but to an original germ, wisely organised for great ends. For metaphysics, in its fundamental features, perhaps more than any other science, is placed in us by nature itself, and cannot be considered the production of an arbitrary choice or a casual enlargement in the progress of experience from which it is quite disparate.

Reason with all its concepts and laws of the understanding, which suffice for empirical use, i.e. within the sensible world, finds in itself no satisfaction because ever-recurring questions deprive us of all hope of their complete solution. The transcendental ideas, which have that completion in view, are such problems of reason. But it sees clearly that the sensuous world cannot contain this completion, neither consequently can all the concepts, which serve merely for understanding the world of sense, such as space and time, and whatever we have adduced under the name of pure concepts of the understanding. The sensuous world is nothing but a chain of appearances connected according to universal laws; it has therefore no subsistence by itself; it is not the thing in itself, and consequently must point to that which contains the basis of this experience, to beings which cannot be cognised merely as phenomena, but as things in themselves. In the cognition of them alone reason can hope to satisfy its desire of completeness in proceeding from the conditioned to its conditions.

We have above (§§ 33, 34) indicated the limits of reason with regard to all cognition of mere creations of thought. Now, since the transcendental ideas have urged us to approach them, and thus have led us, as it were, to the spot where the occupied space (viz., experience) touches the void (that of which we can know nothing, viz., noumena), we can determine the bounds of pure reason. For in all bounds there is something positive (e.g. a surface is the boundary of corporeal space, and is therefore itself a space, a line is a space, which is the boundary of the surface, a point the boundary of the line, but yet always a place in space), whereas limits contain mere negations. The limits pointed out in those paragraphs are not enough after we have discovered that beyond them there still lies something (though we can never cognise what it is in itself). For the question now is, What is the attitude of our reason in this connexion of what

112

we know with what we do not, and never shall, know? This is an actual connexion of a known thing with one quite unknown (and which will always remain so), and though what is unknown should not become the least more known – which we cannot even hope – yet the notion of this connexion must be definite, and capable of being rendered distinct.

We must therefore accept an immaterial being, a world of understanding, and a Supreme Being (all mere noumena), because in them only, as things in themselves, reason finds that completion and satisfaction, which it can never hope for in the derivation of appearances from their homogeneous grounds, and because these actually have reference to something distinct from them (and totally heterogeneous), as appearances always presuppose an object in itself, and therefore suggest its existence whether we can know more of it or not.

But as we can never cognise these beings of understanding as they are in themselves, that is, definitely, yet must assume them as regards the sensible world, and connect them with it by reason, we are at least able to think this connexion by means of such concepts as express their relation to the world of sense. Yet if we represent to ourselves a being of the understanding by nothing but pure concepts of the understanding, we then indeed represent nothing definite to ourselves, consequently our concept has no significance; but if we think it by properties borrowed from the sensuous world, it is no longer a being of understanding, but is conceived as an appearance, and belongs to the sensible world. Let us take an instance from the notion of the Supreme Being.

Our deistic conception is quite a pure concept of reason, but represents only a thing containing all realities, without being able to determine any one of them; because for that purpose an example must be taken from the world of sense, in which case we should have an object of sense only, not something quite heterogeneous, which can never be an object of sense. Suppose I attribute to the Supreme Being understanding, for instance; I have no concept of an understanding other than my own, one that must receive its perceptions (*Anschauung*) by the senses, and which is occupied in bringing them under rules of the unity of consciousness. Then the elements of my concept would always lie in the appearance; I should however by the insufficiency of the appearance be necessitated to go beyond them to the concept of a being which neither depends upon appearance, nor is bound up with them as conditions of its

113

determination. But if I separate understanding from sensibility to obtain a pure understanding, then nothing remains but the mere form of thinking without perception (*Anschauung*), by which form alone I can cognise nothing definite, and consequently no object. For that purpose I should conceive another understanding, such as would directly perceive its objects,[1] but of which I have not the least notion; because the human understanding is discursive, and can (not directly perceive, it can) only cognise by means of general concepts. And the very same difficulties arise if we attribute a will to the Supreme Being; for we have this concept only by drawing it from our internal experience, and therefore from our dependence for satisfaction upon objects whose existence we require; and so the notion rests upon sensibility, which is absolutely incompatible with the pure concept of the Supreme Being.

Hume's objections to deism are weak, and affect only the proofs, and not the deistic assertion itself. But as regards theism, which depends on a stricter determination of the concept of the Supreme Being which in deism is merely transcendent, they are very strong, and as this concept is formed, in certain (in fact in all common) cases irrefutable. Hume always insists that by the mere concept of an original being, to which we apply only ontological predicates (eternity, omnipresence, omnipotence), we think nothing definite, and that properties which can yield a concept *in concreto* must be superadded; that it is not enough to say it is Cause, but we must explain the nature of its causality, for example, that of an understanding and of a will. He then begins his attacks on the essential point itself, i.e. theism, as he had previously directed his battery only against the proofs of deism, an attack which is not very dangerous to it in its consequences. All his dangerous arguments refer to anthropomorphism, which he holds to be inseparable from theism, and to make it absurd in itself; but if the former be abandoned, the latter must vanish with it, and nothing remain but deism, of which nothing can come, which is of no value, and which cannot serve as any foundation to religion or morals. If this anthropomorphism were really unavoidable, no proofs whatever of the existence of a Supreme Being, even were they all granted, could determine for us the concept of this Being without involving us in contradictions.

If we connect with the command to avoid all transcendent judgments of pure reason, the command (which apparently conflicts with

---

[1] *Der die Gegenstände anschaute.*

it) to proceed to concepts that lie beyond the field of its immanent (empirical) use, we discover that both can subsist together, but only at the boundary of all lawful use of reason. For this boundary belongs as well to the field of experience, as to that of the creations of thought, and we are thereby taught, as well, how these so remarkable ideas serve merely for marking the bounds of human reason. On the one hand they give warning not boundlessly to extend cognition of experience, as if nothing but world[1] remained for us to cognise, and yet, on the other hand, not to transgress the bounds of experience, and to think of judging about things beyond them, as things in themselves.

But we stop at this boundary if we limit our judgment merely to the relation which the world may have to a Being whose very concept lies beyond all the knowledge which we can attain within the world. For we then do not attribute to the Supreme Being any of the properties in themselves, by which we represent objects of experience, and thereby avoid dogmatic anthropomorphism; but we attribute them to his relation to the world, and allow ourselves a symbolical anthropomorphism, which in fact concerns language only, and not the object itself.

If I say that we are compelled to consider the world, as if it were the work of a Supreme Understanding and Will, I really say nothing more than that a watch, a ship, a regiment, bears the same relation to the watchmaker, the shipbuilder, the commanding officer, as the world of sense (or whatever constitutes the substratum of this complex of appearances) does to the Unknown, which I do not hereby cognise as it is in itself, but as it is for me or in relation to the world, of which I am a part.

§ 58.   Such a cognition is one of analogy, and does not signify (as is commonly understood) an imperfect similarity of two things, but a perfect similarity of relations between two quite dissimilar things.[2] By means of this analogy, however, there remains a concept

---

[1] The use of the word "world" without article, though odd, seems to be the correct reading, but it may be a mere misprint. – Ed.

[2] There is e.g. an analogy between the juridical relation of human actions and the mechanical relation of motive powers. I never can do anything to another man without giving him a right to do the same to me on the same conditions; just as no mass can act with its motive power on another mass without thereby occasioning the other to react equally against it. Here right and motive power are quite dissimilar things, but in their relation there is complete similarity. By means of such an analogy I can obtain a notion of the relation of things which absolutely are unknown to me. For instance, as the promotion of the welfare of children (= a) is to the love of parents (= b), so the welfare

of the Supreme Being sufficiently determined *for us*, though we have left out everything that could determine it absolutely or in itself; for we determine it as regards the world and as regards ourselves, and more do we not require. The attacks which Hume makes upon those who would determine this concept absolutely, by taking the materials for so doing from themselves and the world, do not affect us; and he cannot object to us, that we have nothing left if we give up the objective anthropomorphism of the concept of the Supreme Being.

For let us assume at the outset (as Hume in his *Dialogues* makes Philo grant Cleanthes), as a necessary hypothesis, the deistical concept of the First Being, in which this Being is thought by the mere ontological predicates of substance, of cause, etc. This must be done, because reason, actuated in the sensible world by mere conditions, which are themselves always conditional, cannot otherwise have any satisfaction, and it therefore can be done without falling into anthropomorphism (which transfers predicates from the world of sense to a Being quite distinct from the world), because those predicates are mere categories which, though they do not give a determinate concept of God, yet give a concept not limited to any conditions of sensibility. Thus nothing can prevent our predicating of this Being a causality through reason with regard to the world, and thus passing to theism, without being obliged to attribute to God in himself this kind of reason, as a property inhering in him. For as to the former, the only possible way of prosecuting the use of reason (as regards all possible experience, in complete harmony with itself) in the world of sense to the highest point, is to assume a supreme reason as a cause of all the connexions in the world. Such a principle must be quite advantageous to reason and can hurt it nowhere in its application to nature. As to the latter, reason is thereby not transferred as a property to the First Being in himself, but only to his relation to the world of sense, and so anthropomorphism is entirely avoided. For nothing is considered here but the cause of the form of reason which is perceived everywhere in the world, and reason is attributed to the Supreme Being, so far as it contains the ground of this form of reason in the world, but according to

of the human species (= c) is to that unknown [quantity which is] in God (= x), which we call love; not as if it had the least similarity to any human inclination, but because we can suppose its relation to the world to be similar to that which things of the world bear one another. But the concept of relation in this case is a mere category, viz., the concept of cause, which has nothing to do with sensibility.

analogy only, that is, so far as this expression shows merely the relation, which the Supreme Cause unknown to us has to the world, in order to determine everything in it conformably to reason in the highest degree. We are thereby kept from using reason as an attribute for the purpose of conceiving God, but instead of conceiving the world in such a manner as is necessary to have the greatest possible use of reason according to principle. We thereby acknowledge that the Supreme Being is quite inscrutable and even unthinkable in any definite way as to what he is in himself. We are thereby kept, on the one hand, from making a transcendent use of the concepts which we have of reason as an efficient cause (by means of the will), in order to determine the Divine Nature by properties, which are only borrowed from human nature, and from losing ourselves in gross and extravagant notions, and on the other hand from deluging the contemplation of the world with hyperphysical modes of explanation according to our notions of human reason, which we transfer to God, and so losing for this contemplation its proper application, according to which it should be a rational study of mere nature, and not a presumptuous derivation of its appearances from a Supreme Reason. The expression suited to our feeble notions is, that we conceive the world as if it came, as to its existence and internal plan, from a Supreme Reason, by which notion we both cognise the constitution, which belongs to the world itself, yet without pretending to determine the nature of its cause in itself, and on the other hand, we transfer the ground of this constitution (of the form of reason in the world) upon the relation of the Supreme Cause to the world, without finding the world sufficient by itself for that purpose.[1]

Thus the difficulties which seem to oppose theism disappear by combining with Hume's principle – "not to carry the use of reason dogmatically beyond the field of all possible experience" – this other principle, which he quite overlooked: "not to consider the field of experience as one which bounds itself in the eye of our reason." The *Critique of Pure Reason* here points out the true mean between dogmatism, which Hume combats, and scepticism, which he would substitute for it – a mean which is not like other means that we

---

[1] I may say that the causality of the Supreme Cause holds the same place with regard to the world that human reason does with regard to its works of art. Here the nature of the Supreme Cause itself remains unknown to me: I only compare its effects (the order of the world) which I know, and their conformity to reason, to the effects of human reason which I also know; and hence I term the former reason, without attributing to it on that account what I understand in man by this term, or attaching to it anything else known to me, as its property.

find advisable to determine for ourselves as it were mechanically (by adopting something from one side and something from the other), and by which nobody is taught a better way, but such a one as can be accurately determined on principles.

§ 59.   At the beginning of this annotation I made use of the metaphor of a boundary, in order to establish the limits of reason in regard to its suitable use. The world of sense contains merely appearances, which are not things in themselves, but the understanding must assume these latter ones, viz., noumena. In our reason both are comprised, and the question is, How does reason proceed to set boundaries to the understanding as regards both these fields? Experience, which contains all that belongs to the sensuous world, does not bound itself; it only proceeds in every case from the conditioned to some other equally conditioned object. Its boundary must lie quite without it, and this field is that of the pure beings of the understanding. But this field, so far as the determination of the nature of these beings is concerned, is an empty space for us, and if dogmatically determined concepts alone are in question, we cannot pass out of the field of possible experience. But as a boundary itself is something positive, which belongs as well to that which lies within, as to the space that lies without the given complex, it is still an actual positive cognition, which reason only acquires by enlarging itself to this boundary, yet without attempting to pass it; because it there finds itself in the presence of an empty space, in which it can conceive forms of things, but not things themselves. But the setting of a boundary to the field of the understanding by something, which is otherwise unknown to it, is still a cognition which belongs to reason even at this standpoint, and by which it is neither confined within the sensible, nor straying without it, but only refers, as befits the knowledge of a boundary, to the relation between that which lies without it, and that which is contained within it.

Natural theology is such a concept at the boundary of human reason, being constrained to look beyond this boundary to the Idea of a Supreme Being (and, for practical purposes to that of an intelligible world also), not in order to determine anything relatively to this pure creation of the understanding, which lies beyond the world of sense, but in order to guide the use of reason within it according to principles of the greatest possible (theoretical as well as practical) unity. For this purpose we make use of the reference of the world of sense to an independent reason, as the cause of all its connexions. Thereby we do not purely invent a being, but, as beyond the sensible world there must be something that can only be thought by the pure understanding, we determine that something in this particular way, though only of course according to analogy.

And thus there remains our original proposition, which is the *résumé* of the whole *Critique*: "that reason by all its *a priori* principles never teaches us anything more than objects of possible experience, and even of these nothing more than can be cognised in experience." But this limitation does not prevent reason leading us to the objective boundary of experience, viz., to the reference to something which is not itself an object of experience, but is the ground of all experience. Reason does not however teach us anything concerning the thing in itself: it only instructs us as regards its own complete and highest use in the field of possible experience. But this is all that can be reasonably desired in the present case, and with which we have cause to be satisfied.

§ 60. Thus we have fully exhibited metaphysics as it is actually given in the natural predisposition of human reason, and in that which constitutes the essential end of its pursuit, according to its subjective possibility. Though we have found that this merely natural use of such a predisposition of our reason, if no discipline arising only from a scientific critique bridles and sets limits to it, involves us in transcendent, either apparently or really conflicting, dialectical syllogisms; and this fallacious metaphysics is not only unnecessary as regards the promotion of our knowledge of nature, but even disadvantageous to it: there yet remains a problem worthy of solution, which is to find out the natural ends intended by this disposition to transcendent concepts in our reason, because everything that lies in nature must be originally intended for some useful purpose.

Such an inquiry is of a doubtful nature; and I acknowledge, that what I can say about it is conjecture only, like every speculation about the first ends of nature. The question does not concern the objective validity of metaphysical judgments, but our natural predisposition to them, and therefore does not belong to the system of metaphysics but to anthropology.

When I compare all the transcendental Ideas, the totality of which constitutes the particular problem of natural pure reason, compelling it to quit the mere contemplation of nature, to transcend all possible experience, and in this endeavor to produce the thing (be it knowledge or fiction) called metaphysics, I think I perceive that the aim of this natural tendency is to free our notions from the fetters of experience and from the limits of the mere contemplation of nature so far as at least to open to us a field containing mere objects for the pure understanding, which no sensibility can reach, not indeed for the purpose of speculatively occupying ourselves with them (for there we can find no ground to stand on), but because practical principles, which, without finding some such scope for their necessary expectation and hope, could not expand to the universality which reason unavoidably requires from a moral point of view.

So I find that the Psychological Idea (however little it may reveal to me the nature of the human soul, which is higher than all concepts of experience), shows the insufficiency of these concepts plainly enough, and thereby deters me from materialism, the psychological notion of which is unfit for any explanation of nature, and besides confines reason in practical respects. The Cosmological Ideas, by the obvious insufficiency of all possible cognition of nature to satisfy reason in its lawful inquiry, serve in the same manner to keep us from naturalism, which asserts nature to be sufficient for itself. Finally, all natural necessity in the sensible world is conditional, as it always presupposes the dependence of things upon others, and unconditional necessity must be sought only in the unity of a cause different from the world of sense. But as the causality of this cause, in its turn, were it merely nature, could never render the existence of the contingent (as its consequent) comprehensible, reason frees itself by means of the Theological Idea from fatalism (both as a blind natural necessity in the coherence of nature itself, without a first principle, and as a blind causality of this principle itself), and leads to the concept of a cause possessing freedom, or of a Supreme Intelligence. Thus the transcendental Ideas serve, if not to instruct us positively, at least to destroy the rash assertions of Materialism, of Naturalism, and of Fatalism, and thus to afford scope for the moral Ideas beyond the field of speculation. These considerations, I should think, explain in some measure the natural predisposition of which I spoke.

The practical value, which a merely speculative science may have, lies without the bounds of this science, and can therefore be considered as a scholion merely, and like all scholia does not form part of the science itself. This application however surely lies within the bounds of philosophy, especially of philosophy drawn from the pure sources of reason, where its speculative use in metaphysics must necessarily be at unity with its practical use in morals. Hence the unavoidable dialectics of pure reason, considered in metaphysics, as a natural tendency, deserves to be explained not as an illusion merely, which is to be removed, but also, if possible, as a natural provision as regards its end, though this duty, a work of supererogation, cannot justly be assigned to metaphysics proper.

The solutions of these questions which are treated in the chapter on the Regulative Use of the Ideas of Pure Reason[1] should be considered a second scholion which however has a greater affinity with the subject of metaphysics. For there certain rational principles are expounded which determine *a priori* the order of nature or rather of the understanding, which seeks nature's laws through experience. They seem to be constitutive and legislative with regard to experience, though they spring from pure reason, which cannot be considered, like the understanding, as a principle of possible experience. Now whether or not this harmony rests upon the fact, that just as nature does not inhere in appearances or in their source (the sensibility) itself, but only in so far as the latter is in relation to the understanding, as also a systematic unity in applying the understanding to bring about an entirety of all possible experience can only belong to the understanding when in relation to reason; and whether or not experience is in this way mediately subordinate to the legislation of reason: may be discussed by those who desire to trace the nature of reason even beyond its use in metaphysics, into the general principles of a history of nature; I have represented this task as important, but not attempted its solution, in the book itself.[2]

And thus I conclude the analytical solution of the main question which I had proposed: How is metaphysics in general possible? by ascending from the data of its actual use in its consequences, to the grounds of its possibility.

---

[1] *Critique of Pure Reason*, II., chapter III, § 7.

[2] Throughout the *Critique* I never lost sight of the plan not to neglect anything, were it ever so recondite, that could render the inquiry into the nature of pure reason complete. Everybody may afterwards carry his researches as far as he pleases, when he has been merely shown what yet remains to be done. It is this duty which must reasonably be expected of him who has made it his business to survey the whole field, in order to consign it to others for future cultivation and allotment. And to this branch both the scholia belong, which will hardly recommend themselves by their dryness to amateurs, and hence are added here for connoisseurs only.

SCHOLIA

Solution of the General Question of the Prolegomena, "How is Metaphysics Possible as a Science?"

Metaphysics, as a natural disposition of reason, is actual, but if considered by itself alone (as the analytical solution of the third principal question showed), dialectical and illusory. If we think of taking principles from it, and in using them follow the natural, but on that account not less false, illusion, we can never produce science, but only a vain dialectical art, in which one school may outdo another, but none can ever acquire a just and lasting approbation.

In order that as a science metaphysics may be entitled to claim not mere fallacious plausibility, but insight and conviction, a *Critique of Reason* must itself exhibit the whole stock of *a priori* concepts, their division according to their various sources (Sensibility, Understanding, and Reason), together with a complete table of them, the analysis of all these concepts, with all their consequences, especially by means of the deduction of these concepts, the possibility of synthetical cognition *a priori*, the principles of its application and finally its bounds, all in a complete system. Critique, therefore, and critique alone, contains in itself the whole well-proved and well-tested plan, and even all the means required to accomplish metaphysics, as a science; by other ways and means it is impossible. The question here therefore is not so much how this performance is possible, as how to set it going, and induce men of clear heads to quit their hitherto perverted and fruitless cultivation for one that will not deceive, and how such a union for the common end may best be directed.

This much is certain, that whoever has once tasted Critique will be ever after disgusted with all dogmatical twaddle which he formerly put up with, because his reason must have something, and could find nothing better for its support.

Critique stands in the same relation to the common metaphysics of the schools as chemistry does to alchemy, or as astronomy to the astrology of the fortune-teller. I pledge myself that nobody who has read through and through, and grasped the principles of, the *Critique* even in these *Prolegomena* only, will ever return to that old and sophistical pseudo-science; but will rather with a certain delight look forward to metaphysics which is now indeed in his power, requiring no more preparatory discoveries, and now at last affording permanent satisfaction to reason. For here is an advantage upon which, of all possible sciences, metaphysics alone can with certainty reckon: that it can be brought to such completion and fixity as to be incapable of further change, or of any augmentation by new discoveries; because here reason has the sources of its knowledge in itself, not in objects and their observation (*Anschauung*), by which latter its stock of knowledge cannot be further increased. When therefore it has exhibited the fundamental laws of its faculty completely and so definitely as to avoid all misunderstanding, there remains nothing for pure reason to cognise *a priori*, nay, there is even no ground to raise further questions. The sure prospect of knowledge so definite and so compact has a peculiar charm, even though we should set aside all its advantages, of which I shall hereafter speak.

All false art, all vain wisdom, lasts its time, but finally destroys itself, and its highest culture is also the epoch of its decay. That this time is come for metaphysics appears from the state into which it has fallen among all learned nations, despite all the zeal with which other sciences of every kind are prosecuted. The old arrangement of our university studies still preserves its shadow; now and then an Academy of Science tempts men by offering prizes to write essays on it, but it is no longer numbered among thorough sciences; and let anyone judge for himself how a man of genius, if he were called a great metaphysician, would receive the compliment, which may be well-meant, but is scarce envied by anybody.

Yet, though the period of the downfall of all dogmatical metaphysics has undoubtedly arrived, we are yet far from being able to say that the period of its regeneration is come by means of a thorough and complete *Critique of Reason*. All transitions from a tendency to its contrary pass through the stage of indifference, and this moment is the most dangerous for an author, but, in my opinion, the most favorable for the science. For, when party spirit has died out by a total dissolution of former connexions, minds are in the best state

to listen to several proposals for an organisation according to a new plan.

When I say that I hope these *Prolegomena* will excite investigation in the field of critique and afford a new and promising object to sustain the general spirit of philosophy, which seems on its speculative side to want sustenance, I can imagine beforehand that everyone, whom the thorny paths of my *Critique* have tired and put out of humor, will ask me, upon what I found this hope. My answer is, upon the irresistible law of necessity.

That the human mind will ever give up metaphysical researches is as little to be expected as that we should prefer to give up breathing altogether, to avoid inhaling impure air. There will therefore always be metaphysics in the world; nay, everyone, especially every man of reflexion, will have it, and for want of a recognised standard, will shape it for himself after his own pattern. What has hitherto been called metaphysics, cannot satisfy any critical mind, but to forgo it entirely is impossible; therefore a *Critique of Pure Reason* itself must now be attempted or, if one exists, investigated, and brought to the full test, because there is no other means of supplying this pressing want, which is something more than mere thirst for knowledge.

Ever since I have come to know critique, whenever I finish reading a book of metaphysical contents, which, by the preciseness of its notions, by variety, order, and an easy style, was not only entertaining but also helpful, I cannot help asking, "Has this author indeed advanced metaphysics a single step?" The learned men, whose works have been useful to me in other respects and always contributed to the culture of my mental powers, will, I hope, forgive me for saying that I have never been able to find either their essays or my own less important ones (though self-love may recommend them to me) to have advanced the science of metaphysics in the least, and why?

Here is the very obvious reason: metaphysics did not then exist as a science, nor can it be gathered piecemeal, but its germ must be fully preformed in the *Critique*. But in order to prevent all misconception, we must remember what has been already said, that by the analytical treatment of our concepts the understanding gains indeed a great deal, but the science (of metaphysics) is thereby not in the least advanced, because these dissections of concepts are nothing but the materials from which the intention is to carpenter our science. Let the concepts of substance and of accident be ever so well dissected and determined, all this is very well as a preparation for

some future use. But if we cannot prove that in all which exists the substance endures, and only the accidents vary, our science is not the least advanced by all our analyses.

Metaphysics has hitherto never been able to prove *a priori* either this proposition or that of sufficient reason, still less any more complex theorem, such as belongs to psychology or cosmology, or indeed any synthetical proposition. By all its analysing therefore nothing is affected, nothing obtained or forwarded, and the science, after all this bustle and noise, still remains as it was in the days of Aristotle, though far better preparations were made for it than of old, if the clue to synthetical cognitions had only been discovered.

If anyone thinks himself offended, he is at liberty to refute my charge by producing a single synthetical proposition belonging to metaphysics, which he would prove dogmatically *a priori*, for until he has actually performed this feat, I shall not grant that he has truly advanced the science; even should this proposition be sufficiently confirmed by common experience. No demand can be more moderate or more equitable, and in the (inevitably certain) event of its non-performance, no assertion more just, than that hitherto metaphysics has never existed as a science.

But there are two things which, in case the challenge be accepted, I must deprecate: first, trifling about probability and conjecture, which are suited as little to metaphysics as to geometry; and secondly, a decision by means of the magic wand of common sense, which does not convince everyone, but which accommodates itself to personal peculiarities.

For as to the former, nothing can be more absurd, than in metaphysics, a philosophy from pure reason, to think of grounding our judgments upon probability and conjecture. Everything that is to be cognised *a priori* is thereby announced as apodeictically certain, and must therefore be proved in this way. We might as well think of grounding geometry or arithmetic upon conjectures. As to the doctrine of chances in the latter, it does not contain probable, but perfectly certain, judgments concerning the degree of probability of certain cases, under given uniform conditions, which, in the sum of all possible cases, infallibly happen according to the rule, though it is not sufficiently determined in respect to every single chance. Conjectures (by means of induction and of analogy) can be suffered in an empirical science of nature only, yet even there the possibility at least of what we assume must be quite certain.

The appeal to common sense is even more absurd, when concept

and principles are announced as valid, not in so far as they hold with regard to experience, but even beyond the conditions of experience. For what is common sense? It is normal good sense, so far as it judges right. But what is normal good sense? It is the faculty of the knowledge and use of rules *in concreto*, as distinguished from the speculative understanding, which is a faculty of knowing rules *in abstracto*. Common sense can hardly understand the rule "that every event is determined by means of its cause," and can never comprehend it thus generally. It therefore demands an example from experience, and when it hears that this rule means nothing but what it always thought when a pane was broken or a kitchen-utensil missing, it then understands the principle and grants it. Common sense therefore is only of use so far as it can see its rules (though they actually are *a priori*) confirmed by experience; consequently to comprehend them *a priori*, or independently of experience, belongs to the speculative understanding, and lies quite beyond the horizon of common sense. But the province of metaphysics is entirely confined to the latter kind of knowledge, and it is certainly a bad index of common sense to appeal to it as a witness, for it cannot here form any opinion whatever, and men look down upon it with contempt until they are in difficulties, and can find in their speculation neither in nor out.

It is a common subterfuge of those false friends of common sense (who occasionally prize it highly, but usually despise it) to say, that there must surely be at all events some propositions which are immediately certain, and of which there is no occasion to give any proof, or even any account at all, because we otherwise could never stop inquiring into the grounds of our judgments. But if we except the principle of contradiction, which is not sufficient to show the truth of synthetical judgments, they can never adduce, in proof of this privilege, anything else indubitable, which they can immediately ascribe to common sense, except mathematical propositions, such as twice two make four, between two points there is but one straight line, etc. But these judgments are radically different from those of metaphysics. For in mathematics I myself can by thinking construct whatever I represent to myself as possible by a concept: I add to the first two the other two, one by one, and myself make the number four, or I draw in thought from one point to another all manner of lines, equal as well as unequal; yet I can draw one only, which is like itself in all its parts. But I cannot, by all my power of thinking, extract from the concept of a thing the concept of something else, whose existence is necessarily connected with the former, but I must call in experience. And though my understanding furnishes me *a priori* (yet only in reference to possible experience) with the concept of such a connexion (i.e. causation), I cannot exhibit it, like the concepts of mathematics, by (*Anschauung*) visualising them, *a priori*, and so show its possibility *a priori*. This concept, together with the principles of its application, always requires, if it shall hold *a priori* – as is requisite in metaphysics – a justification and deduction of its possibility, because we cannot otherwise know how far it holds good, and whether it can be used in experience only or beyond it also.

Therefore in metaphysics, as a speculative science of pure reason, we can never appeal to common sense, but may do so only when we are forced to surrender it, and to renounce all purely speculative cognition, which must always be knowledge, and consequently when we forego metaphysics itself and its instruction, for the sake of adopting a rational faith which alone may be possible for us, and sufficient to our wants, perhaps even more salutary than knowledge itself. For in this case the attitude of the question is quite altered. Metaphysics must be science, not only as a whole, but in all its parts, otherwise it is nothing; because, as a speculation of pure reason, it finds a hold only on general opinions. Beyond its field, however, probability and common sense may be used with advantage and justly, but on quite special principles, of which the importance always depends on the reference to practical life.

This is what I hold myself justified in requiring for the possibility of metaphysics as a science.

APPENDIX

On what can be done to make metaphysics actual as a science

Since all the ways heretofore taken have failed to attain the goal, and since without a preceding critique of pure reason it is not likely ever to be attained, the present essay now before the public has a fair title to an accurate and careful investigation, except it be thought more advisable to give up all pretensions to metaphysics, to which, if men but would consistently adhere to their purpose, no objection can be made.

If we take the course of things as it is, not as it ought to be, there are two sorts of judgments: (1) one a judgment which precedes investigation (in our case one in which the reader from his own metaphysics pronounces judgment on the *Critique of Pure Reason* which was intended to discuss the very possibility of metaphysics); (2) the other a judgment subsequent to investigation. In the latter the reader is enabled to waive for a while the consequences of the critical researches that may be repugnant to his formerly adopted metaphysics, and first examines the grounds whence those consequences are derived. If what common metaphysics propounds were demonstrably certain, as for instance the theorems of geometry, the former way of judging would hold good. For if the consequences of certain principles are repugnant to established truths, these principles are false and without further inquiry to be repudiated. But if metaphysics does not possess a stock of indisputably certain (synthetical) propositions, and should it even be the case that there are a number of them, which, though among the most specious, are by their consequences in mutual collision, and if no sure criterion of the truth of peculiarly metaphysical (synthetical) propositions is to be met with in it, then the former way of judging is not admissible, but the investigation of the principles of the critique must precede all judgments as to its value.

ON A SPECIMEN OF A JUDGMENT OF THE CRITIQUE PRIOR TO ITS EXAMINATION

This judgment is to be found in the *Göttingischengelehrten Anzeigen*, in the supplement to the third division, of January 19, 1782, pages 40 et seq.

When an author, who is familiar with the subject of his work and endeavors to present his independent reflexions in its elaboration, falls into the hands of a reviewer who, in his turn, is keen enough to discern the points on which the worth or worthlessness of the book rests, who does not cling to words, but goes to the heart of the subject, sifting and testing more than the mere principles which the author takes as his point of departure, the severity of the judgment may indeed displease the latter, but the public does not care, as it gains thereby; and the author himself may be contented, as an opportunity of correcting or explaining his positions is afforded to him at an early date by the examination of a competent judge, in such a manner, that if he believes himself fundamentally right, he can remove in time any stone of offence that might hurt the success of his work.

I find myself, with my reviewer, in quite another position. He seems not to see at all the real matter of the investigation with which (successfully or unsuccessfully) I have been occupied. It is either impatience at thinking out a lengthy work, or vexation at a threatened reform of a science in which he believed he had brought everything to perfection long ago, or, what I am unwilling to imagine, real narrowmindedness, that prevents him from ever carrying his thoughts beyond his school-metaphysics. In short, he passes impatiently in review a long series of propositions, by which, without knowing their premises, we can think nothing, intersperses here and there his censure, the reason of which the reader understands just as little as the propositions against which it is directed; and hence (his report) can neither serve the public nor damage me, in the judgment of experts. I should, for these reasons, have passed over this judgment altogether, were it not that it may afford me occasion for some explanations which may in some cases save the readers of these *Prolegomena* from a misconception.

In order to take a position from which my reviewer could most easily set the whole work in a most unfavorable light, without venturing to trouble himself with any special investigation, he begins and ends by saying:

"This work is a system of transcendent (or, as he translates it, of higher) Idealism."[1]

A glance at this line soon showed me the sort of criticism that I had to expect, much as though the reviewer were one who had never seen or heard of geometry, having found a Euclid, and coming upon various figures in turning over its leaves, were to say, on being asked his opinion of it: "The work is a textbook of drawing; the author introduces a peculiar terminology, in order to give dark, incomprehensible directions, which in the end teach nothing more than what everyone can effect by a fair natural accuracy of eye, etc."

Let us see, in the meantime, what sort of an idealism it is that goes through my whole work, although it does not by a long way constitute the soul of the system.

The dictum of all genuine idealists from the Eleatic school to Bishop Berkeley is contained in this formula: "All cognition through the senses and experience is nothing but sheer illusion, and only, in the ideas of the pure understanding and reason there is truth."

The principle that throughout dominates and determines my Idealism is on the contrary: "All cognition of things merely from pure understanding or pure reason is nothing but sheer illusion, and only in experience is there truth."

But this is directly contrary to idealism proper. How came I then to use this expression for quite an opposite purpose, and how came my reviewer to see it everywhere?

The solution of this difficulty rests on something that could have been very easily understood from the general bearing of the work, if the reader had only desired to do so. Space and time, together with all that they contain, are not things nor qualities in themselves, but belong merely to the appearances of the latter: up to this point I am one in confession with the above idealists. But these, and amongst them more particularly Berkeley, regarded space as a mere empirical presentation that, like the phenomenon it contains, is only

[1] By no means "*higher*." High towers, and metaphysically great men resembling them, round both of which there is commonly much wind, are not for me. My place is the fruitful *bathos*, the bottom-land, of experience; and the word transcendental, the meaning of which is so often explained by me, but not once grasped by my reviewer (so carelessly has he regarded everything), does not signify something passing beyond all experience, but something that indeed precedes it *a priori*, but that is intended simply to make cognition of experience possible. If these conceptions overstep experience, their employment is termed transcendent, a word which must be distinguished from transcendental, the latter being limited to the immanent use, that is, to experience. All misunderstandings of this kind have been sufficiently guarded against in the work itself, but my reviewer found his advantage in misunderstanding me.

known to us by means of experience or perception, together with its determinations. I, on the contrary, prove in the first place, that space (and also time, which Berkeley did not consider) and all its determinations *a priori*, can be cognised by us, because, no less than time, it inheres in our sensibility as a pure form before all perception or experience and makes all intuition of the same, and therefore all its phenomena, possible. It follows from this that as truth rests on universal and necessary laws as its criteria, experience, according to Berkeley, can have no criteria of truth, because its phenomena (according to him) have nothing *a priori* at their foundation; whence it follows, that they are nothing but sheer illusion; whereas with us, space and time (in conjunction with the pure conceptions of the understanding) prescribe their law to all possible experience *a priori*, and at the same time afford the certain criterion for distinguishing truth from illusion therein.[1]

My so-called (properly critical) Idealism is of quite a special character, in that it subverts the ordinary idealism, and that through it all cognition *a priori*, even that of geometry, first receives objective reality, which, without my demonstrated ideality of space and time, could not be maintained by the most zealous realists. This being the state of the case, I could have wished, in order to avoid all misunderstanding, to have named this conception of mine otherwise, but to alter it altogether was impossible. It may be permitted me however, in future, as has been above intimated, to term it the formal, or better still, the critical Idealism, to distinguish it from the dogmatic Idealism of Berkeley, and from the sceptical Idealism of Descartes.

Beyond this, I find nothing further remarkable in the judgment of my book. The reviewer criticises here and there, makes sweeping criticisms, a mode prudently chosen, since it does not betray one's own knowledge or ignorance; a single thorough criticism in detail, had it touched the main question, as is only fair, would have exposed, it may be my error, or it may be my reviewer's measure of insight into this species of research. It was, moreover, not a badly conceived plan, in order at once to take from readers (who are accustomed to

[1]Idealism proper always has a mystical tendency, and can have no other, but mine is solely designed for the purpose of comprehending the possibility of our cognition *a priori* as to objects of experience, which is a problem never hitherto solved or even suggested. In this way all mystical idealism falls to the ground, for (as may be seen already in Plato) it inferred from our cognitions *a priori* (even from those of geometry) another intuition different from that of the senses (namely, an intellectual intuition), because it never occurred to anyone that the senses themselves might intuite *a priori*.

form their conceptions of books from newspaper reports) the desire to read the book itself, to pour out in one breath a number of passages in succession, torn from their connexion, and their grounds of proof and explanations, and which must necessarily sound sense-less, especially considering how antipathetic they are to all school-metaphysics; to exhaust the reader's patience *ad nauseam*, and then, after having made me acquainted with the sensible proposition that persistent illusion is truth, to conclude with the crude paternal moralisation: to what end, then, the quarrel with accepted language, to what end, and whence, the idealistic distinction? A judgment which seeks all that is characteristic of my book, first supposed to be metaphysically heterodox, in a mere innovation of the nomenclature, proves clearly that my would-be judge has understood nothing of the subject, and in addition, has not understood himself.[1]

My reviewer speaks like a man who is conscious of important and superior insight which he keeps hidden; for I am aware of nothing recent with respect to metaphysics that could justify his tone. But he should not withhold his discoveries from the world, for there are doubtless many who, like myself, have not been able to find in all the fine things that have for long past been written in this department, anything that has advanced the science by so much as a finger-breadth; we find indeed the giving a new point to definitions, the supplying of lame proofs with new crutches, the adding to the crazy-quilt of metaphysics fresh patches or changing its pattern; but all this is not what the world requires. The world is tired of metaphysical assertions; it wants the possibility of the science, the sources from which certainty therein can be derived, and certain criteria by which it may distinguish the dialectical illusion of pure reason from truth. To this the critic seems to possess a key, otherwise he would never have spoken out in such a high tone.

But I am inclined to suspect that no such requirement of the science has ever entered his thoughts, for in that case he would have directed his judgment to this point, and even a mistaken attempt in

---

[1]The reviewer often fights with his own shadow. When I oppose the truth of experience to dream, he never thinks that I am here speaking simply of the well-known *somnio objective sumto* of the Wolffian philosophy, which is merely formal, and with which the distinction between sleeping and waking is in no way concerned, and in a transcendental philosophy indeed can have no place. For the rest, he calls my deduction of the categories and table of the principles of the understanding, "common well-known axioms of logic and ontology, expressed in an idealistic manner." The reader need only consult these *Prolegomena* upon this point to convince himself that a more miserable and historically incorrect judgment could hardly be made.

such an important matter would have won his respect. If that be the case, we are once more good friends. He may penetrate as deeply as he likes into metaphysics, without anyone hindering him; only as concerns that which lies outside metaphysics, its sources, which are to be found in reason, he cannot form a judgment. That my suspicion is not without foundation, is proved by the fact that he does not mention a word about the possibility of synthetic knowledge *a priori*, the special problem upon the solution of which the fate of metaphysics wholly rests, and upon which my *Critique* (as well as the present *Prolegomena*) entirely hinges. The Idealism he encountered, and which he hung upon, was only taken up in the doctrine as the sole means of solving the above problem (although it received its confirmation on other grounds), and hence he must have shown either that the above problem does not possess the importance I attribute to it (even in these *Prolegomena*), or that by my conception of appearances it is either not solved at all, or can be better solved in another way; but I do not find a word of this in the criticism. The reviewer, then, understands nothing of my work, and possibly also nothing of the spirit and essential nature of metaphysics itself; and it is not, what I would rather assume, the hurry of a man incensed at the labor of plodding through so many obstacles, that threw an unfavorable shadow over the work lying before him, and made its fundamental features unrecognisable.

There is a good deal to be done before a learned journal, it matters not with what care its writers may be selected, can maintain its otherwise well-merited reputation, in the field of metaphysics as elsewhere. Other sciences and branches of knowledge have their standard. Mathematics has it, in itself; history and theology, in profane or sacred books; natural science and the art of medicine, in mathematics and experience; jurisprudence, in law books; and even matters of taste in the examples of the ancients. But for the judgment of the thing called metaphysics, the standard has yet to be found. I have made an attempt to determine it, as well as its use. What is to be done, then, until it be found, when works of this kind have to be judged of? If they are of a dogmatic character, one may do what one likes; no one will play the master over others here for long, before someone else appears to deal with him in the same manner. If, however, they are critical in their character, not indeed with reference to other works, but to reason itself, so that the standard of judgment cannot be assumed but has first of all to be sought for, then, though objection and blame may indeed be permitted, yet a certain degree of leniency is indispensable, since the need is common to us all, and the lack of the necessary insight makes the high-handed attitude of judge unwarranted.

In order, however, to connect my defense with the interest of the philosophical commonwealth, I propose a test, which must be decisive as to the mode, whereby all metaphysical investigations may be directed to their common purpose. This is nothing more than what formerly mathematicians have done, in establishing the advantage of their methods by competition. I challenge my critic to demonstrate, as is only just, on *a priori* grounds, in his way, a single really metaphysical principle asserted by him. Being metaphysical it must be synthetic and cognised *a priori* from conceptions, but it may also be any one of the most indispensable principles, as for instance, the principle of the persistence of substance, or of the necessary determination of events in the world by their causes. If he cannot do this (silence however is confession), he must admit, that as metaphysics without apodeictic certainty of propositions of this kind is nothing at all, its possibility or impossibility must before all things be established in a critique of the pure reason. Thus he is bound either to confess that my principles in the *Critique* are correct, or he must prove their invalidity. But as I can already foresee, that, confidently as he has hitherto relied on the certainty of his principles, when it comes to a strict test he will not find a single one in the whole range of metaphysics he can bring forward, I will concede to him an advantageous condition, which can only be expected in such a competition, and will relieve him of the *onus probandi* by laying it on myself.

He finds in these *Prolegomena* and in my *Critique* (chapter on the "Theses and Antitheses of the Four Antinomies") eight propositions, of which two and two contradict one another, but each of which necessarily belongs to metaphysics, by which it must either be accepted or rejected (although there is not one that has not in this time been held by some philosopher). Now he has the liberty of selecting any one of these eight propositions at his pleasure, and accepting it without any proof, of which I shall make him a present, but only one (for waste of time will be just as little serviceable to him as to me), and then of attacking my proof of the opposite proposition. If I can save this one, and at the same time show, that according to principles which every dogmatic metaphysics must necessarily recognise, the opposite of the proposition adopted by him can be just as clearly proved, it is thereby established that metaphysics has a hereditary failing, not to be explained, much less set aside, until we ascend to its birth-place, pure reason itself, and thus my *Critique* must either be accepted or a better one take its place; it must at least be studied, which is the only thing I now require. If, on the other hand, I cannot save my demonstration, then a synthetic proposition *a priori* from dogmatic principles is to be reckoned to the score of my opponent, then also I will deem my impeachment of ordinary metaphysics as unjust, and pledge myself to recognise his stricture on my *Critique* as justified (although this would not be the consequence by a long way). To this end it would be necessary, it seems to me, that he should step out of his incognito. Otherwise I do not see how it could be avoided, that instead of dealing with one, I should be honored by several problems coming from anonymous and unqualified opponents.

PROPOSALS AS TO AN INVESTIGATION OF THE CRITIQUE UPON WHICH A JUDGMENT MAY FOLLOW

I feel obliged to the honored public even for the silence with which it for a long time favored my *Critique*, for this proves at least a postponement of judgment, and some supposition that in a work, leaving all beaten tracks and striking out on a new path, in which one cannot at once perhaps so easily find one's way, something may perchance lie, from which an important but at present dead branch of human knowledge may derive new life and productiveness. Hence may have originated a solicitude for the as yet tender shoot, lest it be destroyed by a hasty judgment. A test of a judgment, delayed for the above reasons, is now before my eye in the *Gothaischen gelehrten Zeitung*, the thoroughness of which every reader will himself perceive, from the clear and unperverted presentation of a fragment of one of the first principles of my work, without taking into consideration my own suspicious praise.

And now I propose, since an extensive structure cannot be judged of as a whole from a hurried glance, to test it piece by piece from its foundations, so thereby the present *Prolegomena* may fitly be used as a general outline with which the work itself may occasionally be compared. This notion, if it were founded on nothing more than my conceit of importance, such as vanity commonly attributes to one's own productions, would be immodest and would deserve to be repudiated with disgust. But now, the interests of speculative philosophy have arrived at the point of total extinction, while human reason hangs upon them with inextinguishable affection, and only after having been ceaselessly deceived does it vainly attempt to change this into indifference.

In our thinking age it is not to be supposed but that many deserving men would use any good opportunity of working for the common interest of the more and more enlightened reason, if there were only some hope of attaining the goal. Mathematics, natural science, laws, arts, even morality, etc., do not completely fill the soul; there is always a space left over, reserved for pure and speculative reason, the vacuity of which prompts us to seek in vagaries, buffooneries, and myticism for what seems to be employment and entertainment, but what actually is mere pastime; in order to deaden the troublesome voice of reason, which in accordance with its nature requires something that can satisfy it, and not merely subserve other ends or the interests of our inclinations. A consideration, therefore, which is concerned only with reason as it exists for it itself, has as I may reasonably suppose a great fascination for everyone who has attempted thus to extend his conceptions, and I may even say a greater than any other theoretical branch of knowledge, for which he would not willingly exchange it, because here all other cognitions, and even purposes, must meet and unite themselves in a whole.

I offer, therefore, these *Prolegomena* as a sketch and textbook for this investigation, and not the work itself. Although I am even now perfectly satisfied with the latter as far as contents, order, and mode of presentation, and the care that I have expended in weighing and testing every sentence before writing it down, are concerned (for it has taken me years to satisfy myself fully, not only as regards the whole, but in some cases even as to the sources of one particular proposition); yet I am not quite satisfied with my exposition in some sections of the doctrine of elements, as for instance in the deduction of the conceptions of the Understanding, or in that on the paralogisms of pure reason, because a certain diffuseness takes away from their clearness, and in place of them, what is here said in the *Prolegomena* respecting these sections, may be made the basis of the test.

It is the boast of the Germans that where steady and continuous industry are requisite, they can carry things farther than other nations. If this opinion be well founded, an opportunity, a business, presents itself, the successful issue of which we can scarcely doubt, and in which all thinking men can equally take part, though they have hitherto been unsuccessful in accomplishing it and in thus confirming the above good opinion. But this is chiefly because the science in question is of so peculiar a kind, that it can be at once brought to completion and to that enduring state that it will never be able to be brought in the least degree farther or increased by later discoveries, or even changed (leaving here out of account adornment by greater clearness in some places, or additional uses), and this is an advantage no other science has or can have, because there is none so fully isolated and independent of others, and which is concerned with the faculty of cognition pure and simple. And the present moment seems, moreover, not to be unfavorable to my expectation, for just now, in Germany, no one seems to know wherewith to occupy himself, apart from the so-called useful sciences, so as to pursue not mere play, but a business possessing an enduring purpose.

To discover the means how the endeavors of the learned may be united in such a purpose, I must leave to others. In the meantime, it is my intention to persuade anyone merely to follow my propositions, or even to flatter me with the hope that he will do so; but attacks, repetitions, limitations, or confirmation, completion, and extension, as the case may be, should be appended. If the matter be but investigated from its foundation, it cannot fail that a system, albeit not my own, shall be erected, that shall be a possession for future generations for which they may have reason to be grateful.

It would lead us too far here to show what kind of metaphysics may be expected, when only the principles of criticism have been perfected, and how, because the old false feathers have been pulled out, she need by no means appear poor and reduced to an insignificant figure, but may be in other respects richly and respectably adorned. But other and great uses which would result from such a reform strike one immediately. The ordinary metaphysics had its uses, in that it sought out the elementary conceptions of the pure understanding in order to make them clear through analysis, and definite by explanation. In this way it was a training for reason, in whatever direction it might be turned; but this was all the good it did; service was subsequently effaced when it favored conceit by venturesome assertions, sophistry by subtle distinctions and adornment, and shallowness by the ease with which it decided the most difficult problems by means of a little school-wisdom, which is only the more seductive the more it has the choice, on the one hand, of taking something from the language of science, and on the other from that of popular discourse, thus being everything to everybody, but in reality nothing at all. By criticism, however, a standard is given to our judgment, whereby knowledge may be with certainty distinguished from pseudo-science, and firmly founded, being brought into full operation in metaphysics; a mode of thought extending by degrees its beneficial influence over every other use of reason, at once infusing into it the true philosophical spirit. But the service also that metaphysics performs for theology, by making it independent of the judgment of dogmatic speculation, thereby assuring it completely against the attacks of all such opponents, is certainly not to be valued lightly. For ordinary metaphysics, although it promised the latter much advantage, could not keep this promise, and moreover, by summoning speculative dogmatics to its assistance, did nothing but arm enemies against itself. Mysticism, which can prosper in a rationalistic age only when it hides itself behind a system of school-metaphysics, under the protection of which it may venture to rave with a semblance of rationality, is driven from this, its last hiding-place, by critical philosophy. Last, but not least, it cannot be otherwise than important to a teacher of metaphysics, to be able to say with universal assent, that what he expounds is Science, and that thereby genuine services will be rendered to the commonweal.

A PRUSSIAN HUME AND A SCOTTISH KANT

Lewis White Beck

In a letter to Herder written in 1781, Hamann said of Kant: "He certainly deserves the title, 'a Prussian Hume.' "[1] No one, so far as I know, has had the temerity to state explicitly that Hume deserves the title, "a Scottish Kant." But almost. One trend in contemporary Hume interpretation may finally lead someone to make this claim, or accusation. H. H. Price refers to "a Scottish version of Kant's Copernican Revolution."[2] Robert Paul Wolff finds that Hume's propensities "play a role quite similar to that of the categories in the *Critique of Pure Reason.*"[3] W. H. Walsh says of the Humean imagination that it is "simply the Kantian understanding in disguise."[4]

The traditional notion that Kant and Hume are diametrically opposed, and that whatever merit Kant's philosophy has depends upon his having given a cogent "answer to Hume," does not seem as obvious as it used to. While no one would deny that the great divide between naturalism and transcendentalism[5] in the theory of knowledge separates these two thinkers, even that divide is not as clear-cut as it once appeared, and is now rendered somewhat obscure by emphasis upon a pragmatism[6] believed to be pervasive in their constructions of a common world out of private experiences. With growing attention to the role of normative structures in Hume's analysis of experience, and to the possibility of relativizing the hard, fixed categorial lines found in Kant's analysis, it becomes possible to see Kant and Hume as engaged in a common project.[7] I do not wish to go too far and talk as if the differences were less important than the similarities between these two men. But I do wish to make it appear meet, fitting, and seemly to talk about Kant in a gathering called to celebrate the life and work of Hume – something that would, I think, have appeared thirty or forty years ago to be in bad taste.

The problem of causation has traditionally been seen as the bone of contention between Hume and Kant. I shall, on the contrary, argue that it is precisely here that a surprising degree of accommodation between them is possible. To this end, I shall first recount Kant's stand on the conception of causality both before and after Hume awoke him from his dogmatic slumber.[8] I shall then show that Kant misunderstood Hume's views in the *Treatise*, but that this misunderstanding was a fruitful one. Finally I shall try to show that something in fact needed by Hume but not supplied in the *Treatise* was given by Kant when he attempted to refute the point he erroneously believed to have been argued for by Hume.

Kant's treatment of the problem of causation goes through three distinct phases, which I shall call the pre-Humean, the quasi-Humean, and the post-Humean.[9]

1. In 1755, the year Sulzer translated Hume's *Enquiry Concerning Human Understanding*, Kant was busy criticizing Wolff's derivation of the causal principle from that of sufficient reason, and Wolff's derivation of the latter from the principle of contradiction. But in the work Kant wrote that year, the *Nova dilucidatio*, he attempted to give a rationalistic proof of the principle of efficient causality. This proof is vulnerable to Hume's refutation of all such arguments, which is to be found in the *Treatise*, Book I, Part iii, Chapter 3, but Kant was at that time, and perhaps always, ignorant of Hume's refutation.

2. In 1763, in the essay *Versuch, den Begriff der negativen Grössen in die Weltweisheit einzuführen*, Kant gave up his rationalistic arguments to demonstrate the logical necessity of causal judgments. Logical necessity, he says, depends upon identity and contradiction; but any causal judgment may be denied without contradiction, and no statement of identity entails a causal connection between things not identical: "The rain never follows the wind because of the law of identity."[10] Now admittedly this does sound like Hume, and by this time he had certainly read Sulzer's translation. But one cannot be sure that these new ideas are to be attributed to his reading of Hume, for there was another philosopher nearer home who had definitely influenced Kant and whose thoughts moved in the same

direction. This was Christian August Crusius, an anti-Wolffian who had taught (if I may use later Kantian terminology) that the principle of causation, like every specific causal judgment, is synthetic and not analytic; and that the principle of causation, unlike any specific causal judgment, is a priori and not known as a result of induction. While Crusius had given an account of the proclivity of the mind to think causally – not wholly unlike that given later by Thomas Reid – Kant then and always rejected Crusius's explanation because it required, he thought, a belief in a pre-established harmony and permitted a subjective necessity to masquerade as an objective necessity.[11] In 1763, however, Kant had little to say about his own theory of causation, and what he says is obscure and tentative.

Three years later, in the *Träume eines Geistersehers*, Kant writes in an ironic, semi-skeptical manner strongly reminiscent of Hume. He insists that causal connections are not intelligible, that is to say, founded on reason, but appear to us to be intelligible simply because they are made familiar to us through repetitive experience. "That my will is capable of moving my arm is no more comprehensible to me than if someone told me he could stop the moon in its orbit."[12] "The grounds of reason, whether used as an argument for or against the possibility or impossibility of a thing, are absolutely irrelevant. The right of decision must be left to experience [*Erfahrungen*] alone."[13] The ultimate and irreducible causes of things, the *Grundkräfte*, are either unknown or unintelligible to us, and the a posteriori contingency of every causal judgment demands that the way be left open for continual revision of our putative causal knowledge. Kant, in good Humean idiom though citing only Voltaire, appeals to mankind to remain within the limits of experience, since specific causal knowledge is founded on and extends only as far as experience.

While the sentiments in this ironical work resemble those we would expect Hume to express in the face of the fantastic stories of Swedenborg, once again there is no decisive reason to ascribe this essay to Hume's influence on Kant. Such ideas as those I have mentioned were widely accepted in Germany at this time, among natural scientists like Maupertuis and anti-Wolffian philosophers like Crusius and his extensive school, and Berlin enlighteners.[14] The skeptical conclusions which are so prominent a feature of Hume's *Enquiry* are here hardly more than *obiter dicta*; there is no argument that causal inferences depend upon irrational propensities in the mind and are instinctive. Most of the Humean ideas in this essay were very much in the air in Germany, and it would be difficult or impossible to trace them to one source.[15]

3. The post-Humean phase of Kant's treatment of causation is well known. As I shall repeatedly have to refer to it in later parts of this paper, a brief historical account will suffice at this time. We must consider three events of the years 1770 and 1772.

(a) In 1770 Kant published his Inaugural Dissertation, which sharply separated the sensible from the rational faculties in man, distinguished between the sensible or phenomenal world and the intelligible or noumenal world, and formulated the a priori forms of both. The proper method of metaphysics, which is now seen as the systematic knowledge of the intelligible world, requires preventing the ascription of the forms of sensible knowledge (space and time) to the objects of pure reason; space and time are the subjective ways things look to human beings, but metaphysics is to deal with things as they are, and most errors in metaphysics arise from the surreptitious application of spatial and temporal predicates to purely intelligible things. Though Kant is copious in his elaboration of the forms of sensibility – so much so that this treatment passes over almost without change into the transcendental aesthetic of the *Critique of Pure Reason* – he finds comparatively little to say about pure intelligible forms. What he does say is hardly more than a warmed-over version of some parts of Wolff's ontology, and this little is jettisoned when he comes to write the Dialectic of the *Critique of Pure Reason*, for by then he has realized that there is no synthetic knowledge of what is not spatial and temporal. But this was not his belief in 1770, and he confidently expected to proceed immediately with his metaphysical writings which would expound the principles of pure reason in their application to a purely intelligible world.

Toward the end of the Dissertation, however, he introduces a strangely hybrid form of principle, principles which have a *purely subjective though purely intellectual origin*: "They are commended to us only by the special nature of the intellect, owing to their convenience for its free and extended employment . . . upon conditions under which the intellect seems to itself to make easy and ready use of its insight." They are "principles of convenience" or "rules of judgment, to which we willingly submit and to which we cling as if they were axioms [which they are not], solely for the reason that if we gave them up, scarcely any judgment about a given object would be possible to our intellect."[16] The first of these is the principle of causality according to the law of nature.

(b) In his famous letter of 21 February 1772, to Marcus Herz, Kant refers to an objection which had been raised by Lambert[17] to the Inaugural Dissertation's application of theoretical concepts (presumably including the concept of causation) to purely intelligible objects. He confesses that in writing what he is now engaged upon, the *Critique of Pure Reason*, he noticed that "something essential was lacking" in his account of how purely intelligible concepts which originate a priori in the mind can refer to objects: "If such intellectual conceptions depend on our inner activity, whence comes the agreement that they are supposed to have with objects?"[18] He rejects the answers given by Plato, Malebranche, and Crusius, but does not give his own answer; rather he claims to have found a rule or rules for the discovery of such concepts. To use the later terminology of the *Critique*, he has discovered the root of the metaphysical deduction of the categories, and presumably thought that it could do the work later assigned to the transcendental deduction of the categories,[19] for he expresses confidence that the book will be finished in three months.

(c) What led to the extension of the three months to nine years? The third event is more conjectural, but I believe there is sufficient evidence to substantiate it. At Easter time, 1772, there was published a German translation of Beattie's *Essay on the Nature and Immutability of Truth*.[20] Suddenly, through copious quotations, there was opened to Kant many of the riches of Hume's *Treatise of Human Nature*. Kant now realized that Hume had not confined his skeptical attacks to the putative necessity and intelligibility of specific causal judgments − attacks which he himself had participated in − but had raised a serious problem about the causal principle itself. In Beattie's words, "Our opinion of the necessity of a cause to the production of everything which hath a beginning, is by Mr. Hume supposed to arise from observation and experience."[21]

It was this suggestion (*Erinnerung*[22]) of Hume which awoke Kant from his "dogmatic slumber."[23] He was "far from following [Hume] in the conclusions he arrived at by regarding, not the whole of his problem, but a part"; he "generalized" Hume's problem and found that "the connection of cause and effect was by no means the only concept by which the understanding thinks the connections of things a priori."[24] Thus was born the fundamental question: "How are synthetic judgments possible a priori?" He finds Hume to be correct in rejecting the possibility of necessary synthetic judgments which go beyond experience, but he thinks Hume was in error in failing to see the difference between a priori in the sense of "going beyond possible experience" and a priori in the sense of "underlying possible experience."[25] As heretofore, he accepts Hume's conclusion that all specific causal judgments are contingent, but under the tutelage of Beattie he states, "Hume was in error in inferring from the contingency of our determinations in accordance with the law [of causality] the contingency of the law itself."[26]

Had Beattie not said that Hume treated the causal principle in the same way, and with the same skeptical conclusions,[27] that he had dealt with specific causal laws, there would have been no interruption of Kant's dogmatic slumber. But I shall now attempt to show that Beattie, though he could have documented his statement (he did not) with at most two or three quotations[28] from the *Treatise*, may have misled Kant into thinking that there was an argument to which he needed to reply, not just an "opinion." There is no such argument, and Hume's implicit account of the causal principle is much more like Kant's own than Kant had any reason to suspect. This suggests that we owe the inception of the *Critique of Pure Reason* to a fortunate historical error.

Hume distinguishes two questions concerning necessary connection: (a) "For what reason do we pronounce it *necessary*, that everything whose existence has a beginning, should also have a cause?", and (b) "Why we conclude, that such particular causes must *necessarily* have such particular effects."[29] I shall simplify and restate these by referring to them respectively as the question (a) why every event necessarily has some cause, and (b) why the same cause necessarily has the same effect? Still more briefly, I shall refer to the two principles Hume is investigating as (a) every-event-some-cause, and (b) same-cause-same-effect.

Hume concludes that the principle every-event-some-cause is not known by intuition or reason, and hence that "that opinion must necessarily arise from observation and experience," but I look in vain for an answer to the question Hume now formulates: "How experience gives rise to such a principle?". Having asked this question he not only never answers it, he does not even discuss it again.

He finds that it will be "more convenient" to answer the question why same-cause-same-effect and then to "sink" the question why every-event-some-cause in it, in the expectation that "'T will, perhaps, be found in the end, that the same answer will serve both questions."[30] This conjecture leads us to expect a Mill-like argument that the former principle is an induction from cases falling under the latter, an induction from successful inductions, for that is the only way in which the principle every-event-some-cause could possibly arise from observation and experience. But, as we shall see, Hume does not anticipate Mill's argument and, in fact, never answers the first question at all. Though he says "It is universally allowed that nothing exists without a cause of its existence."[31] he also grants that it is easy to conceive "that there is no absolute nor metaphysical necessity, that every beginning of existence should be attended with [a cause]."[32] Question (a), having once been sunk in question (b), never re-emerges.

Rather, I shall try to show that the principle every-event-some-cause remains on dry land, ready to rescue the principle same-cause-same-effect when the latter is threatened by recalcitrant experience. Hume availed himself of the principle every-event-some-cause precisely in those cases where the intimate connection he had discovered among regular sequence, contiguity, association, belief, and causation can get no purchase on experience because regular sequence is lacking.

Had the application of the two principles always had the same occasion and outcome, naturally Hume would have preferred to use the second, which he does fully account for. But where they do not, he uses the first to permit the extrapolation of the second beyond and even against the teachings of experience, and he gives much the same kind of practical justification for so using it that he had already given for using the principle same-cause-same-effect. Usually Hume warns against giving causal explanations where there is no association of ideas and induction to back them up, thinking that that is the operation of fancy. But there is at least one instance of the proper use of causal explanation which is both counter-associational and practically justified.

I refer to Hume's account of the porter coming into his room. Hume is sitting in his chamber when on a sudden he hears a noise as of a door opening and a little after sees a porter advance upon him with a letter. "This gives occasion to many new reflexions and reasonings," as follows:

> To consider these phaenomena of the porter and the letter in a certain light, they are contradictions to common experience [in which the sound of a door opening is commonly associated with the sight of its opening], and may be regarded as

objections to those maxims, which we form concerning the connexions of causes and effects. I am accustom'd to hear such a sound, and see such an object in motion at the same time. I have not receiv'd in this particular instance both these perceptions. These observations are contrary.[33]

The conclusion is that:

as all reasoning concerning matters of fact arises only from custom, and custom can only be the effect of repeated perceptions, the extending of custom and reasoning beyond the perceptions can never be the direct and natural effect of the constant repetition and connexion, but must arise from the co-operation of some other principles.[34]

Before considering what these other principles are, we must say something about the role of principles and general rules in Hume's philosophy.[35] Hume often writes, and is usually read, as if belief and causal belief are created in us passively by the mechanism of association. Yet Hume is not content to explain why we believe as we do; he wants to give rules for the correction of our beliefs. These rules, of course, do not have a transcendental origin or sanction, though they function normatively as if they were a priori regulative. What they are is revealed by Hume's contrasting the functions of the imagination whereby we may believe mere coincidences to be causally connected, with "the general and more establish'd properties of the imagination" (which is the understanding[36]) whereby the brute-custom origin of causal beliefs is refined by more cautious inquiry, and superstition is made to give way to science. The human mind is in constant battle with itself[37] – there is a struggle between its instinctive inference to causation from mere association which may be accidental, and its reflective weighing of evidence to achieve a conception of the world less affected by the vagaries of accidental experience. Hume remarks that "reflection on *general rules* keeps us from augmenting our belief upon every increase of the force and vivacity of our ideas."[38]

What is needed in the case of the porter is the inverse of this consideration: A reflexion on the general rule every-event-some-cause keeps us from *reducing* our belief in same-cause-same-effect upon every diminution of force and vivacity of our ideas which occurs when the impression generally associated with an idea is lacking. Regrettably, Hume does not cite this general rule, which cannot have originated in the same way as the generalization which is contradicted by the case of the porter. Rather, he cites explicitly only the general rule that objects intermittently perceived should be ascribed continued existence when thought governed by this rule will increase the coherence of experience. Presumably he cited only this rule because of his predominant concern in that chapter with the status of unobserved objects.[39] The general rule arises from the following consideration:

> Objects have a certain coherence even as they appear to our senses; but this coherence is much greater and more uniform, if we suppose the objects to have a continu'd existence; and as the mind is once in the train of observing an uniformity among objects, it naturally continues, till it renders the uniformity as compleat as possible.[40]

This gives rise to the theory of double existence, which he says has the backing neither of reason nor of imagination.[41] It does not follow from the standard Humean analysis of causation; it follows rather from Hume's (and the common man's) conviction that if the cause of an event is not found within experience it must be feigned to lie outside it. That is why I said that the first principle, instead of being sunk in the second, is used to rescue the second when experience "contradicts" it.

The description Hume gives of the objects perceived is, in Locke's terminology, in terms of coexistence, not of causation. "Objects have a certain coherence," he says; but the constancy of conjunction of simultaneous properties is not essentially different from the constancy of conjunction of serial properties. In both there is association and consequent belief.

In Hume's observing the porter entering his room, there is a manifest absence of coherence. He knows that an opening door (as seen) is associated with a particular sound. But here one is present to his senses and the other absent. If coherence and causation were based exclusively on association of impressions, this would be a negative instance. It would lead the pure inductivist to say that the association between the sight and the sound is weaker than it had been, and the probability of the causal judgment less than it had been. He might even deny that the noise had a cause. Neither Hume nor the common man will draw such a conclusion. Both claim that had they been looking, they would have seen the door open. Why? Because they believe that every event has some cause even if the preceding impression is not the same. "There is nothing existent, either externally or internally, which is not to be consider'd either as a cause or an effect."[42]

The counterfactual claim is supported by *two* principles: every-event-some-cause and same-cause-same-effect. It would be of little use to assert the former without the latter, for to get any practical benefit we must use the latter. But while the first is independent of the second, we cannot maintain the second without the first, since the case before us is counterexample to the second taken alone.

Thus Hume did not "sink" the first question in the second so successfully that the first question need not be raised again. Hume's principle same-cause-same-effect is an induction from his answer to simpler questions about what causes what. But he has no answer to the question about every-event-some-cause, since that is not an induction from the second; rather, it comes into its own where the second breaks down. The principle every-event-some-cause permits us to reinstate the principle same-cause-same-effect in the face of negative instances. We reinstate it for the sake of our need to make our experiential coherence "much greater and more uniform" than the intermittent perceptions we actually have; but it cannot itself be the result of associations of perceptions because it functions precisely where our perceptions are *not* regular enough to support associations, causal beliefs, and the principle same-cause-same-effect.

This reading of Hume takes at least a small step toward justifying the epithet "the Scottish Kant." It shows that Hume distinguished the a posteriori causal laws induced from the experience of regular sequences from a quite different causal law which is not based on mere association and thus not vulnerable to disconfirmation when the sequence of impressions is not uniform. It is a principle of a higher order which regulates our ascription of causality in the absence of association and even where association and expectation are flouted by the actual course of our impressions. Naturally Hume does not have a theory that one of the conceptions of causation is a priori and the other a posteriori; but a priori is as a priori does, and when a principle is called upon to correct experience, it is functioning in an a priori manner regardless of its origin. It is at least debatable whether Kant's a priori principles have any higher function in spite of their nobler ancestry.

This reading of Hume also throws interesting light on Kant's theory of causation and the true nature of his "answer to Hume." It has often been objected that Kant's second analogy does nothing to support the principle same-cause-same-effect.[43] This is true, but it was not Kant's purpose there to support *that* principle; he was concerned only with the principle every-event-some-cause, and did not "sink" this principle in same-cause-same-effect. He says:

> The accepted view is that only through perception and comparison of events repeatedly following in a uniform manner upon preceding appearances are we enabled to discover a rule according to which certain events always follow upon certain appearances, and that this is the way in which we are first led to construct for ourselves the concept of cause.[44]

Kant accepts the first of these tenets. The discovery of what is the cause of what is exactly the same for Kant as for Hume. Kant makes no claim that we can discover by reason, or know a priori, the connection of any specific cause with a specific effect and understand its necessity.[45] Even the principle same-cause-same-effect is not known a priori to be true. For Kant, it is a regulative principle,[46] functioning like the principle Hume postulates that unobserved causes must be like observed ones.[47] So far there is little dispute between Kant and Hume. The big difference lies in the second clause of the "accepted belief," namely, that the concept of cause arises in the same manner as the knowledge of what is the cause of some event. Kant insists that the first principle cannot arise in the way the second principle does according to Beattie's reading of Hume, but is rather an a priori condition for the discovery and use of the second.

I shall try to show why Hume did not agree with this, and how Kant supported it. Every reader of Hume is baffled by his repeatedly and arbitrarily shifting back and forth between talking about objects and events and talking about impressions.[48] Sometimes he tries to justify this[49] and sometimes he anticipates Kant in distinguishing between them in a phenomenalistic way.[50] But usually, I think, he is just careless and profits from this carelessness. Because he does not clearly maintain the distinction, in setting up his problem he fails to distinguish between his awareness of a sequence of states in a perceived object and a sequence of mere impressions of a perceived object. He believes he can see objective events, distinguish them from mental events, feel a "gentle force" among the latter which is absent from the former, and by repeated observation of ordered pairs of objective events come to read the gentle force into them.

But if Hume had rigorously employed the phenomenalistic

language to which he is alone entitled, he would not have been able to draw his prima facie distinction between a sequence of impressions and a sequence of perceived objective events, as if the latter were as directly given as the former. He would have seen that the sequence of impressions of a house and the sequence of impressions of a moving ship require rules for interpreting one sequence of impressions as the perception of a stationary permanent object and the other sequence as the perception of a sequence of states or positions of a changing object. Until these rules are made and justified, Hume has no right to use the concept of objective event in classifying some impressions as impressions of events which are observed to occur in ordered pairs, so that same-cause-same-effect could appear to be an empirical generalization from these observations. But Hume does not see that he must justify the use of the concept of objective event before he can establish, even in his own way, the principle same-cause-same effect. Objective events are not "just given"; as much goes into their construction as Hume properly saw goes into the construction of an identical object intermittently perceived.

Kant's second analogy is meant to provide precisely this justification for talk about objective events, and he sees the connection of the two problems by coupling it with the first analogy, which deals with continued existence. He shows that the concepts of objective event and cause and effect are related to each other necessarily, and not by mere association. Only much later, in an essentially Humean kind of argument, does he deal with the question of the justification of the principle same-cause-same-effect. He is explicitly following a line of argument which I have suggested that Hume actually followed, in contradistinction to the one which Beattie said Hume followed.

Looked at in this way, the charge that "Kant begged Hume's question" and ended up in the same boat with Reid, Oswald, and Beattie is easily answered. Kant's argument in the second analogy does not simply dignify as a priori a principle which Hume, according to Beattie, believed to be a posteriori and therefore uncertain. Rather, it begins with an assumption that Hume never thought of doubting, namely, that we can distinguish between a sequence of impressions of an enduring object and a sequence of impressions which indicates that an objective change is occurring. Hume's answer to how we know same-cause-same-effect could never have been given without this assumption. But Kant raises a question which neither Hume nor any other philosopher before him had seen, namely, how do we distinguish between the two kinds of sequence?

Kant's answer is that any sequence which is taken to represent an objective change of states of affairs, or an event, must be taken as a necessary sequence, and that the concept of a necessary sequence is the concept of causation. Without possessing the concept of causation we could not distinguish between objective events and subjective sequences, and therefore the concept of a causal connection between objective events cannot arise from observation of them, but rather must be presupposed in recognizing them. Given the first principle, every-event-some-cause, which fixes our realm of discourse, we can then, in good Humean fashion, go about finding uniform ordered pairs of events by straightforward observation and induction. Kant does not challenge this; he only argues that his principle, the second analogy of experience, like Hume's principle, every-event-some-cause, is a necessary condition for Hume's second principle, which we know by repeated observation.[51]

I have argued that, once we modify or reject Beattie's interpretation, we can see that such an argument is not wholly unlike Hume's own procedure when faced with the example of the porter, however little inclined Hume would be to use the language of a priori judgments and transcendental principles.

NOTES

1 *Hamann Briefwechsel*, ed. Henkel, IV, 293.
2 *Hume's Theory of the External World*, p. 9. See also F. W. Dauer, "Towards a Copernican Reading of Hume," *Nous* 9 (1975), 269–95.
3 "Hume's Theory of Mental Activity," in *Hume*, ed. V. C. Chappell, p. 127.
4 "Hume's Concept of Truth," in *Reason and Reality* (Royal Institute of Philosophy Lectures 1970–71), pp. 99–116, at end.
5 R. A. Mall, "Humes Prinzipien- und Kants Kategoriensystem," *Kant-Studien* 62 (1971), 319–34; and the same author's "Naturalismus und Kritizismus: Hume und Kant," *Akten des IV. Internationalen Kant Kongresses* (1974), Part II, pp. 30–41.
6 G. B. Mathur, "Hume, Kant, and Pragmatism," *Journal of the History of Ideas* 16 (1955), 198–208. But see, to the contrary, W. L. Robison, "On the Consequential Claim that Hume is a Pragmatist," *Journal of Critical Analysis* 4 (1974), 141–53.
7 The most comprehensive treatment of the relations between Hume and Kant is to be found in Henri Lauener's *Hume und Kant: Systematische Gegenüberstellung einiger Hauptpunkte ihrer Lehren* (Bern and Munich, 1969); but this well-balanced book does not, in my opinion, break any new ground.

See also Hansgeorg Hoppe, "Kants Antwort auf Hume," *Kant-Studien* 62 (1971), 335–50.

8 The theory of affinity will have to be omitted from this discussion both because of lack of space and because of its perplexing obscurity. Its bearing upon Hume's "pre-established harmony between the course of nature and the succession of our ideas" repays careful study. See Henry E. Allison, "Transcendental Affinity – Kant's Answer to Hume," *Proceedings of the Third International Kant Congress* (1970), pp. 303–11.

9 It seems hardly possible to formulate an account of Kant's gradually increasing knowledge of Hume which fits *all* the apparent facts. For a long time there has been extensive controversy concerning it. The account given here is a summary of my narrative in *Early German Philosophy*, pp. 424–25, 451–53, 465–67, which, in turn, is in general agreement with Vaihinger, *Kommentar zu Kants Kritik der reinen Vernunft*, I, 344–47. Vaihinger surveys all the polemical literature before his time, and most of his conclusions seem to me not to have been rendered less plausible by significant work done since his time. See L. Robinson, "Contributions à l'histoire de l'évolution philosophique de Kant," *Revue de Métaphysique et de morale* 31 (1924), 269–353, esp. 303 ff. See also below, n. 23.

10 Ak. II, 203.

11 Letter to K. L. Reinhold, 19 May, 1789 (Zweig, *Correspondence*, p. 144); *Reflexionen* 4375, 4446 (Ak. XVII, 492, 554).

12 Ak. II, 370 (trans. Manolesco, p. 95). Almost the same example used for the same purpose, is to be found in Hume's *Enquiry* (ed. Hendel) p. 77: "planets in their Orbit."

13 Ak. II, 371 (Manolesco, p. 96).

14 Mendelssohn (*Gedanken über die Wahrscheinlichkeit, Ges. Schriften* [1929], I, 156) says that Sulzer's translation of the *Enquiry* is "in everyone's hands."

15 This is the conclusion reached by Giorgio Tonelli, "Die Anfänge von Kants Kritik der Kausalbeziehungen und ihre Voraussetzungen im 18, Jahrhundert," *Kant-Studien* 57 (1966), 417–60. (I am indebted to Professor Tonelli also for a personal communication on how widespread was the knowledge of Hume's works in Germany.)

16 *Form and Principles of the Sensible and Intelligible Worlds*, § 30.

17 See "Lambert and Hume in Kant's Development from 1769 to 1772."

18 In Zweig, *Correspondence*, p. 72.

19 See H. J. de Vleeschauwer, *La déduction transcendentale dans l'oeuvre de Kant*, I, 171, 217 ff., for a different interpretation of the order of discovery.

20 Vaihinger (*Kommentar zu Kants Kritik*, I, 347) seems to have been the originator of this hypothesis. It is defended most fully by Robert Paul Wolff, "Kant's Debt to Hume via Beattie," *Journal of the History of Ideas* 21 (1960), 117–23. It is possible that Kant had not hitherto known even of the existence of Hume's *Treatise*; Tetens, whose knowledge of things English (and of the English language) was better than Kant's, referred to Hume and to "the heroic skeptic, the author of the *Treatise of Human Nature*" as if they were two different men (*Ueber die allgemeine spekulativische Philosophie* [1775], ed. Uebele [Berlin, 1913], p. 12). Karl Groos ("Hat Kant Humes Treatise Gelesen?" *Kant-Studien* 5 [1901], 177–81) points to some striking resemblances, partly verbal and partly substantive (dealing with existence as a predicate),

between the *Treatise* and Kant's *Einzig moglicher Beweisgrund zu einer Demon-
stration des Daseins Gottes* (1763) and proffers them as evidence (against
Benno Erdmann's "Kant und Hume um 1762," *Archiv für Geschichte der
Philosophie*, I [1887], 62–77, 216–30) that Kant had been influenced by the
Treatise; but Wolff (p. 122) has located possible common sources for both
Hume and Kant.

Upon reading Beattie in 1772, Kant was oddly selective in what he
learned, saying that Hume had examined only part of his problem, that
concerned with cause and effect (*Prolegomena*, IV, 260). Yet from Beattie he
could have learned of the following topics in the *Treatise* absent from the
Enquiry: the status of material objects and the identity of the self. He might
have learned too that Hume was a skeptic about geometry, from a cryptic
note in Beattie (p. 162; German trans. 125 n.), but he continued to ascribe
to Hume only the mathematical teaching of the *Enquiry* (see *Critique of
Practical Reason*, Ak. V, 14 [Beck, p. 14]). In spite of this, there is so striking
a resemblance between Kant's explanation of why "A straight line is the
shortest distance between two points" is not analytic (*Critique of Pure Reason*,
B. 16) and Hume's explanation of why it is not a definition (*Treatise*, ed.
Selby-Bigge, pp. 49–50) that one can hardly believe that Kant did not know
of Hume's argument; yet the passage in question is not in Beattie.

21 Beattie, *Essay on the Nature and Immutability of Truth* (1770), p. 108. German
   translation (Copenhagen and Leipzig, 1772), p. 85. I do not wish to challenge Beattie's statement that this was Hume's opinion, though it is not, so
   far as I can see, ever explicitly argued for in the *Treatise* or elsewhere. A
   reader properly primed by an earlier reading of the *Treatise* might perhaps
   discern the view in *Enquiry* (ed. Hendel), p. 49, 3 lines from bottom of
   page, but the *Enquiry* so conflates the two questions formally separated in
   the *Treatise* that it is never clear (even in the passage just alluded to) that
   Hume is discussing the causal maxim and not some specific causal generalization. In the letter to John Stewart of 1754 (Greig, *Letters of David Hume*,
   I, 187), he asserts that the certainty of the falsity of the proposition that
   anything might arise without a cause proceeds "neither from Intuition nor
   Demonstration; but from some other Source" – presumably experience. But
   this remains a presumption based solely on the exclusion of the two alternatives Hume does discuss and is never supported by any positive argument.

22 In my edition of the *Prolegomena* (New York, 1951) I translated *Erinnerung*
   as if it referred to Kant's recollection of what Hume had said, not to Hume's
   suggestion or hint, and explained my choice in a footnote. In *Early German
   Philosophy*, p. 465, n. 104, I waivered; now I wish to renounce that translation
   not merely on grammatical grounds (the 1951 reading was strained) but on
   the grounds that Kant could not, in 1772, have "recollected" what Hume
   had said.

23 Kant used the metaphor "dogmatic slumber" several times. In *Prolegomena*,
   § 50, he says that the antinomy is "a very powerful agent to arouse philosophy from its dogmatic slumber." Robinson ("Contributions à l'histoire de
   l'évolution philosophique," p. 305) has concluded that the allusion to Hume
   in the Introduction is not meant to be historically accurate, but is an "exposé
   d'un caractère préconcue et plutôt systématique du rapport de sa doctrine
   avec celle de Hume." This I find hardly credible, especially since the tone

of the Introduction passage, unlike that of § 50, is autobiographical. Benno
Erdmann, in his edition of the *Prolegomena* (Leipzig, 1878, pp. lxxxv–lxxxvi),
argues that the passage in § 50 refers to 1769, the year that "brought great
light" and prepared the way for the Inaugural Dissertation, which showed
that intelligible objects are not spatial (the first consequence of the
antinomy); that the allusion to Hume in the Introduction refers to the very
different problem which arose after the Dissertation; and that the two
passages were allowed to stand in the *Doppelredaktion* that the *Prolegomena*
underwent as a result of the Garve-Feder review. According to Erdmann's
stratification of the text, § 50 was in the original manuscript and the Hume
passage in the Introduction was added in the revision.

But in a letter to Garve (21 September 1798; Zweig (*Correspondence*,
p. 252) the autobiographical claim, missing from § 50, is supplied when
Kant says that the antinomy "is what first aroused me from my dogmatic
slumber." This is indeed puzzling. Can it be due to a lapse of memory?
The letter is filled with complaints about Kant's declining health and mental
abilities.

The relation between Kant and Hume has continued to be the object
of controversy; and since this article was first published in 1978 there have
been at least three books continuing a controversy that began more than a
century ago: see e.g. Manfred Kuehn, *Scottish Common Sense* 1768–1800;
Günter Gawlick and Lothar Kreimendahl, *Hume in der deutschen Aufklärung*;
Kreimendahl, *Kant – Der Durchbruch von 1769*.

24 *Prolegomena*, Ak. IV, 260.
25 *Critique of Pure Reason*, A 765 = B 793.
26 Ibid., A 766 = B 794.
27 Beattie, of course, believed that the principle was known intuitively.
28 I refer to the last paragraphs in *Treatise*, Book I, Part iii, Sections ii and iii
(Selby-Bigge, pp. 78, 82). Dr John Bricke has subsequently called my attention to Section xii (Selby-Bigge, p. 132) as at least marginally appropriate.
29 *Treatise of Human Nature* (ed. Selby-Bigge), p. 78.
30 Ibid., p. 82.
31 *Enquiry Concerning Human Understanding* (ed. Hendel), p. 104. See also letter
to John Stewart, February 1754 (*Greig, Letters of David Hume*, I, 187).
32 *Treatise*, p. 172.
33 Ibid., p. 196.
34 Ibid., p. 198.
35 See Walsh, "Hume's Concept of Truth"; Thomas K. Hearn, Jr., ' "General
Rules' in Hume's *Treatise*," *Journal of the History of Philosophy* 8 (1970),
405–22; P. V. Vanterpool, "Hume's Account of General Rules," *Southern
Journal of Philosophy* 12 (1974), 481–92.
36 *Treatise*, pp. 267, 440.
37 Ibid., p. 147. Similarly, in moral judgment there is a conflict between
immediate sympathy and "general establish'd maxims," pp. 293–94.
38 Ibid., p. 632.
39 Price (*Hume's Theory*, p. 8) complains about the order in which Hume
discusses necessary connection and the existence of objects, which misleads
the reader into failing to notice that the discussion of the former requires
to be formulated in the light of the latter. Price says it is as confusing as if

Kant had put the analogies before the transcendental deduction; I would say, rather, the second analogy before the first (See p. 128).

40 *Treatise*, p. 198.

41 Ibid., p. 212.

42 Ibid., p. 75.

43 For example, A. O. Lovejoy, "On Kant's Reply to Hume," *Archiv für Geschichte der Philosophie*, 1960, reprinted in Gram (1967), pp. 284–308, at 300–1.

44 *Critique of Pure Reason*, A 195 = B 240–41. What is puzzling about this passage is that Kant calls what he now thinks is Hume's view "the accepted view." *This* view can hardly have been widely accepted in Germany.

45 Kant repeatedly asserts that empirical laws cannot be derived from a priori principles of the understanding, yet he believed some of them to be necessary. Those are the ones involved in an overall theory whose principles are derived from the a priori principles of "rational science" or "pure physics." See *Critique of Pure Reason*, A 127–28; A 270 = B 252; B 165; A 216 = B 263. Where the overall theory is lacking (as in chemistry), the principles are only empirical and the laws are only "laws of experience" without any "consciousness of necessity" attaching to them. The body of knowledge containing them should be called "a systematic art" and not a "science." *Metaphysical Foundations of Natural Science*, Ak. IV, 468 (trans. Ellington, p. 4).

46 *Critique of Pure Reason*, A 657 = B 686.

47 *Treatise*, p. 104.

48 Kant is equally at fault; see "A Reading of the Third Paragraph in B," in *Essays on Kant and Hume* (Beck, 1978).

49 *Treatise*, pp. 67, 118, 218.

50 Ibid., pp. 108, 242.

51 The argument given all too dogmatically in this paragraph is based on a fuller treatment I give in "Once More unto the Breach: Kant's Answer to Hume, Again" and in "A Non Sequitur of Numbing Grossness?" (Beck, 1978). I would modify only one point in the former article: in the last paragraph on p. 133. I accept Beattie's statement at face value, as Kant did, whereas in this paper I give reasons to reject it.

KANT'S CONCEPTION OF "HUME'S PROBLEM"

Manfred Kuehn

I

In 1783, forty-four years after the appearance of Hume's *Treatise of Human Nature*, and thirty-five years after that of his *Enquiry concerning Human Understanding*, a Prussian philosopher named Immanuel Kant found it necessary to "openly confess" that "the suggestion of David Hume was the very thing which many years ago first interrupted [his] dogmatic slumber and gave [his] investigations in the field of speculative philosophy a quite new direction."[1] In fact, Kant went so far as to characterize his then very controversial *Critique of Pure Reason* as "the execution of Hume's problem in its widest extent."[2] In making this confession, he seems to be responding to Hume, who in the Conclusion of Book I of his *Treatise* expressed as his "only hope" that he would "contribute a little to the advancement of knowledge, by giving in some particulars of a different turn to the speculations of philosophers, and pointing out to them more distinctly those subjects, where alone they can expect assurance and conviction."[3]

Kant's confession certainly has had – and just as certainly will have – an important influence upon the way in which philosophers see both Hume and Kant. Moreover, there is no scarcity of papers which deal with Kant's relation to Hume. Most of these papers deal with Kant's supposed "answer to Hume."[4] Yet there is hardly any agreement on what was the "question" and what was Kant's "answer." It is indeed a "scandal of philosophical scholarship that after nearly two centuries the question must still be debated: *What was Kant's answer to Hume?*"[5] But it is perhaps even a greater scandal that the true extent of Hume's "question" for Kant has never been investigated satisfactorily, and that Kant's conception of Hume's problem has never been formulated in its entirety. For, only after it has been decided what the question for Kant was, can we hope to evaluate the answer or solution.

Kant's relation to Hume is puzzling indeed. Their positions are intimately related on many issues, but on the whole, they seem quite different from each other. The standard view of the Hume-Kant relation emphasizes the differences. Hume and Kant are located on opposite sides of the spectrum of philosophical positions. The Scot's empiricism, sensationalism, skepticism and naturalism are separated by a deep gulf from the German's criticism, intellectualism, anti-skepticism, and anti-naturalism. Hume's problem, according to this view, is simply identical with the problem of causality. Hume, the skeptic, *par excellence*, attacked the principle of causality and questioned its objective validity. Kant, who saw the grave consequences of this attack for all of science and especially for metaphysics, came to the rescue, saved the causal principle as one of the genuinely rational furnishings of the mind, and thus "answered" Hume, disproving skepticism. According to this standard view, Hume's problem is of rather limited importance for the understanding of Kant and Hume.

But this view leaves out almost everything that makes the Hume-Kant relation philosophically interesting. Recent discussions have shown that the traditional picture is really an over-simplification and suggested that the differences between Hume and Kant are much more subtle than has been assumed commonly.[6] This has been done mainly by means of a careful comparative analysis of Hume's texts and Kant's critical writings. I believe, however, that any consistent and thorough account must start not with Kant's fully developed critical thought, but must attempt to establish what "Hume's problem" was for Kant at the early stages of his development of the critical philosophy. Kant's *Entwicklungsgeschichte* may very well provide further clues for piecing together the puzzle that is the Hume-Kant relation. Accordingly, this paper is not intended as another contribution to the discussion of Kant's supposed "answer" to Hume. Instead, I want to show that Kant's original conception of Hume's problem is far broader than various discussions suggest. For this reason, I shall first give a short account of the major sources of Kant's knowledge of Hume, and say a few things about the date at which Hume's problem became urgent for Kant. Then, I shall show that Hume's problem had a distinct dialectical dimension for Kant and is, accordingly, important for the understanding of the antinomy of pure reason. Finally, I shall indicate some of the consequences which this reconstruction of Kant's conception of Hume's problem has for the interpretation of Kant and Hume.

II

It is not well known – because little research has been done on the subject – but Hume's philosophy was very successful in Germany after the middle of the eighteenth century.[7] Whereas his reputation in France rested mainly upon his historical, political, and literary writings, the Germans appreciated Hume's metaphysical investigations at least as much as his more popular essays.[8] It may be asked why the Germans were so interested in Hume's philosophy so early already. The reason is to be found in the philosophical situation in Germany during the 1750s. When Christian Wolff died in 1754, his philosophy, which had dominated the German schools almost uncontested for the preceding three decades, had begun to decline in influence. It no longer possessed the binding authority which it had exerted during the earlier stages of its career. Wolffianism appeared stale and stagnant. But no new German philosophy of similar stature or authority had arisen. It was in this situation that the Germans turned to foreign, and especially British, models.[9] One of these models clearly was Hume.[10]

Hume's first *Enquiry* appeared in German as the second volume of the *Vermischte Schriften* in 1755, the very year in which Kant began to teach at the University of Königsberg.[11] Johann Georg Sulzer, the editor of the German translation of the first *Enquiry*, gives Hume high praise as a philosophical writer. Hume can write clearly and elegantly about the most profound and difficult problems of metaphysics. "Thoroughness and pleasantness seem to fight for priority." Hume is the model for a truly popular philosopher, and Sulzer hopes the Germans will imitate Hume in this regard.[12] Closely connected with the problematic of a popular philosophical style is for Sulzer – as well as most of his contemporaries – the problem of common sense. In fact, popular expression is seen only as the external expression of the principle of common sense.[13] Therefore, Hume's philosophy is also a model for philosophers who want to combine philosophical reasoning with common sense.

But one of Sulzer's most important reasons for publishing the translation is his belief that philosophers whom nobody criticizes become lax and superficial and that the German philosophers are in this situation. They have allowed their weapons to become blunt and rusty "during the long peace." Hume could be useful as a critic of German philosophers. Sulzer hopes that "the publication of this work will *interrupt their leisurely slumber* and give them *a new occupation*."[14]

Kant clearly alluded to this passage in his *Prolegomena* almost thirty years later. But he knew and appreciated Hume from 1755 onwards. Ludwig Ernst Borowski, who attended Kant's very first lectures between 1755 and 1756, testified that Hume and Hutcheson were already important to Kant during that period.[15] Johann Georg Hamann wrote a letter to Kant in 1759 that suggests they had already talked about Hume's doctrine of belief before.[16] Kant's *Observations on the Feeling of the Beautiful and Sublime* of 1764 contains a quote from Hume's *Moral and Political Essays*.[17] Johann Gottfried Herder, who attended Kant's lectures between 1762 and 1764, mentions Hume as one of the most important philosophers discussed by Kant.[18] Kant's "Announcement" of his lectures for the winter of 1765–66 calls attention to the importance of Hume's moral philosophy, and his *Träume eines Geistersehers* of 1766 make abundantly clear how important Hume had become for Kant by that time.[19] It appears, therefore, that Kant knew Hume's philosophy very well from 1755 onwards and that every similarity between Kant and Hume is indeed the result of influence.[20]

In the light of this evidence, one may ask why Kant did not "wake up" as early as 1755 or 1766. It appears to me that the reason may be found again the the philosophical situation in Germany during that time. German philosophers, although opening up to British empiricism, were still very much part of the rationalistic tradition. Hume had based causality upon "habit," "custom," and "imagination." The Germans felt that all of these principles could be reduced to reason and thus be rendered more secure. Sulzer, Mendelssohn, and most others believed that Hume could easily be refuted in this way and therefore did not worry too much about it.[21] Others, like Kant in 1766, accepted Hume's analysis of causation and became moderate skeptics. They felt that the attack upon the principle of causality was not fatal for all of human thinking. Hume's analysis only revealed the frailty of the human understanding and the impossibility of the grandiose metaphysical dreams and schemes in the Wolffian tradition.

Moreover, Hume's popular first *Enquiry* does not stress the skeptical conclusions that may be drawn from the Humean analysis of causality. Hume himself suggests that with regard to the causal principle it is more "conformable to the ordinary wisdom of nature to secure so necessary an act of the mind, by some instinct or mechanical tendency, which may be infallible in its operation . . . and may be independent of all the laboured deductions of the understanding."[22] Moderate skepticism with regard to matters metaphysical and reliance upon common sense to orient oneself in thinking became the prevailing characteristics of many philosophers during the 1760s and 1770s. Kant was clearly one of them, at least during the 1760s.[23]

Later Kant calls this philosophical persuasion "indifferentism," and while he characterizes it as a refusal "to be any longer put off with illusory knowledge" and as "obviously the effect not of levity but of the matured judgment of the age," he also finds that "it is idle to fein indifference to such enquiries, the object of which can never be indifferent to our human nature."[24] Furthermore, he later recognises that all "pretended indifferentists . . . inevitably fall back, in so far as they think at all, into those very metaphysical assertions which they profess so greatly to despise."[25] Accordingly, the "stage of indifference . . . is the most dangerous for an author." But it is, according to Kant, at the same time "the most favorable for the science. For when party spirit has died out by a total dissolution of former connections, minds are in the best state to listen to several proposals for an organization according to a new plan."[26] Being at this stage in 1766, Kant was ready to be "aroused from his dogmatic slumber."

But when did Kant finally "wake up" or realize that indifferentism was not a solution? Something changed Kant's mind; and the question is when this happened and what occasioned it. In the *Prolegomena* Kant tells us that after he was "aroused," he "*first* tried whether Hume's objection could not be put into a general form" and then found "soon" that the concept of causality was only one among many a priori concepts of the understanding and that all of metaphysics consisted of them.[27] This clearly indicates the early 1770s, for in a letter to J. Bernoulli, dated 16 November 1781, Kant says: "In the year 1770 I was already able to distinguish the *sensibility* in human knowledge from the *intellectual*. . . . But then the problem of the *source of the intellectual* elements in our knowledge created new and unforeseen difficulties."[28] By 21 February 1772 Kant is already well advanced in the solution of this problem. He has "reduced the transcendental philosophy (that is to say, all concepts belonging to completely pure reason) to a certain number of categories."[29] Therefore, Hume's problem must have been conceived by Kant at some time between 1770 and 1772.

However, the matter is greatly complicated by the fact that Kant gives also another, quite different and apparently contradictory, account of how he first conceived of the problem of critical philosophy. Even in the *Prolegomena* he claims that the antinomy of pure reason "serves as a very powerful agent to rouse philosophy from its dogmatic slumber and to stimulate it to the arduous task of undertaking a critical examination of reason itself."[30] In a very late letter to Garve, Kant turns this into an autobiographical account, saying: "the antinomy of pure reason . . . that is what first aroused me from my dogmatic slumber and drove me to the critique of reason itself, in order to resolve the scandal of ostensible contradiction of reason with itself."[31] Furthermore, in one of his notes he tells us that he first grasped the doctrine of critical philosophy "only obscurely" and proved "propositions and their opposites" because he suspected that "there was an illusion of the understanding." He ends by saying that the year 1769 gave him "great light."[32] This, taken together with Kant's communication to Mendelssohn that the *Critique* "is the product of nearly twelve years of reflection," suggests not only that Kant had discovered the critical problem in 1769 already, but also that Hume had very little to do with it.

In accordance with these two, apparently contradictory, claims by Kant, two different theories have been developed. One has Kant "roused" by the problem of the antinomies in 1769. It emphasizes other sources than Hume.[33] The other argues for 1772 as the date for Kant's "waking up" and emphasizes James Beattie's *Essay on Truth* as the source of Kant's knowledge of Hume's *Treatise* and the occasion of his awakening.[34] I now believe that both theories are equally false, or, at best, equally inadequate, since both fail to take into account all the evidence.

Kant could not have awakened in 1769, because his Inaugural Dissertation is still the expression of dogmatic metaphysical reveries. In fact, this work is more dogmatic than the earlier *Träume eines Geistersehers*.[35] Perhaps the Inaugural Dissertation represents the "falling back into dogmatism" which is inevitable for the pretended indifferentist, according to Kant. This does not preclude, however, Kant's being aware of some of the elements of his later critical philosophy. The transcendental aesthetic, in any case, is there almost completely.[36] Nor does Kant's description of the "great light" of 1769 preclude Hume's influence on Kant at that time.[37] But however this may be, to say that Kant had discovered *the* antinomies in 1769 is more than the evidence allows us to say. Kant's very formulation of what he did during that year suggests that he had *not* discovered the antinomies, but only proved "some" propositions and their opposites.[38]

But Kant could not have been aroused by Hume after March or April 1772 either. When the German translation of Beattie's *Essay* appeared, Kant had "generalized" Hume's problem already, as the letter of 21 February 1772 makes clear.[39] If we take Kant's own account of his philosophical development seriously, 1772 must be eliminated as well. Kant must have conceived of Hume's problem independently of Beattie's *Essay* at some time between 1770 and February 1772.[40]

If the two traditional theories are false, we must ask: What was it that occasioned Kant's awakening? Perhaps the analogy of awakening is somewhat misleading. It suggests a sudden change in Kant's outlook, a radical conversion from dogmatism to criticism. But the change may have been a gradual readjustment of philosophical doctrines and a slow realisation that there was a much more fundamental problem than most indifferentists thought. Kant evidently liked the analogy of sleeping and dreaming for metaphysical speculation. The very title of his *Dreams of a Spirit-Seer, Illustrated by Dreams of Metaphysics* testifies to that. He simply may not have been able to resist a play with words in his famous confession. There need not have been one decisive and exactly datable moment at which Kant realized that he had discovered Hume's problem. It may very well be that during the period from 1769 to the summer of 1772 Kant slowly – and under increasing influence of Hume – worked out what he later considered to be the problem of critical philosophy.

This account is quite compatible with the view that Kant's interest in Hume and the problem of causality "peaked" at certain decisive and datable times, and that these fixed themselves in Kant's mind. One such peak clearly was 1772, when he read Beattie's *Essay* and became more closely acquainted with certain doctrines of Hume that are not to be found in the first *Enquiry*. Another peak may have been 1769, when he realized the importance of differentiating between sensibility and understanding. The last section of Hume's *Enquiry* may have been important then.[41] But it appears to me that 5 and 12 July 1771 are even more important than either one of the dates given above. For in July 1771 there appeared in the *Königsberger Zeitung* a German translation of the last chapter of Book I of Hume's

Treatise.[42] The translator was Hamann, and the piece was appropriately entitled "Night-Thoughts of a Skeptic." I believe that these "Night-Thoughts" disturbed Kant in his "dogmatic slumber" and finally woke him.

III

In the Conclusion of Book I of the *Treatise* Hume also discusses the causal principle. But the thrust of his discussion here is entirely different from that of the first *Enquiry.* While Hume attempts to show in the *Enquiry* that our knowledge of any particular causal connection cannot be based upon reasonings a priori, but "arises entirely from experience, when we find that particular objects are constantly conjoined with each other," in the Conclusion of Book I of the *Treatise* he emphasizes that the connection between the cause and effect "lies merely in ourselves" and that it is "nothing but" a "determination of the mind."[43] In the *Enquiry* it could appear that the causal connection, though itself not objective, was somehow based upon the objects themselves. In this passage Hume clearly claims that the causal relation is entirely subjective. We may want to "push our enquiries, till we arrive at the original and ultimate principle" of any phenomena, but we cannot. The discovery of the subjective character of the causal relation "not only cuts off all hope of ever attaining satisfaction, but even prevents our very wishes; since it appears that when we desire to know the ultimate and operating principle, as something, which resides in the external object, we either contradict ourselves, or talk without a meaning."[44] Here the question of the very possibility of metaphysics is asked in the context of a discussion of the causal principle.

Kant agrees with Hume that the connection or tie between cause and effect is a "determination of the mind." Though he finds this determination in the understanding and not in the imagination, his problem is the same as Hume's: How can we go from "that in us which we call 'representation' to the object?"[45] It is exactly this problem that still occupies Kant in February 1772. Though he has "generalized" Hume's problem, he is far from having solved it (and he knows it). If anything, the generalization of the problem has made it more pressing than ever. If Hume's analysis is correct, we must ask "How is pure natural science possible?"; "How is metaphysics in general possible?" and "How is metaphysics as a science possible?" Accordingly, the solution to the problem posed by Hume's analysis is seen by Kant as constituting "the key to the whole secret of hitherto still obscure metaphysics."[46]

But Hume's problem is not exhausted by this, for in the Conclusion of Book I of the *Treatise* the problem of causality is placed in a wider context. It is not just the understanding that forces us to "either contradict ourselves, or talk without a meaning." Hume also finds fault with his fundamental principle of imagination. It also leads "us into error when implicitly follow'd (as it must be)." For this principle "makes us reason from causes and effects" and

> convinces us of the continu'd existence of external objects, when absent from the senses. But tho' these two operations be equally natural and necessary in the human mind, yet in some circumstances they are directly contrary, nor is it possible for us to reason justly and regularly from causes and effects, and at the same time believe the continu'd existence of matter. How then shall we adjust these principles together.[47]

If "antinomy" is defined as a contradiction between the basic principles of the human mind, then this passage clearly does contain an antinomy.[48] Kant's antinomy of pure reason must be compared with Hume's antinomy of the imagination. This clearly shows that there is a dialectical dimension to Hume's problem. The principles of the human mind upon which we *must* rely lead us to "embrace a manifest contradiction." Both the imagination and the understanding are without "any degree of solidity and satisfaction."[49] This shows that the problem of the antinomies is just another aspect of the problem of Hume.

That the problem of causality is closely connected with that of the antinomies may even be seen from Kant's account in the *Prolegomena*. Kant defends Hume against his Scottish critics by arguing that the question never was whether the concept of cause was "right, useful, and even indispensable for our knowledge of nature, for this Hume had never doubted." Hume's true problem concerns the ultimate justification of the concept of cause, namely, "whether it could be thought by reason a priori ... whether it possessed an inner truth, independent of all experience, implying a perhaps more extended use not restricted merely to objects of experience."[50] Quite clearly, the antinomies involve what Kant calls here "extended use." One of the most important doctrines of the *Critique of Pure Reason*, is that such an extended use of any of our concepts of principles, while unavoidable and in accordance with common sense, leads reason to contradict itself.[51] Something rather similar can be observed in Hume's work. He argues that the extended use that has been made of the causal principle by arguing from the world as an effect to the existence of God as its cause is illegitimate, because it transcends the proper sphere of this principle, namely, experience.[52] Kant certainly found this argument important. For in the Transcendental Dialectic of the first *Critique* he opposes the "dogmatism of pure reason" of the theses with the "pure empiricism" of the antitheses.[53] That the pure empiricism of the antitheses represents Hume's empiricism is fairly clear from the context of the discussion, though Kant mentions by name Epicurus only. (But this is certainly significant, as Hume in section XI of the first *Enquiry*, "Of a Particular Providence and of a Future State," uses Epicurus as the mouthpiece for his views.)[54] Later Kant not only identifies Hume's doctrine as "empiricism," but also alludes to a passage of Hume's first *Enquiry.*[55]

But Kant himself tells us that "it was not the investigation of the existence of God, immortality, and so on, but rather the antinomy of pure reason – the world has a beginning; it has no beginning, and so on – right up to the fourth (sic): 'There is freedom in man, versus there is no freedom.' " that "first aroused" him.[56] It is here that Beattie's *Essay* becomes important. Beattie also finds that the causal principle is the "foundation" of the argument that God is the creator of the universe, and he attacks Hume's analysis of causality mainly because he wants to save this "most important argument that ever employed human reason."[57]

For Beattie the causal principle is an "axiom" and a "principle of common sense, which every rational mind does and must acknowledge to be true; not because it can be proved, but because the law of nature determines us to believe it without proof." He further holds that the argument for the existence of God "from the works that are created . . . as far as it resolves itself into this axiom, is properly a demonstration, being a clear deduction from self-evident principle."[58] Beattie then goes on to argue that many things we observe have had a beginning and must, therefore, have been caused.

> That the whole sensible universe has to us the appearance of an effect . . . cannot be denied: and that it is, what it appears to be, an effect, that it had a beginning, and was not from eternity, is proved by every species of evidence the subject will admit.[59]

The entire universe is a vast system of works and effects. It is like a chain in which every link is supported by another link. Everything has a beginning. Accordingly, the whole chain cannot be thought unsupported either, and it must have had a beginning in time.

But this is not all Beattie has to say. After having presented his arguments for his view that the world has a beginning (and was thus caused), he presents arguments to the contrary to show the antithesis to his thesis:

> The reader, if he happens to be acquainted with Mr. Hume's *Essay on a particular providence and a future state* will see, that these remarks are intended as an answer to a very strange argument there advanced against the belief of Deity. "The universe," we are told, "is an object quite singular and unparalleled; no other object that has fallen under our observation bears any similarity to it; neither it nor its cause can be comprehended under any known species; and therefore we can form no rational conclusion at all concerning the cause of the universe."[60]

In all fairness to Beattie – and Beattie has been treated rather unfairly by philosophers – it must be said that this representation of Hume's position is free from any distortion and shows it at its strongest. Beattie does not take the easy way out. He tries to reduce Hume's claim *ad absurdum*: Each thing in the universe

> had a beginning. ... What thing in the universe exists uncaused? Nothing. Is this a rational conclusion? So it seems then, that though it be rational to assign a cause to everything in the universe; yet to assign a cause to the universe is not rational.[61]

The clash of the two positions is as apparent as the strength of the arguments for each of them. Beattie's discussion calls attention to the circumstances that both conclusions, "the world has a beginning" and "the world has no beginning", are equally rational. Kant says somewhat later in his *Enzyklopädievorlesungen* (1775) and in the context of a reference to Oswald: "these propositions are equally clear, but they still contradict each other."[62]

To be sure, the final version of the first antinomy does not resemble Beattie's discussion as much as does the version of the *Enzyklopädievorlesungen*. For, whereas the lectures make a clear connection between the temporal beginning and the causal principle, the final version of the first *Critique* refers only to space and time.

But even in the *Critique* there are passages that remind one of Beattie. Thus Kant uses an argument to establish the first part of the thesis (the limitedness of the world with regard to time) that is also hinted at by Beattie when he claims that the "Atheist will never be able to elude the force of this argument, till he can prove, that every thing in nature exists necessarily, independently, and *from eternity*."[63] Kant argues for the thesis by trying to disprove that the world has no beginning, i.e. exists from eternity; and he believes that he has shown that the theory must be false because it implies that "up to every given moment an eternity has elapsed."[64]

The "dogmatists" who defend the different theses of the antinomies against the "pure empiricists" or "skeptics" and who are later identified as "the defenders of the good cause" certainly resemble Beattie and Oswald: "Ridicule and boasting form [their] whole armory, and these can be laughed at, as mere child's play." We should not follow them, for

> if we resort to other means than those of untrammeled reason, if we raise the cry of high treason, and act as if we were summoning the vulgar . . . who have no understanding of such subtle enquiries – we make ourselves ridiculous.[65]

We should be "peaceable onlookers" and not rush into the fight, "sword in hand," because there can be no victors. The dialectical debate between Hume, Priestley, and the dogmatic defenders of the good cause is acknowledged to be relevant for the dialectic of pure practical reason by Kant himself.

But however that may be, it should be fairly clear by now that Hume's problem was the occasion not only for the metaphysical deduction of Kant's transcendental logic, but also for the antinomy of pure reason of his transcendental dialectic. The traditional views concerning the origin of Kant's criticism are just as inadequate in their systematic interpretation as they are wrong in their historical account. Their assumption that it must have been *either* the problem of causality *or* the problem of the antinomies that occasioned Kant's criticism is simply not justified. The exclusive "or" is quite inappropriate in the light of the actual evidence. Kant's two accounts of the origin of his philosophy do not contradict but supplement each other. The contradiction has been created by scholars who read distinctions of Kant's fully developed criticism into the early problem. But this is, to borrow a concept from biology, phylogenetically wrong. The specific parts of Kant's system evolved from a problem that was at first quite undifferentiated. If only for this reason, *all* of the specific doctrines of Kant's critical enterprise are intimately bound up with Hume's influence upon Kant.

IV

However, it would be impossible to show this in any detail here. For this reason I shall restrict myself to the discussion of some of the more general consequences which this reading has for the interpretation of the thought of Kant and Hume. In order to be able to do this, I have to introduce another, though closely related, aspect of Kant's relation to Hume, namely, "Hume's principle."[66]

Though the Kant-Hume relation cannot be understood without Hume's principle, it has received rather less attention than Hume's problem. Closer attention to this principle would also have drawn attention to the importance of Hume for Kant's antinomy, for it forbids us, in Kant's words, "to carry the use of reason dogmatically beyond the field of all possible experience."[67] It is also identical with Kant's "original proposition, which is the résumé of the whole *Critique*: 'Reason by all is a priori principles never teaches us anything more than objects of possible experience, and even of these nothing more than can be known in experience.' "[68] This fundamental agreement between Kant and Hume is surprising in at least two different respects.

First of all, this agreement shows that Kant and Hume aim at the very same thing (or, at least, that Kant believed he was aiming at the very same thing as was Hume), namely, the determination of the limits of metaphysics and human knowledge in general. Kant clearly felt that he was the executor of Hume's philosophical will. This means, however, that Kant was not primarily concerned with "answering" Hume or refuting skepticism.[69] His critical philosophy is in a fundamental sense a justification of Hume's principle.

But having said this, I must hasten to point out that Kant's justification or defense of Hume is limited. Kant subscribes as little to Hume's "radical empiricism" or skepticism as he accepts "the dogmatism which Hume combats."[70] This may also be seen from the way in which he supplements Hume's principle with another principle which Hume, according to Kant, "quite overlooked," namely, "not to consider the field of experience as one which bounds itself in the eyes of our reason."[71] Experience itself does not have bounds for Kant. "That which bounds it must lie quite without it."[72] While we may not be said to know, strictly speaking, what lies outside of experience and bounds it, we are somehow aware of it too. The second principle advises us thus to be more tolerant than Hume's principle alone would allow us. Kant discusses this most fully in his *Critique of Practical Reason*, and it is there, accordingly, that we must look for Kant's full answer to Hume.[73] But Kant's theoretical philosophy, as a limited defense of Hume and a "generalization" of Hume's problem (in the transcendental logic *and* the transcendental dialectic), can contain only a limited answer to Hume. Since scholarship on Kant and Hume has concentrated long enough on this limited answer, it may be time now to look at Kant's limited defense of Hume.

But Kant's agreement to Hume's principle is curious in another respect as well. For Kant's acceptance of this principle goes back much further than his awareness of Hume's problem.[74] Thus Kant's basic stance towards Hume did not change when he realized the fundamental importance of Hume's problem. The *Critique* is, therefore, the continuation of an older enterprise.

But it is a continuation of this enterprise by different means. What did change as a result of Kant's discovery of Hume's problem was his approach to the establishment or justification of Hume's principle. In 1766 Kant was more or less satisfied with Hume's own foundation of this principle, but by the beginning of 1772 he felt that another foundation of it had to be given. Kant then rejected the "indifferentist" view of Hume. Whereas before he agreed that the proposition "all human reasoning is informal" is "informally acceptable," after 1771 Kant reverted to a formal analysis. His *Critique* is the attempt to show how metaphysics is possible as a (formal and strict) science. It is also the attempt of a "thorough," that is, formal foundation of Hume's principle.[75]

Kant's stance towards Hume can thus serve to emphasize the continuity in Kant's thinking. If we are looking for Kant's "metaphysical motives" and "systematic intentions," we will find them here and not anywhere else.[76] Kant did not radically change when he embarked on his critical enterprise and his criticism is in some sense the development of a metaphysical system, but neither Kant's precritical period nor the development of his critical metaphysics can be understood apart from Hume's influence upon Kant.

The relationship of Kant and Hume is much more intricate than the traditional account suggests. The differences and similarities are very subtle. The dialectic and "Hume's principle" show, in any case, that they have much more in common than the clumsy labels empiricism/rationalism, sensationalism/intellectualism, skepticism/ anti-skepticism, and naturalism/anti-naturalism suggest. Previous discussions of Hume and Kant have shown that "the system of principles in Humean philosophy plays a role similar to the system of the categories in Kantian" philosophy and that Kant's understanding and Hume's imagination have almost identical functions.[77] It appears to me that this reconstruction of Kant's conception of Hume's problem shows that it is not inappropriate to speak of an "antinomy of the imagination" in Hume. Attention to the dialectical dimension of Hume's problem takes thus a further "step toward justifying the epithet 'the Scottish Kant' " and gives more credence to a "Copernican reading of Hume."[78]

NOTES

1 This is a slightly revised version of a paper read at the 10th Hume Conference, Trinity College, Dublin, Ireland, 25–28 August 1981. I would like to thank Reinhard Brandt, Antony Flew, David Fate Norton, and John W. Yolton for their useful criticisms and suggestions.

Professor Flew, in the opening session, made an observation that appears to me especially relevant to the matters discussed in this paper, namely that many recent students of Hume seem to be working with a "defective copy" of Hume's *Treatise*, i.e. a copy that does not include the Conclusion of Book I, and that this may result in a distorted picture of Hume. It is perhaps somewhat ironic that this paper shows that Kant, one of the most important students of Hume, also worked with a "defective copy" of the *Treatise*. However, Kant's copy consisted almost entirely of a translation of the Conclusion that suffers such neglect today.

I hope that this paper will contribute to a renewal of philosophical interest in this part of Hume's work and go some way towards showing that Hume was much more of a skeptic than the more recent naturalistic interpretation of Hume suggests. In this I am certainly influenced by my former teacher David Fate Norton, whose *David Hume, Common Sense Moralist, Sceptical Metaphysician* (Princeton, New Jersey: Princeton University Press, 1982) – which I knew long before its publication – serves to re-emphasize the skeptical dimension of Hume.

2 *Prolegomena*, pp. 33f. I have substituted "suggestion" for "recollection." For the reasons, see Lewis White Beck, "A Prussian Hume and a Scottish Kant," reprinted in this volume, pp. 139–55.

3 David Hume, *A Treatise of Human Nature*, ed. L. A. Selby-Bigge (Oxford: The Clarendon Press, 1968), p. 273. To show that Kant is indeed responding to this passage of the *Treatise* and that it is wrong categorically to deny Kant knowledge of this work will be among the aims of this paper.

4 See, for instance, Arthur Lovejoy, "On Kant's Reply to Hume," *Archiv für Geschichte der Philosophie* 19 (1906), 380–407; E. W. Schipper, "Kant's Answer

to Hume's Problem," *Kant-Studien* 53 (1961), 68–74; M. E. Williams, "Kant's Reply to Hume," *Kant-Studien* 55 (1965), 71–8; R. A. Mall, "Hume's Prinzipien und Kant's Kategoriensystem," *Kant-Studien* 62 (1971), 319–34; Hansgeorg Hoppe, "Kants Antwort auf Hume," *Kant-Studien* 62 (1971), 335–50. Most important are Lewis White Beck's various papers on this topic, the majority of which can be found in his *Essays on Kant and Hume*, 1978).

5 Lewis White Beck, "Once More unto the Breach: Kant's Answer to Hume, Again," *Ratio* 9 (1967), 33–7 (reprinted in *Essays on Kant and Hume*).

6 See R. P. Wolff, "Hume's Theory of Mental Activity," in *Hume*, ed. V. C. Chappell (Garden City, New York: Doubleday & Co., Inc., 1966), pp. 99–128; Mall, "Hume's Prinzipien und Kant's Kategoriensystem;" F. W. Dauer, "Towards a Copernican Reading of Hume," *Noûs* 9 (1975), 269–95; Nicholas Capaldi, "The Copernican Revolution in Hume and Kant," *Proceedings of the Third International Kant-Congress*, ed. Lewis White Beck (Dordrecht, Holland: D. Reidel Publishing Co., 1972), pp. 234–240; Beck, "A Prussian Hume and a Scottish Kant."

7 Even the *Treatise* was reviewed in German philosophical journals. (See Ernest C. Mossner, "The Continental Reception of Hume's *Treatise*, 1739–1741," *Mind* 56 (1947), 31–43; see also Mossner, *The Life of David Hume* (Austin, Texas: University of Texas Press, 1954), pp. 124f.). But Hume's success really began during the mid-1750s. Hume's influence in Germany may be divided into roughly four different periods. The first period lasted from the early 1750s until the early 1770s; the second from the early 1770s until about 1783, the appearance of Kant's *Prolegomena*; the third from 1784 until roughly 1792, the appearance of Gottlob Ernst Schulze's *Aenesidemus*; the fourth from 1793 until the success of Hegel in the early nineteenth century. What makes Hume's influence in Germany so interesting is that it corresponds in its duration almost exactly to the period of Kant's philosophical development, the success of his critical philosophy and its demise. Kant had just become a teacher at the University of Königsberg, when Hume's first *Enquiry* appeared in German (1755), and Hume's philosophical reputation faded together with that of Kant. In fact, the philosophical destinies of these two men were intricately bound up with each other from the beginning to the end.

About the first period of Hume's influence in Germany, very little is known. It is certain that by 1760 all of Hume's major philosophical publications, the (anonymous) *Treatise* excepted, were translated into German. Giorgio Tonelli claims in his "Die Anfänge von Kant's Kritik der Kausalbeziehungen und ihre Voraussetzungen im 18. Jahrhundert" (*Kant-Studien* 57 (1966), 417–60) that Humean ideas were very much in the air in Germany during this period and hence all these ideas cannot be traced back to Hume. This appears wrong, especially because certain philosophers whom he refers to as having put forth Humean ideas were clearly influenced by Hume, such as Maupertuis and Basedow. (See L. Grossmann, "Berkeley, Hume and Maupertuis," *French Studies* 14 (1960), 304–24, for instance.)

It appears that during this early period Hume's influence was strongest in Berlin, the capital of Prussia and the center of the German enlightenment. Johann Georg Sulzer, a German-speaking member of the Berlin Academy and a well-known philosopher, was the editor of the German translation of the first *Enquiry*. F. G. Resewitz, a close friend of Moses Mendelssohn, was the German translator of the *Four Dissertations*, which appeared in 1759, and Moses Mendelssohn himself published as early as 1755 an essay on probability, in which he set out to disprove some of Hume's skeptical conclusions. He tells us in that essay that Hume's first *Enquiry* is "in everyone's hands."

This appears to have had a significant influence upon the French reception of the work. The translator of the *Oeuvres philosophiques* of Hume, which began to appear in 1758 with the first *Enquiry* as Volume I, was the perpetual secretary of the Berlin Academy, J. B. Merian, and the writer of the Preface was another prominent member of this institution, namely J. H. S. Formey. The entire enterprise is said to go back to a suggestion by Maupertuis, the president of the Berlin Academy. Given the fact that translations were at that time usually made from English into French first, and only after into German (often from the French rather than from the English), it is certainly significant that in the case of Hume's first *Enquiry* a German translation appeared first. (See M. Blassneck, *Frankreich als Vermittler englisch-deutscher Einflüsse im 17. und 18. Jahrhundert*, Bochum-Langendreer, 1934.)

But the interest in Hume's philosophy during this period clearly was not restricted to Berlin. Johann Georg Hamann in distant Königsberg, for instance, found Hume very important and useful as well. This is clearly shown by his *Socratic Memorabilia* of 1759. (See Philip Merlan, "From Hume to Hamann," *The Personalist* 32 (1951), 11–18; Merlan, "Hamann et les Dialogues de Hume," *Revue de Metaphysique* 59, 285–9; and Charles W. Swain, "Hamann and the Philosophy of David Hume," *Journal of the History of Philosophy* 5 (1967), 343–51.) This suggests, I believe, that Hume was much more important in Germany during the 1750s and 1760s than Tonelli would have us believe.

The second period of Hume's influence in Germany is characterized by a growing influence of Scottish common sense philosophy in Germany as *the* enemy of Hume's skepticism and Berkeley's idealism. This period covers almost exactly the same period as Kant's "silent years," i.e. those years in which he worked out his critical philosophy. How closely Hume and Reid, Oswald and Beattie are connected in Kant's mind is shown by his *Prolegomena*. (I have investigated the Scottish influence in Germany in my *Scottish Common Sense in Germany, 1768–1800; A Contribution to the History of Critical Philosophy* (Montreal, McGill University, 1980). Hume's effects upon German thought during that period certainly would deserve a separate treatment.)

The third period of Hume's influence begins with the appearance of Kant's *Prolegomena*. Many German philosophers more or less identified Kant and Hume and criticized or praised both in much the same way. This period saw a first translation of Hume's *Treatise of Human Nature* (1790–92). The translator was Ludwig Heinrich Jakob, one of the earliest followers of Kant.

The better knowledge of Hume certainly contributed significantly to the further reception of Kant's philosophy. The difference between Kant and Hume came to be seen more and more clearly. Thus in 1792 Gottlob Ernest Schulze argued in his very influential *Aenesidemus* that Kant had not and could not possibly have answered Hume's skepticism. Hume's skepticism and Reid's critique of phenomenalism were turned against Kant and his adherents; and it appears to have been this skepticism that led to the demise of Kantianism and the rise of idealism.

8 For Hume's French connection, see especially Rudolf Metz, "Les Amitiés françaises de Hume," *Revue de Littérature Comparée* 9 (1929), 644–713.

9 See Johann Gottlieb Buhle, *Geschichte der neuern Philosophie seit der Epoche der Wiederherstellung der Wissenschaften*, 6 vols, Göttingen, 1800–1805, vol. VI, pp. 503f., see also vol. V, pp. i–x. Most contemporaries were very much aware of the British influence, while many of the more recent historical accounts of the period neglect it somewhat.

10 See below. But Hume was by no means the only one whom the Germans considered important. Shaftesbury, Hutcheson, Lord Kames, Adam Ferguson, and Adam Smith, among others, were considered to be at least as important.

11 See note 7.

12 David Hume, *Philosophische Versuche über die Menschliche Erkenntnis*, Hamburg and Leipzig, 1755, Vorrede. That Sulzer is not the translator is clear from the following: "Es haben mich zwei Gründe zu der Bekanntmachung dieser Übersetzung bewogen, die ich durch einen blossen Zufall in die Hände bekommen habe."

13 Hume, *Philosophische Versuche*.

14 Ibid. Because the translation is rare and the passage of great interest, I quote the German as well: "Ich hoffe, dass die Bekanntmachung dieses Werkes sie [die deutschen Philosophen] aus ihrer müssigen Ruhe ein wenig aufwecken, und ihnen eine neue Thätigkeit geben werde. Dieses ist einer von den Gründen, die mich zur Herausgebung dieses Werkes bewogen haben." (The emphasis in the translation is mine.)

15 B. Erdmann, "Kant und Hume um 1762," *Archiv für Geschichte der Philosophie* I (1887–8), 62–77, 216–30, 67.

16 Immanuel Kant, *Philosophical Correspondence, 1759–99*, ed. and trans. Arnulf Zweig (Chicago: University of Chicago Press, 1967), pp. 41f. This is the very same year in which Hamann's *Socratic Memorabilia* appeared.

17 Compare Erdmann, "Kant and Hume um 1762," 63f.

18 Ibid., 6f. See also the long quotation from Herder in Beck's "Sketch of Kant's Life and Work" in Kant, *Prolegomena*, ed. Beck, pp. xxii, and Herder's notes taken from lectures by Kant between 1762–64 (Kant, *Werke*, Akademie Ausgabe, vol. 28, 1).

19 Compare Beck, "A Prussian Hume and a Scottish Kant," 65f. Beck aptly calls this phase of Kant's thought "quasi-Humean."

20 Erdmann argues in his "Kant and Hume um 1762" against a fundamental influence of Hume upon Kant around 1762. It seems to me that Erdmann is somewhat too skeptical here. He also points out that Kant probably did not know the German translation of the *Four Dissertations*, because they are nowhere mentioned by Kant. But there is a conspicuous parallel to Hume's "Natural History of Religion" in Kant's *Prolegomena*. Compare Hume: "the mind of man appears of so loose and unsteady a texture, that, even at present, when so many persons find an interest in continually employing on it the chissels and the hammer, yet they are not able to engrave theological tenets with any lasting impression" (section XII) and Kant: "I should think

that Hume might fairly have laid as much claim to common sense as Beattie and, in addition, to a critical reason ... which keeps common sense in check and prevents it from speculating, or, if speculations are under discussion, restrains the desire to decide. ... By this means alone can common sense remain sound. Chisels and hammers may suffice to work a piece of wood, but for etching we require an etcher's needle" (*Prolegomena*, ed. Beck, p. 7).

21 Sulzer supplied extensive notes to the text of the German translation. He acknowledges that the fourth essay (concerning causality) is the most fundamental for Hume's skepticism and thus attempts to give a refutation. But this refutation is remarkable only for the persistence with which it misses the point.

22 David Hume, *Enquiries concerning the Human Understanding and concerning the Principles of Morals*, ed. L. A. Selby-Bigge, 2nd. edn. (Oxford: The Clarendon Press, 1970), p. 55.

23 See note 19.

24 Immanuel Kant, *Critique of Pure Reason*, trans. Norman Kemp Smith (New York: St. Martin's Press, 1965), Ax.

25 Ibid.

26 Kant, *Prolegomena*, p. 123–4.

27 Ibid., p. 33.

28 Kant, *Correspondence*, trans. Zweig, p. 97.

29 Ibid., p. 73.

30 Kant, *Prolegomena*, p. 99 see also *Critique of Pure Reason*, A757/B785 and A769/B797.

31 Kant, *Correspondence*, trans. Zweig, p. 252.

32 Immanuel Kant, *Gesammelte Schriften*, ed. Königlich Preussische Akademie der Wissenschaften (Berlin, 1902), vol. 18, p. 69.

33 Various sources for Kant's antinomies have been suggested. It is impossible to discuss all or even some of them adequately here. The theory that is perhaps most generally accepted today traces Kant's antinomies back to the correspondence of Leibniz and Clarke. The theory I put forward in the following need not contradict the view that the dispute between Newtonians and Leibnizians provides the general framework for the antinomies.

34 For a summary of the evidence for this theory, see Robert Paul Wolff, "Kant's Debt to Hume via Beattie," *Journal of the History of Ideas* 21 (1960), 117–23. See also Lewis White Beck, "Lambert and Hume in Kant's Development," *Essays on Kant and Hume*, pp. 101–10. I accepted this theory in my *Scottish Common Sense in Germany*. The account below does not so much contradict the systematic claims of this theory as it modifies and supplements them.

35 But perhaps the sharp indictment of dogmatism of the *Träume eines Geistersehers* is somewhat out of character. In a letter to Mendelssohn, dated 8 April 1766, Kant apologizes for the tone of his "little book."

36 Kant changed his account of the forms of sensibility only slightly in the first *Critique*.

37 If we assume – as I believe we must – that the most important discovery of 1769 was that of the limiting marks of the sensible and the intelligible in our knowledge, then Hume's *Enquiry* could as well have served as a

starting point for Kant as could any other of the sources mentioned thus far. Section XII of the first *Enquiry* deals with objectives "against the evidence of *sense*" and "against all abstract *reasonings*." Hume finds, for instance, that "no priestly *dogmas* . . . ever shocked common sense more than the doctrine of the infinite divisibility of space" and "the absurdity of these bold determinations of the abstract sciences seem to become, if possible, still more palpable with regard to time." In fact, Hume claims, "nothing can be more sceptical . . . than this scepticism itself, which arises from some of the paradoxical conclusions of geometry or the science of quantity." There are "clear and distinct idea[s which] contain circumstances, contradictory to [themselves]." Julius Janitsch, *Kants Urteile über Berkeley* (Strassburg, 1879) suggests that the last section of the *Enquiry* may have been important for Kant's discovery of the antinomies in 1769. He does not, however, explicate the consequences of this for Kant's conception of Hume's problem. Moreover, the Conclusion of Book I of the *Treatise* appears to me more important and 1769 is too early (see note 38).

38 See note 48. However, Norbert Hinske has shown that the antinomies have roots that reach far back in Kant's development. See his "Kant's Begriff der Antinomie und die Etappen seiner Ausarbeitung," *Kant-Studien* 55 (1966), 485–96.

39 Kant, *Correspondence*, trans. Zweig, pp. 70–6, especially 73.

40 This does not mean, however, that Beattie was unimportant for Kant's development, as will be seen from the following. In any case, Kant could have known of Beattie's *Essay on Truth* through a review in the *Göttingische Anzeigen von gelehrten Sachen*, which appeared on 28 January 1771. The reviewer of this work (most probably Johann Georg Heinrich Feder) finds "many correct and exact *thetic and antithetic remarks*" in Beattie, but concludes that, on the whole, "somebody like Hume would still have an easy game with him, when he asserts, for instance, that the principle 'everything that happens has a cause' has a further ground (*einen weitern Grund*) than experience" (p. 94, emphasis mine, and p. 92).

41 See notes 37 and 38. Even if the last section of the first *Enquiry* was not important for Kant in 1769, when he re-read it later it must have provided an important confirmation of his theory.

42 Apparently this has been established first by Swain in "Hamann and the Philosophy of David Hume." See also Helmut Holzhey, *Kant's Erfahrungsbegriff* (Basel/Stuttgart, 1970), p. 146n. and p. 153, who mentions however only the first installment of Hamann's translation. To my knowledge, nobody has yet drawn the obvious conclusion for Kant's development. That Kant did indeed know that this passage was from Hume is shown by his allusion to Hume, who "ran his ship ashore for safety's sake, landing on skepticism, there to let it lie and rot" *Prolegomena*, ed. Beck, p. 10, compare *Treatise*, pp. 263ff.).

Karl Grios, "Hat Kant Hume's Treatise gelesen?" *Kant-Studien* 5 (1901), 177–81, argued on the basis of this parallel that Kant knew the *Treatise*. Erdmann tried to show in his "Kant and Hume um 1762" that even Hamann did not know the *Treatise* before 1781 (see especially p. 65). But the translation clearly shows that Erdmann is wrong and that Groos is right. Kant knew at the very least the Conclusion of Book I of the *Treatise*.

Since Hamann and Kant were friends and discussed philosophy at times, it is very likely that Kant learned about other aspects of the *Treatise* from Hamann. In any case, Hamann preferred this early work of Hume, and he freely gave his opinion about all of Hume's philosophy. Krauss, another good friend of Kant and Hamann, was very thankful to Hamann for introducing him to this work. He knew, according to Hamann, the *Treatise* "by heart." Kant and Krauss regularly undertook long walks and frequently dined together. Kant could have learned everything about the contents of the *Treatise* from Krauss, his colleague and former student. Thus, even if Kant could not speak or read a word of English, he could have had a rather intimate acquaintance with Hume's *Treatise*.

43 Hume, *Enquiry*, p. 27 and *Treatise*, p. 266.
44 Hume, *Treatise*, pp. 266f.
45 Kant, *Correspondence*, trans. Zweig, p. 71.
46 Ibid.
47 Hume, *Treatise*, pp. 265f.
48 For the critical Kant an antinomy is a contradiction of the laws of reason. It does not just consist in the contradiction of two propositions that can both be proved, but in a contradiction of "laws, principles or maxims" (see Hinske, "Kants Begriff der Antinomie," p. 488). Thus Hume's contradiction within his "*principle* of imagination" certainly would meet some important criteria of "antinomy" in Kant's sense of the term. Lately John Bricke in his *Hume's Philosophy of Mind* (Princeton: Princeton University Press, 1980), pp. 9–10, 13, 21, 24, 96, 152, has also spoken of an "unavoidable antinomy" in Hume. I have tried to clarify this issue further in my "Hume's Antinomies", *Hume Studies* 8, 1983.
49 Hume, *Treatise*, p. 266.
50 Kant, *Prolegomena*, pp. 32.
51 See Kant, *Critique of Pure Reason*, Avii, for instance.
52 Hume, *Enquiry*, section XI, "Of a Particular Providence and of a Future State." See also his "Natural History of Religion." Both works are very important for a proper understanding of the extent of the problem of causality (or "Hume's problem"). Neither one has received the attention it would deserve.
53 Kant, *Critique of Pure Reason*, A462ff./B490ff.
54 Hume, *Enquiry*, pp. 132–42. See also Kant, *Prolegomena*, pp. 114ff.
55 Kant, *Critique of Pure Reason*, A739ff./B767ff., especially A745/B773. Compare A474/B502 with Hume, *Enquiry*, p. 41.
56 Kant, *Correspondence*, trans. Zweig, p. 252.
57 James Beattie, *An Essay on the Nature and Immutability of Truth*, Facsimile-Reprint of the first edition, Edinburgh, 1770, ed. F. O. Wolf (Stuttgart-Bad Canstatt: Friedrich Frommann Verlag (Günther Holzboog), 1973), p. 111.
58 Ibid.
59 Ibid., p. 113.
60 Ibid., p. 115.
61 Ibid.
62 Immanuel Kant, *Vorlesungen über Philosophische Enzyklopädie*, ed. G. Lehmann (Berlin: Akademie Verlag, 1961), p. 59.
63 Beattie, *Essay on Truth*, p. 118.

64 Kant, *Critique of Pure Reason*, A426/454.
65 Kant, *Critique*, A743/B771, A746/B774, A757/B785, A769/B797 make very clear the connection with Hume.
66 Kant, *Prolegomena*, p. 117.
67 Ibid.
68 Ibid., p. 119.
69 The importance of the anti-skeptical tendency of Kant's criticism, which is clearly there, can be easily exaggerated.
70 Kant, *Prolegomena*, p. 117.
71 Ibid.
72 Ibid., p. 118.
73 See Immanuel Kant, *Critique of Practical Reason*, trans. Lewis White Beck (Indianapolis, New York: The Bobbs Merrill Co., Inc., 1956), pp. 52ff. It is impossible to say more about this here.
74 See, for instance, his *Träume eines Geistersehers*. There he finds that the metaphysician has to find out whether the task of inquiring into the hidden qualities of things "be within the limits of our knowledge," and to determine the relations of this task "to conceptions derived from experience; for these must always be the foundation of all our judgments. To this extent metaphysics is *the science of the boundaries of human reason*." The translation of this passage is taken from Lewis White Beck, *Early German Philosophy* (Cambridge, Massachusetts: Harvard University Press, 1969), p. 445.
75 Kant, *Prolegomena*, p. 33. "Yet even he [Hume] did not suspect such a formal science. . . ." The formulation of the indifferentist position is taken from Nicholas Capaldi's Introduction to the *McGill Hume Studies*, "The Problem of Hume and Hume's Problem," p. 12. Capaldi's outline of Hume's problem may be enlightening for Hume, but it appears to me that Kant is located wrongly, for he clearly rejected "A₁" ("All human reasoning is informal") after having become aware of Hume's problem.
76 The metaphysical or ontological school of Kant-interpretation (which comprises such philosophers as Martin Heidegger, Max Wundt, Heinz Heimsoeth, and Gottfried Martin) uses the continuity between Kant's pre-critical and critical period as well as an emphasis upon Kant's so-called "metaphysical motives" in order to show that Kant was a metaphysician in fairly much the same way as Leibniz, Fichte, and Hegel. This reconstruction of Kant's view of Hume's problem and principle suggests that Kant belongs to a quite different metaphysical tradition, and that Kant is closer to Hume than to Leibniz.
77 See Wolff, "Hume's Theory of Mental Activity" and Mall, "Humes Prinzipien- und Kants Kategoriensystem."
78 See Beck, "A Prussian Hume and a Scottish Kant," and Dauer, "Towards a Copernican Reading of Hume."

CHANGING THE NAME OF THE GAME

Kant's cognitivism versus Hume's psychologism

Patricia Kitcher

I KANT'S REPLY: THE PROBLEM

Teaching the history of modern philosophy can be a trial. After weeks of anticipation, we come, finally, to one of the most exciting episodes: Kant's brilliant and unprecedented reply to Hume. The students are dumbfounded, but for the wrong reason. After all, they have been carefully taught that the difficulty with Hume – why he failed where Kant will succeed – is that he mistakenly turned philosophical questions into psychological ones. Instead of providing a philosophical defense of the concept of personal identity or causation, for example, he contented himself with psychological accounts of the origin of these ideas. Students are "majorly perplexed," as they put it, because Kant's reply seems like more of the same. He does not seem to answer Hume so much as to extend his psychological accounts and change the names – and not for the better. In place of reasonably familiar psychological notions, such as habit and resemblance, they are confronted with "forms of intuition," "syntheses of apprehension," and a great deal more transcendental paraphernalia.

This problem is not restricted to students. Kant versus Hume scholarship has often come to just about the same conclusion. The most popular means for distinguishing the Kantian and Humean projects can be captured in two claims:

1 Kant tries to provide a normative analysis of cognition, whereas Hume's account was intended to be naturalistic, even genetic.
2 Hume's philosophy not only ends in skepticism, but in failure

178

within its own terms, because empiricist psychology is inadequate to permit even a genetic explanation of cognition. By abandoning the strictures of empiricism, Kant is able to provide a better account of knowledge.

Upon closer inspection, however, these differences have not seemed so clear. A number of prominent scholars have defended Hume's normative epistemological interest.[1] From the other direction, Mall has argued that Kant's critical theory is a species of Humean naturalism.[2] Norman Kemp Smith and Robert Paul Wolff have called the second mode of demarcation into question, by insisting that Hume's psychological arsenal has important resources beyond those usually listed.[3] On the other side, although Kant's freeing himself from the shackles of empiricism is often regarded as virtuous, it is not very clear how it helps. If this move is understood solely in terms of willingness to endorse a priori or necessary truths, then it cannot provide a resolution of the problems Hume raises; it simply begs the question against him. However, scholars are almost unanimous in denying that it helps by allowing Kant to invoke psychological principles beyond the empiricists' law of association. On this point, the experts and the students agree. Trying to ground the law of association by invoking a transcendental faculty of imagination (A 100–2), for example, makes an account of cognition no less psychological and considerably more obscure.

My aim is to argue against this position shared by experts and carefully taught students. The essential difference between Hume and Kant is precisely that the latter is willing to go beyond the empiricists' picture of mental life and consider what types of faculties are necessary for cognition and how their existence might be established. That is why Kant succeeds (to the degree that he does) where Hume failed. Since my approach flies in the face of current orthodoxy, it may be useful to enlist some unlikely (and perhaps unwilling) allies to overcome initial resistance.

I begin at the most general level. In recent years, many epistemologists have argued that the Fregean proscription against mingling with psychology was a mistake.[4] A substantial portion of this group believes that epistemology can retain its normative character, even while drawing on theoretical and empirical results in psychology.[5] Given these developments, the possibility that Kant's reflections on cognitive faculties might contribute to the resolution of epistemological problems should not be dismissed out of hand. Further, these epistemologists note that for most of its modern existence, their discipline has been heavily influenced by psychology.

Second, since Kant's work falls within the psychological tradition of epistemology, my approach is a natural one. Although this should not be controversial, it has been, so I will adduce two historical and two contemporary authorities. In 1871, just prior to the Fregean revolution in epistemology, Jürgen Bona-Meyer devoted an entire book to the problem of *Kant's Psychologie*.[6] Kuno Fischer's famous commentary (1866) presents the central problem of the *Critique* as explaining the fact of cognition. He continues:

> If there be such knowledge at all, both the faculties of our reason must contribute, each in its own way; and, therefore, to explain knowledge each of these faculties must be investigated. But the character of a power or faculty can only be ascertained by its effects. Hence, the nature and action of the cognitive faculties can only be discovered by learning in what the fact of cognition and its possibility consists.[7]

Much more recently, P. F. Strawson sums up what he takes to be Dieter Henrich's important new insight into the methodology of the transcendental deduction:

> A [juridical] deduction in the relevant sense aims to justify an acquired title, or claim of right, by tracing it back to *origins*, to origins which are such as to confer legitimacy on it. In application to the *Critique* this is a matter of elucidating crucial *basic facts* by virtue of which our *knowledge-claims* are justified and upon which our possession of knowledge depends. These basic facts relate to *specific cognitive capacities* of which we have, in reflection, an *implicit* awareness or knowledge. The deduction is then said to proceed, not by linear demonstration, but by a variety of argumentative strategies that will systematize and render explicit the functioning of our cognitive capacities and, in doing so, will, it is hoped, exhibit the necessary "validity of the categories for all objects of experience." (Original emphasis; in the last phrase, Strawson is quoting Henrich.)[8]

This account of Henrich's position is accurate and Strawson seems to endorse it as a description of how the deduction is *supposed* to go. In the past, both Henrich and Strawson have prided themselves on avoiding psychological entanglements when dealing with the *Critique*.[9] I take these new papers as evidence that they no longer

180

think this is possible while remaining even moderately faithful to the text.

Finally, I am not alone in thinking that a critical difference between Hume and Kant is that the latter delved more deeply into the prerequisites of our basic cognitive capacities. Lewis White Beck, the dean of American Kant scholars and no friend of psychology, points out that Hume's error about causation lay in taking the ability to recognise the difference between one event and another for granted, rather than trying to analyze it.[10] The same theme echoes throughout Hansgeorg Hoppe's essay, "Kant Antwort auf Hume" ("Kant's Answer to Hume"). For instance, Hoppe observes that:

> Hume presupposes the objective validity of our impressions, that is, the fact that they relate to enduring matters of fact, from which they are distinct, or [that they] are even identical with the objects. . . .
>
> His question about the continuing existence of objects comes, to that extent, too late. (my translation)[11]

Hoppe goes on to note that by reflecting on such errors in Hume, we can truly appreciate Kant's point in describing his own investigations as being concerned with the possibility of experience, with the problem of how we go beyond impressions (*Vorstellungen*) as mere modifications of the subject to these as impressions indicating things and matters of fact.[12]

In a well-known paper, Robert Paul Wolff describes what Hume's theory would look like had he been willing to abandon the attempt to explain cognition solely in terms of the contents of mental states and appeal instead to mental activities.[13] The resulting account is both more plausible and more Kantian. This is a reconstruction, however. Wolff alters the ground rules of Hume's enterprise by freeing it from the bounds of associationism and then provides him with a vocabulary of faculties. I take the success of Wolff's reconstructive project as significant evidence that the relative weakness of Hume's system lies in its inadequate treatment of the processes involved in cognition.[14]

So much for a preliminary defense of the strategy. Since I wish to launch (if not fully defend) a general thesis, I need to analyze several Kantian replies to Humean challenges. I consider three topics that would be included in every list of Hume's skeptical theses: personal identity, the existence of continuing and independent objects, and causation. These are large issues and my discussions are not meant to be exhaustive. Rather, I try to show only that on natural readings of Hume's problems and Kant's solutions (sometimes supplied by me, sometimes by others), there is a clear pattern to the interchanges. For all three cases, I argue that Hume is led into unwonted skepticism or a less satisfactory account by restricting himself to the theoretical constructs of empiricism: impressions, ideas, and their association. By contrast, Kant approaches these issues in the framework of a normative endeavor to determine what conditions are required for us to achieve various kinds of cognition, given our basic cognitive constitution. In pursuing this goal, he draws reasonably freely on psychological constructs that are anathema to empiricists: mental faculties and mental rules explicitly characterized as being independent of sensory data and its association by spatio-temporal contiguity. Thus I will defend the two standard ways of explaining how Kant's reply to Hume works – his epistemology is normative and unfettered by empiricist psychology – by taking the second point very seriously. The problem of Kant's reply to Hume arises, I believe, only because current interpreters have been unwilling to pay more than lip-service to this second, completely obvious difference between their approaches.

II HEAPS AND SYNTHESES

Personal identity or mental unity is not usually regarded as a matter of dispute between Hume and Kant. Kant does not mention Hume's position explicitly, and the topic is only dealt with in the *Treatise*, which was not translated into German before the appearance of the *Critique*. I have argued elsewhere, however, that there is ample external evidence that Kant was aware of Hume's shocking views and ample internal evidence that he tried to refute them.[15] Since Hume changes his mind, to put it mildly, between Book I and the Appendix, I discuss his position in two parts.

'Of personal identity'

Hume embarks on this topic to dispel the metaphysical and popular doctrine that each of us has a self that enjoys perfect simplicity and identity. The ground for this claim, he maintains, is that we are "intimately conscious" of the self, "we feel its existence and continuance in existence" (T 251).[16] His philosophical target is Descartes and the doctrine that each time I think, or more neutrally, each time there is a thought, it is absolutely certain that I exist. Since this intimate consciousness is simply introspection, unsympathetic readers are likely to resist Hume's initial characterization of the relevant evidence. Cartesians need not assume that we are intimately conscious of the self. Their position is that thoughts, ideas, perceptions, *cogitationes*, or whatever you want to call mental states, are incapable of independent existence. Hence, once the "*Cogito*" is granted, so must be the "Sum." Hume does not address the issue in this form, because he rightly has no time for this kind of position. If the claim is that it is part of the meaning of "mental state" that mental states are accidents, then he regards the view as frivolous. One might as well try to argue that all men are married, by noting that "husband" is a correlative term to "wife" (cf. T 82). Since this issue cannot be settled by appealing to the relations of ideas, Hume rejects the possibility that the claim is a just inference.

The remaining possibility is that claims about the simplicity and identity of the soul are supported by factual evidence. Since the soul cannot be observed by any of the five outer senses, we must (as he said) turn to reflection or inner sense. Reflection is the ability to be affected by our own ideas in such a way as to have impressions produced by them (T 8). With considerable relish, Hume undertakes a mock experiment, which he invites the reader to try as well: Use reflection to look at your thoughts and see if you can discern a simple and continuing self. Far from simplicity and identity, what we are actually aware of through inner sense are multiplicity and difference, perceptions that succeed each other with "inconceivable rapidity" whenever "our eyes turn in their sockets" or our thoughts race from one topic to another (T 252). It is important to note that this "introspective report" must be largely theory driven. Inconceivably rapid variations are presumably also imperceptibly rapid. In any case, Hume concludes that the metaphysicians' view is wrong: "There is properly no simplicity in it at one time; nor identity in different" (T 253). Still, something remains to be explained. Even ignoring misguided metaphysicians, why do ordinary people believe in identity and simplicity when the evidence is so contrary?

Although Hume believes that perfect identity through time requires absolute sameness of properties, he notes that we often ascribe identity in the absence of this condition. The most illuminating class of exceptions are cases of animal identity:

with all animals and vegetables [we attribute identity because] . . . not only [do] the several parts have a reference to some general purpose, but also a mutual dependence on, and connexion with each other . . . they stand in the reciprocal relation of cause and effect in all their actions and operations. (T 257)

Hume's general position in Book I is that personal identity is, first, fictitious, and, second, like that we attribute to animals and vegetables. The point of the latter claim is to imply that the origin of this belief must be similar to that of beliefs about animals and vegetables. Before cashing the analogy, Hume interrupts himself to reinforce the first point. Lest the reader be unconvinced by what has gone before, he presents his case as a full-dress argument.

Implicitly we are to recall that the only available data for a claim of mental identity are the rapidly succeeding perceptions viewed through inner sense. The identity claim cannot meld these distinct perceptions into a unity, however. For "every distinct perception . . . is a distinct existence, and is different, and distinguishable, and separable from every other perception . . ." (T 259). So the only remaining question is whether these distinct perceptions are, despite their separateness, really bound together. Here Hume appeals to his general principle that the understanding never observes any real connection among (separate) objects. Rather, when carefully examined, it turns out that the data that lead to a belief in real connection are not *evidence* for that belief at all. Instead, the perceptions are resembling, contiguous in space and time, and/or related by cause and effect, so that the mind comes to associate them together and to *feel* a connection. As a result of this feeling of connection, a connection is projected on to the objects, producing a fictitious belief.

At this point, all that needs to be considered is which of the laws of association gives rise to the feeling of connection among perceptions and so to the belief in a continuing and identical self. Although Hume gives some weight to the resemblance, his well-known hypothesis is that the causal relations among perceptions, the fact that they "mutually produce, destroy, influence, and modify each other" (T 261), lead us (mistakenly) to treat them as a unity. In drawing this conclusion, Hume seems to have given up – almost absentmindedly – part of the analogy with animals and vegetables. Apparently, he finds no common end or purpose in the perceptions of one mind.

Appendicitis

When Hume realized the disastrous implications of his views on personal identity, he reviews the two central issues: Must the self be a substance in order to support perceptions? What is the evidence that perceptions are distinct? He notes that philosophers (that is, empiricists) already acknowledge that we can have no adequate idea of an external substance, but only ideas of particular qualities. Their reasoning (which he does not give) is that we only have sensory access to particular qualities. By the same reasoning, the fact that reflection yields only particular perceptions should lead us away from the doctrine that we have an adequate idea of an enduring inner substance (T 635). Alternatively, the only evidence we have is of particular qualities or particular perceptions, so we cannot justly infer the existence of outer or inner substances.

To bolster his earlier, somewhat cavalier experiment, Hume also offers a direct argument that the impressions of reflection must be of distinct perceptions. Since ideas are borrowed from preceding perceptions, ideas of objects must have this source. He continues: "Consequently, no proposition can be intelligible or consistent with regard to objects, which is not so with regard to perceptions" (T 636). Given that it is intelligible and consistent to say that objects are distinct, Hume feels entitled to conclude the same with regard to perceptions. It cannot be absurd to claim that they are distinct.

Hume's willing slide between "object" and "perception" has often been criticized. That is not the issue here, however. His argument is an implicit *reductio* for the claim that our perceptions must have some mark of distinctness in them. We start from the assumption that we have a clear idea of distinct objects. A table and a chimney are his examples. The next step is unexpressed. Let us suppose, contrary to the *demonstrandum*, that our perceptions are not distinct, but all flow together or bear some sign of real connection across all of them. The crucial point to realize is that there is only one set of contents. We have impressions of a table, a chimney, their being situated next to each other, and their being distinct. Our ideas are copied from these and so have the same contents. Impressions of reflection are impressions of these ideas, however, and so also have the same contents: impressions of the ideas of a table, a chimney, their situation, and their distinctness. If the latter impressions bear a mark of sameness or real connection among them, then so must the ideas and the preceding, resembling impressions of sensation. In which case, we would not, contrary to the assumption, have a clear idea of the table and the chimney as distinct. So, the impressions of reflection cannot bear indications of real connection across all of them, but must, in fact, show some marks of distinctness. It does not matter that we also have ideas and impressions of different aspects of single objects. The reflected impressions of these impressions would, presumably, bear marks of sameness. Hume's point is that so long as what we call a single mind has impressions and ideas of distinct objects, then some impressions of reflection must have marks of distinctness.

As Kemp Smith insists, Hume acknowledges two further elements beyond the contents of perceptions: the relative vivacity of different mental states and the feelings that accompany impressions of reflection. The former factor is supposed to provide the basis for explaining how we are able to differentiate among impressions, ideas, memories, and flights of imagination. Hume appeals to feelings, in part, to explain how we fall into error. For example, since the causal relations among perceptions induce a feeling of connection, we project a connection on to the perceptions and so claim that they all belong to a single subject. This is a confusion, however. It amounts to mixing data about objects (albeit our own perceptions in this case) with data about our reaction to the objects. At this point, Hume has given his final and considered answer to the question about the ordinary and metaphysical view of an enduring self. Given the only possible origin of this idea, which involves a confounding of objective and subjective sources of information, no serious epistemologist could regard it as sound. Alternatively, given the only possible data, namely, the contents of our impressions of reflection, there can be no evidence in favor of a real connection across all the perceptions that we say belong to a single mind. Whatever philosophers and laymen may say about a continuing self, the evidence is otherwise. What we call an individual mind is just a heap of perceptions.

Of course, Hume's bracing confession in the Appendix is that he cannot live with his own results. He now understands that his account of personal identity has led him into hopeless inconsistency. Despite the interpretive disputes on this point, I think it is fairly clear where the inconsistency lies. Hume says that there are two principles that he cannot render consistent:

that all our distinct perceptions are distinct existences, and that

the mind never perceives any real connexion among distinct
existences. (T 636)

Since these two claims are consistent, the obvious strategy is to find
some third claim which he cannot give up which, when combined
with these, produces an inconsistent triad. And the obvious candidate
must be something like: the distinct perceptions we attribute to
single minds really belong to single minds and must be acknowledged
to do so. In Book I, Hume suggests that this could happen in two
different ways. Perceptions might be modifications of an enduring
substance or they might be related by real connections. Since the
first option is explicitly ruled out, the remaining possibility is that
perceptions are and must be acknowledged to be really connected –
a view that is flatly inconsistent with the two principles he cannot
give up.

To understand why Hume is committed to single minds, we need
look no further than the law of association. As Barry Stroud points
out, this most basic psychological assumption itself requires the
assumption of single minds. For what the law says is that if A (type)-
perceptions and B (type)-perceptions are constantly conjoined, then
upon the presentation of a new instance of A, there will be a further
perception or at least idea of the B-type. The catch is that this
statement of the law contains a hidden restriction: All these perceptions must belong to a single mind. For if every time that I have an
A-perception, someone else has a B-perception, then there will be
no thought of B upon the presentation of A. Small wonder that
Hume despaired. The principles of psychology on which he tried
to erect his science of man all make essential (if implicit) use of the
notion of a single mind, and his account of personal identity reveals
that notion to be unsound.

What has gone wrong?

One glaring weakness is that Hume badly misunderstands the nature
of his "data." He does not discover that our perceptions are distinct
and constantly changing in the same way that Dalton discovered that
some people are color-blind. As noted, his "results" are entirely
theory driven. Taking, as always, vision as the paradigm outer sense,
the inconceivably rapid flux of perceptions is no observation, but
a prediction from two assumptions: Since the eye is in constant
motion, the retinal image is constantly changing; perceptions

faithfully replicate sensory data.[17] As we have seen, the independent argument about the data in the Appendix relies explicitly on empiricist psychology. The contents of impressions of reflection reflect the contents of impressions of sensation. Because Hume takes these assumptions of empiricist psychology as bedrock, he misconstrues highly theoretical claims as given data.

To see the second problem, consider a crucial difference between Hume's account of personal identity and his treatment of causation and induction. When we observe a large number of regularities in our perceptions, we come to expect effects upon the presentation of causes and come, more generally, to expect the course of nature to continue to be regular. Thus, our beliefs in causal connections and in the inductive principle are to be explained by reference to a feeling of expectation that naturally arises in the mind when certain patterns of data are presented to it. Although Kant regards the connection between the data and the feeling as merely contingent (B 168), the mechanism of expectation is, as Hume describes it, a reliable indicator of these patterns. Further, the causal and inductive beliefs produced by it can be tempered by general rules – such as the eight he lists – gleaned from experience. Thus, from Hume's point of view, these beliefs are tolerably well justified, although not in the way one might have thought. The beliefs are formed through a mechanism that reliably indicates the presence of pattern in the data and are susceptible to correction by appeal to a much broader database. The only error is that the feeling of necessity which alerts us to the pattern is confounded with the data so that we come to believe in metaphysical necessity.

Hume's problem in explaining our belief in personal identity is that he must appeal to the same mechanism. If the "data" are distinct perceptions standing in causal relations, then the belief should concern causal connection, not identity. Despite their close association, normally, we do not take causes and effects to be identical or parts of a larger whole. Hume is unwilling to fudge on this point. He will not posit another feeling which helpfully arises when we are reflecting on our own perceptions. Neither will he deceive himself into thinking that the resemblance produced by memory is enough to make a significant difference. So, in the end, Hume cannot explain why we have a belief in personal identity at all, let alone why this might be a reasonable belief to have.

Kant's discovery of real connection

Besides the absence of explicit references, Kant's discussion of this issue is so different in appearance from Hume's that it is no wonder it has not struck readers as a reply. Where Hume straightforwardly questions our belief in personal identity, Kant's intricate answer – the transcendental synthetic unity of apperception – seems to descend full-blown on to the text, without any problem ever having been posed. Still, two textual facts make the linkage clear. At A 107, a passage that led Kemp Smith to wonder if Kant were not familiar with Hume's account, we get the following reflection and criticism:

> The consciousness of the self, according to the determination of our state in inner perception, is merely empirical, and always changing. There can be no permanent and continuing self in this flux of inner appearances. . . . What has necessarily to be represented as numerically identical cannot be thought as such through empirical data. To render such a transcendental presupposition valid, there must be a condition which precedes all experience, and which makes experience itself possible. (A 107, amended translation)[18]

Here Kant reviews the problem as it stands in Hume and explains how he is going to succeed where his predecessor failed. He will show that personal or mental identity is a necessary condition for the possibility of (cognitive) experience itself.

The second point of textual contact is the doctrine of synthesis. Hume despaired of finding a real connection to bind perceptions into a single mind. Throughout the deduction, Kant constantly refers to the need for a "synthesis" of cognitive states. As I have argued elsewhere, what Hume means by "real connection" is a relation of existential dependence between the relata and that is precisely what is created by synthesis.[19]

> By *synthesis*, in its most general sense, I understand the act of adding different cognitive states [or their contents] to each other and of comprehending their diverse [elements] in a single representation. (A 77/B 103, my translation)

That is, synthesis is a process whereby the diverse elements of various cognitive states are comprehended – combined and preserved – in a single resultant state. Had the earlier states, with their particular elements, not existed, neither would the resulting synthesized state.

For (as we will see), the content of the resulting state consists in its having been produced from these predecessors and the contents of the preceding states depends on their producing the resulting state.

At this point, we can see the basic outlines of Kant's solution to Hume's problem. He will demonstrate real connection by arguing that a synthesis of cognitive states is necessary for cognitive experience. More specifically, he argues that knowledge requires both intuitions and concepts. Even the most minimal knowledge claim requires that we have some sensory representation of an object and some concept under which we can classify it. His argument is that both intuitions and concepts are impossible without a synthesis of cognitive states. Hume asserts the existence of impressions and ideas, which Kant characterizes more accurately as "intuitions" and "concepts." Kant's argument is not just an *ad hominem*, however: since Hume admits the existence of impressions and ideas and since a real connection among cognitive states is necessary for these, he must grant it as well. Regardless of what empiricists *assert*, his point is the normative one that cognition requires intuitions and concepts – and so real connections and individual minds.

Since I have offered detailed discussions of Kant's arguments that intuitions and concepts require a synthesis of cognitive states elsewhere,[20] I will just summarize them here and then explain how the doctrine of synthesis solves Hume's problem. The critical point about both intuitions and concepts is that they are representational. In essence, Kant's argument about intuitions is that they would not represent anything to the subject were they simply caused by sensory stimulation. To represent something to the subject, they must lead to, that is, be synthesized in, further cognitive states, in particular, conceptual judgments.[21] Otherwise, like the overwhelming majority of Leibniz's *petites perceptions*, they would make no contribution to the cognitive life of the subject and so be nothing to us as cognitive beings. How can concepts represent? Kant realized that the Wolffian alternative of positing a *vis representiva* was just as hopeless as the empiricist claim that ideas represent by virtue of resembling the impressions that give rise to them. Instead, he argues that concepts can only have particular contents in virtue of their generation from, that is, their synthesis from, particular intuitions (A 103).

Kant attributes the process of synthesis to a faculty of "imagination," which is nothing more than a dummy name for whatever it is that carries out syntheses. Synthesis creates a relation of real connection among cognitive states, because the resultant states depend for their contents, and so their identity as particular states, on the states that produced them and conversely. The process of synthesis also depends on a relation among cognitive states, however: they must be connectible by synthesis. It must be possible for elements from state S_1 to be combined with elements from state S_2 in a resulting state S_3. Implicitly, Kant assumes that his must be possible without these elements being transmitted through outer sense.[22]

If both the creation of real connections by synthesis and the dependency of synthesis on a connectibility of cognitive states are borne in mind, then we can understand Kant's doctrine of the way in which diverse cognitive states are yoked together in a single "I think." Start with a set of states such that later ones have been synthesized from earlier ones. All states belong to the same "I think" that are connectible by synthesis with the states in this set.[23] His conclusions about the possibility of cognitive states and synthetic connection are summarized in the dramatic opening statements of the doctrine of apperception in both editions, although the point is somewhat clearer in A:

> We are conscious a priori of the complete identity of the self in respect of all cognitive states which can ever belong to our knowledge, as being a necessary condition of the possibility of all cognitive states. *For in me they can represent something only in so far as they belong with all others to one consciousness, and therefore must at least be capable of being so connected.* (A 116, my emphasis, amended translation)

That is, cognitive states that can represent something and can belong to cognition must all be connectible. In the later edition, Kant stresses the fact that unless cognitive states could be synthetically connected in a single "I think", they would be impossible or nothing to the subject (B 132, 133). He also clarifies his position in B, by explaining that being connectible with an identical "I think" is a matter of being synthetically connectible with each other (B 133).

The real connection Kant finds among cognitive states is the relation of contentual interchange and dependence. Unless cognitive states belonged to systems in which contentual interchange was actual between some states and possible across all of them, they could not be representational states, neither intuitions nor concepts. So we must posit these systems and refer to the diverse states of individual minds, even though Kant agrees with Hume that the self is not a substance or even anything separate from the system of states. This posit is justified, because it is required to explain some very minimal facts of cognition, the existence of intuitions and concepts. Interestingly, Kant solves Hume's problem by considering not just the relations among particular cognitive states, but their common purpose: cognition.

The morals of this exchange are fairly clear. Kant's account of mental unity is more satisfactory than Hume's, for three reasons. First, Kant does not accept the empiricist account of impressions and ideas as given, but questions how such creatures are possible. Second, he is willing to sanction additional mental equipment that is not firmly tied to sensory experience, in particular, a transcendental imagination that synthesizes elements from cognitive states occurring at widely different times. Finally and most importantly, Kant's account is more deeply normative. Although Hume presents the theory of impressions and ideas as if it were a well-tested scientific theory, his support for it is clearly based on normative considerations. Any ideas used in knowledge claims *ought* to be anchored in sensory evidence. Further, his concerns are not just with a descriptive theory of human nature that would explain how our beliefs arise. Despite his packaging of his philosophy, he is more deeply concerned with issues of justification than of genesis (*per se*). Nevertheless, Kant manages to be more normative, because his overriding question about the possibility of cognition enables him to recast individual requests for justification in a larger normative project. In the present case, Hume's question of whether a belief in a simple and identical self is justified becomes: Does cognition (or, better, some aspect of cognition that all will grant, such as the representational character of cognitive states) require the existence of individual minds? It is only by taking this highly original normative approach that Kant cracks the problem. On the other hand, it is not clear that he ever would have considered the need for a synthesis of cognitive states – a doctrine which is the heart of his theory of cognition – had Hume not first denied that any real connection among them was discoverable.

III CONTINUING OBJECTS AND STABLE PERCEPTS

Hume's inquiries into our belief in continuing and distinct objects do not produce terminal inconsistency. Still, he is unpleasantly surprised by his results. As sympathetic commentators remind us, his expressed goal is not to justify our belief in objects that exist independently of our perceptions and continuously, even when unperceived.[24] Rather, it is to explain how we come to this belief, on the basis of internal and constantly perishing perceptions (T 187). In the end, I will dissent from this consensus of special pleaders. Surely it is extraordinary to claim that, in this one case, Hume has no normative agenda at all, even though he raises justificatory questions about our beliefs in God, miracles, necessary causes, a continuing self, moral principles, and every other issue he tackles. For the moment, however, I focus on Hume's genetic account.

The tangled origins of our belief in continuing objects

Ordinary people come to believe in continuing objects as a result of the action of several mental mechanisms. First, they sometimes perceive objects uninterruptedly over a period of time. Because of changes in other aspects of their perceptions, they are aware of the passage of time. So, for example, a person may view a fountain while others come and go around it. Despite these changes, the fountain perception would be invariant in its qualitative character. Hume assumes that we have some way of monitoring the feeling produced by the mind not having to change the qualitative character of (part of) its perception (T 203). For ease in reference, we may call this disposition of the mind the "feeling of invariance." Normally, our perceptions of objects are interrupted; we cannot survey all the furniture of the universe at all times. Further, when we perceive the same object again (as we say), it is often from a different angle or in a different light, so the perception differs qualitatively from previous perceptions. Nevertheless, Hume surmises, there is enough constancy in our perceptions of a desk, for example, that we are put in the same disposition of mind as when continuously viewing the fountain. Then he offers a general principle: whatever ideas place the mind in the same disposition or in a similar one are apt to be confounded. So the idea of invariance through time, which naturally arises in viewing an object without interruption, is extended to objects viewed variously and interruptedly. These too are believed to continue, identically the same, through time. Continuous existence implies distinct existence. This seems to present a problem, since ordinary people confound objects and perceptions. Hence, they are committed to perceptions existing independently of minds. Here, Hume appeals to his account of personal identity to note that, despite appearances, it is quite consistent to imagine perceptions as distinct from and so independent of minds (T 207).

Never mind that ordinary people do not share Hume's views about personal identity. There are still two serious problems with this account, one internal and one external. Given the feeling of invariance, the imagination feigns a continued existence of, for example, a desk object/perception. We are directly aware of our perceptions, however, and what we are aware of are frequent and long interruptions in our perceptions (T 207). Further, perceptions (naturally) command our assent (T 212). Hence the mind's natural powers produce contrary views. The imagination produces a belief in the continuity (and so distinct existence) of object/perceptions; our direct awareness of interrupted perceptions leads us to deny identity and continuity.

We get out of this predicament, Humes argues, because memory and association also produce a belief in sameness. A present impression of the desk conveys its liveliness to memory images which, given their resemblance to the present impression, are taken to be the same with it. That is, due to the action of memory and association, we favor the imagination over direct perception (T 208). The internal problem is that his psychological account implies that we would do the opposite, that the direct awareness of perceptions would compel us to acquiesce in a lack of continuity. Hume manages to line up two sets of mental mechanisms on the continuity side: the feeling of invariance aided by the principle of confounding and memory-association. But he offers no reason to believe that the resulting propensities could overwhelm the force of direct perception. Further, he provides no reason why coming down on the side of discontinuity would be inconsistent or any more paradoxical than the position that perceptions exist independently of minds. It is no good to remind the reader that the *explanandum* is our belief in continuing and distinct objects (T 206). His account of psychological mechanisms does not lead us to expect this outcome, so the explanation fails. Hume virtually acknowledges this point when he reflects that the mechanisms he appeals to are "trivial," too trivial to lead to any solid reasoning (T 217). Presumably he also sees that they are too trivial to counterbalance direct perception.

The external difficulty with Hume's genetic story is that he holds the belief produced to be false. Laymen believe that what they perceive are continuing and independently existing entities. A few simple experiments and a little reflection reveal, however, that our perceptions have no independent existence. By pressing our eyes, we can produce double images; by changing our distance from objects, we can diminish or augment the size of perceptions (T 210–11). Hence the qualities of our perceptions depend very much on our state. To complete the indictment of lay opinion, Hume would need to show that what we are aware of are perceptions. This position was so widely held, however, that he simply assumes it, adverting to it only in other contexts (e.g. T 212).

The difference between the discussion and Hume's treatment of the self is striking. In that case, when he discovers that a common belief is false, he invites us to reject it. Further, the cases are parallel. It is not that the common belief in continuing and distinct objects is unjustified or not justified in the way we might have thought. The belief is false (T 209, 213). I have no grounds for speculating about why Hume does not consign to the flames what he clearly regards as a metaphysical error. My point is only that he is much less sanguine about his results than his commentators. He began by assuming that we should have faith in our senses and (so) that there are independent objects. As he reflects on his discoveries, he acknowledges that "to be ingenuous, I feel myself *at present* of a quite contrary sentiment, and am more inclin'd to repose no faith at all in my senses, or rather imagination" (T 212). Commentators latch on to the "at present" to suggest that Hume does not doubt external objects. Since he concludes his discussion by noting that skepticism always follows profound reflection, but is cured by resuming normal activities, it is easy to read the qualifier as indicating that, like the common person, Hume generally accepts external objects. This is probably true, but certainly irrelevant. His psychological account is still unsatisfactory and his normative position quite unclear.

In his concluding reflections, Hume's concerns are entirely normative. By his account, the constancy and coherence of perceptions produce a belief in continuity. Unfortunately, coherence can do almost nothing; the weakness of this factor was exposed early in the section. One might be tempted to reason as follows: Whenever I hear a certain noise, for example, I have seen a door moving. In the present case, with my back to the door, I hear only the sound. In order to increase the coherence of my views, I assume that this past regularity holds, even though I don't see the door move. That is, I assume the continuity of objects in order to explain the regularities

I observe. Hume's reason for denying this account of the origin of the belief is instructive:

> since nothing is ever really present to the mind, besides its own perceptions, 'tis not only impossible, that any habit should ever be acquir'd otherwise than by the regular succession of these perceptions, but also that any habit shou'd ever exceed that degree of regularity. (T 197)

Since our perceptions are not particularly coherent, but ever fluctuating and gappy, the force of habit cannot itself produce a belief in continuous objects/perceptions. Hence he must turn to constancy and to more exotic psychological mechanisms.

Upon re-examining his account of these mechanisms, however, he finds them to be trivial and the suppositions they produce false. His point is not that the mechanisms are non-rational. That result would be fine. The problem is that they are capricious and unreliable. Through these mechanisms, constancy and coherence give rise to a belief in continuing objects, but "these qualities of perceptions have no perceivable connexion with such an existence" (T 217). And, as noted, the belief is false, a "gross illusion."

The unsatisfactory character of this account is even clearer when we compare these mechanisms with Hume's paradigm of a non-rational, but still trustworthy, mechanism: sympathy. Sympathy leads us to feel the difficulties of others as our own. Although these troubles are not in fact ours, the attitude produced by sympathy is hardly a gross illusion, since other people strongly resemble us in body and mind (T 316–18). Further, sympathy is a remarkable quality (T 316), which accounts for our sense of justice (T 499) and is susceptible to correction by general rules (T 586). Finally, the mechanism of sympathy fits so well with Hume's basic principles about the operations of the understanding and the passions that it offers significant confirmation for these views (T 319). The contrast could hardly be greater. The mechanisms offered to explain our belief in continuing objects are trivial, indicate no relation of any kind between the data and conclusion, are contrary to general rules gleaned from science, and strongly imply that his account of basic psychological forces, in particular the power of direct perception, needs to be modified.

Even if the problems are less acute than with personal identity, the account of continuing objects has no joy for Hume. It is a failure within its own terms. He does not provide a plausible explanation for how the belief in continuous objects arises nor, *a fortiori*, an explanation that reveals that belief to be well if non-rationally grounded.

Constructing objects and percepts

Hume does not challenge our belief in continuing objects, so there is no call for a direct reply. Still, Kant was aware of the problem Hume tried to solve. In the *Inquiry*, he could read Hume's own summation of it.[25] Natural instinct leads people to have faith in their senses and thus to suppose an external world. In so doing, they assume that the very things they are aware of are external objects. Unfortunately, the slightest reflection reveals that we are only aware of perceptions. Worse still, once this is recognised, it becomes clear that it is not possible to argue from perceptions to resembling objects as their causes, since we can never have evidence of anything beyond our perceptions (I 160–62).

Hume raises this issue in a discussion of philosophical skepticism; further, in the "Refutation of Idealism," Kant offers a reply to the very skeptics Hume discusses, Descartes and Berkeley. Nevertheless, this cryptic addition to the second edition does not provide Kant's best response to Hume's problem. That occurs in the exposition of his own views. All philosophers who acknowledged that we have no direct access to objects had to face the problem of explaining how we formed beliefs about objects on the basis of our own cognitive states. Certainly Kant was acutely sensitive to the issue. As with personal identity, he does not confront it directly, however, but by raising the general question of how cognition is possible.

Cognition requires that our senses somehow present the properties of objects to us. The widespread assumption was that this occurs through perception, the forming of sensory images of which we are conscious (A 120, B 160, A 320/B 376). At this point, Kant asks a question that eluded his predecessors (or was relegated by them to psychophysics): How is perception possible? This issue engenders philosophical perplexity once two widely recognised facts are brought together. We have stable perceptions. As Hume noted, we can observe an object for a while with no (apparent) change in our perceptual state. On the other hand, in the normal case, the information that comes in through our senses, paradigmatically the retina, is in constant flux.[26] In Hume's own terms, our different perceptions "succeed each other with inconceivable rapidity" (T 252). Still, we *normally* have stable perceptions.

Kant casts this problem in an illuminating way. In this rapid flux, sensory information comes in at different times (A 99). To form a stable image, temporally distinct information must be combined (A 120). Further, these pieces of information must be brought together in a combination, "such as they cannot have in sense itself" (A 120). The problem is not just that the senses cannot combine information. It is also that the one kind of order they could provide – the temporal order of the acquisition of information – is inadequate to the purpose. For the image of a fountain must represent the top of the fountain as above the rest, whatever the order of viewing.[27] In a note, Kant reflects on why his predecessors missed the need for combination:

> Psychologists have hitherto failed to realise that imagination is a necessary ingredient of perception itself. This is due partly ... to the belief that the senses not only supply impressions but also combine them so as to generate images of objects. For that purpose something more than the mere receptivity of impressions is undoubtedly required, namely, a function for the synthesis of them. (A 120a).

Thus, even perception requires a synthesis by the imagination that goes beyond the sensory data.

Although not intended as such, Kant's analysis of perception offers an ideal solution to Hume's puzzle. Hume rejected coherence as an explanation, because the natural force of association could not produce a belief in greater regularity than was actually present in our perceptions. As a result, he was forced to appeal to much more dubious mechanisms. When Kant examines our ability to represent objects (A 104ff.) and to make judgments about them, as opposed to our own inner states (B 142), he reaches the same conclusion. These cognitive tasks require that data brought in through the senses be combined or synthesized by the imagination according to rules other than the empiricist law of association.[28]

This discovery does not worry Kant or lead him to doubt his senses, however. He has already shown that we must have faculties capable of introducing greater order than is present in sensory impressions even to achieve the stable perceptions granted by all. Indeed, he has already shown that the same or a very similar process, rule-governed synthesis, is required for perception. The relation between Kant's analyses of perception and of object cognition exemplifies a general strategy of his transcendental psychology. We can appreciate that strategy by considering a common criticism: he argues that knowledge is possible, by arguing that we must possess a certain faculty, because knowledge is possible only if we do. A more sophisticated version of the objection is that only regressive arguments, from certain cognitive accomplishments to their necessary conditions, are valid; but only progressive arguments, starting with very minial premises, can avoid begging the question against skeptical opponents. Kant manages to construct valid arguments that do not beg the question, because he investigates *a number of different tasks* that are involved in the overall project of cognition.

In the present case, it is questionable how we are able to form beliefs or judgments about objects, as opposed to our own inner states. An analysis of the task, starting with a perspicuous description of what the task is and an account of the materials all agree are available to perform it, reveals that an additional faculty is required. Doubts about the existence of such a faculty and so about the original task are removed by showing that such a faculty (or a very similar one) must be admitted in order to explain a cognitive task granted by all – perception. Hansgeorg Hoppe's observation cited above is exactly right: "Hume's question about continuing objects comes . . . too late. . . ."[29] Had he realized that perception itself required construction out of sensory data, he would not have jibbed at the suggestion that natural and non-trivial propensities within the mind must also construct beliefs about objects.

Kant's analysis of our belief in objects fits the requirements of Hume's system surprisingly well. He offers no rational deduction for the existence of external objects.[30] Rather, the belief in independent objects is produced by a "natural" faculty that is not obviously untrustworthy and whose pronouncements are subject to correction by wider evidence.[31] This solution is possible, because his approach differs from Hume's in exactly the three respects noted in the case of personal identity. Unlike his predecessor, Kant questions the basic empiricist assumption that impressions or, better, perceptions, are just given. He is willing to appeal to mental equipment beyond the law of association and various feelings, because he sees that this is necessary even for very basic tasks. And his account is more deeply normative. As I argued above, Hume's discussion of this issue is normative, despite his own and his commentators' efforts to disguise this fact. But again, Kant's investigation is more normative – and more successful – because it occurs in an overall project of analyzing the requirements of all levels of cognition.

IV NECESSARY CONNECTION AND EVENT COGNITION

Kant's reply to Hume's denial of the necessity of causation is both a vast and well-trodden territory. To repeat my initial disclaimer, the following account is far from exhaustive. Further, I shorten the discussion by drawing on such interpretive consensus as exists. Parts of my case simply allude to exegetical insights and arguments provided by others. Finally and most importantly. I do not try to argue that Kant's treatment of causation is definitive. My conclusions are much more limited: Kant's defense of a necessitarian concept of causation in the second analogy represents an important advance on Hume's position and it does so because his approach differs from his antagonist's in the three ways already highlighted.

What Hume denies

Although sometimes treated as a timeless contribution, Hume's discussion of causation is widely recognised as belonging in a rich historical context. Descartes, Malebranche, Newton, and Berkeley all pondered the efficacy of causes in a mechanistic world.[32] Hume is clear where his sympathies lie. He finds the idea of Malebranche and the Cartesians that only God can be an active power extraordinary and a distortion of Newton's teachings (I 84 n.). By contrast, he reads Newton as offering a hypothesis that the ether is a real active fluid[33] and seems to endorse the sturdy common sense of Locke, Clarke, and Cudworth in having nothing to do with occasional causes (loc. cit.). At a more general level, he takes the existence of these debates as evidence that no one has solid evidence to support any conjectures about real powers (T 158).

Against this background, Hume offers an account of our belief in causation that renders the mystery of real powers moot. Although his solution to the puzzle about powers is better characterized as a "dissolution," unlike the two previous topics, he has no second thoughts. There is no hint in either the *Treatise* or the *Inquiry* that his account of causal reasoning is anything short of a triumph for his philosophical approach. He lays the approach out at the beginning of his lengthy discussion in the *Treatise*:

200

> 'Tis impossible to reason justly, without understanding perfectly
> the idea concerning which we reason; and 'tis impossible per-
> fectly to understand any idea without tracing it up to its origin,
> and examining the primary impression, from which it arises.
> The examination of the impression bestows a clearness on the
> idea: and the examination of the idea bestows a like clearness
> on all our reasoning. (T 74–75)

To understand and evaluate our causal reasoning, we must examine
the idea of causation. Hume's well-known account is that the
ordinary person's idea of a cause includes three items: causes are
contiguous with their effects, precede them, and are necessarily
connected with them. He sees no particular difficulty in explaining
the first two elements, since he assumes that we have impressions of
contiguity and succession (T 77). He is, however, quite blunt that
contiguity and succession do not add up to causation:

> An object may be contiguous and prior to another, without
> being consider'd as its cause. There is a NECESSARY CON-
> NECTION to be taken into consideration; and that relation
> is of much greater importance (T 77, original emphasis)

Hume proceeds to consider the idea of necessary connection in
causation by examining two nearby issues: why do we believe that
all events necessarily have causes; why do we believe that causes
necessarily have such particular effects? The first question is quickly
dispatched. Surveying the metaphysical defenses of the *ex nihilo*
principle reveals nothing but question-begging rationalization. And,
as noted, he is contemptuous of the suggestion that, since the idea
of "cause" is contained in that of "effect", we can justly reason that
all events have causes (T 82).

Hume devotes much more effort to grappling with the second
question in both the *Treatise* and the *Inquiry*. Watching one instance
of a cause and effect gives us no notion that the effect had to follow
the cause. This is painfully obvious once we recognise that, before the
effect occurs, we are helpless to predict it. Each new instance of
the same cause-effect sequence provides no new outer impressions.
Nevertheless, it is the observation of the repeated succession of the
same event types that leads us to describe instances of the former as
"causes" and instances of the latter as "effects." Since any idea must
arise from precedent impressions and there are no external candidates, he turns to internal impressions (T 155). Frequent observation

of event sequences has two effects. Through the operation of the law and association, the ideas of the events become so linked that when a new impression of the former is presented, we immediately think of the latter and with sufficient vivacity transferred from the impression that the idea is forceful enough to amount to belief. Further, this determination of the mind from the impression of the cause to the idea of the effect can itself be felt as an impression of reflection. Here, at last, is the impression standing behind the idea of necessary connection. In the *Inquiry*, the explanation is truncated somewhat. Without appeal to an impression of determination, Hume simply explains how belief in the effect arises, when we have an impression of the cause.

From this account of the genesis of our belief in necessary connection. Hume extracts three momentous conclusions. First, our idea of necessary connection is too confused to be the basis of any just reasoning. We (mistakenly) project an inner impression on to outer events. Since reasoning is a matter of comparing (clear) ideas to see their relations, such an idea is unsuitable for this task. Second, we never will be able to reason accurately about powers, so the current abstruse metaphysical disputes are to be expected, but should be avoided. All agree that the causal powers of matter lie deep within it and are unrelated to sensible properties. However, only sensible properties can give rise to impressions and only impressions can give rise to ideas and only clear ideas can be the basis of just reasoning. So just reasoning about causal powers is simply beyond our capacities.

Finally, causation needs to be viewed in two different ways. As a philosophical (exact) relation, a cause should be defined as:

> An object precedent and contiguous to another, and where all the objects resembling the former are plac'd in like relations of precedency and contiguity to those objects, that resemble the latter. (T 170, cf. I 87)

As a natural relation,

> A cause is an object precedent and contiguous to another, and so united with it, that the idea of the one determines the mind to form the idea of the other, and the impression of the one to form a more lively idea of the other. (T 170, cf. I 87)

In neither the *Treatise* nor the *Inquiry* does Hume pause to consider whether these two definitions are materially equivalent; both passages race straight to the conclusion. We observe, for example, a fire and a melting candle and say the fire "caused" the wax to melt. On both these definitions, however, the circumstances relevant to the pronouncement "cause" are foreign to causal agent itself (since they refer either to numerous *other* events or to a mental factor). This is as must be, for we can find nothing in the cause which gives its connection with the effect (I 87).

Despite the confusion of subjective and objective, Hume's indictment of causal reasoning is tightly circumscribed. It is not *reasoning*. Rather, by natural instinct, when confronted with certain objective patterns, we generate feelings of determination which lead us to call some things "causes," others "effects," and to infer the one when given an instance of the other. Hume proffers no explanation for why we are so well tuned to constant conjunction. Not being tempted by an appeal to Divine Providence, he describes this fact as "perfectly extraordinary and incomprehensible" (T 172). Nevertheless, he regards the mechanism as both reliable and unavoidable. Further, particular instinctually generated beliefs can be corrected by using general rules drawn from wider experience.

According to Wright, far from being a skeptic about causation, Hume views habit as leading to a belief in causal powers – that there is some hidden, but real inner essence in things that gives them their productive powers – that can be achieved in no other way.[34] This view is somewhat extreme among current interpretations. Further, it is not obvious how knowledge of inner essences would resolve the puzzle of necessary connection, even if it were possible. Still, Wright's position is representative in seeing Hume's skepticism about causation as quite mitigated. We are not enjoined to give up causal reasoning or even told that the belief in necessary connection is false, but only that our idea of connection is not sufficiently clear to be used in demonstrative reasoning.

Brute facts versus cognitive requirements

Kant has two fundamental and interrelated objections to Hume's account of the foundation of our belief in necessary connection. Most obviously, Hume traces the belief to a subjective source. Worse still, he makes it entirely contingent:

> The concept of cause ... would be false if it rested only on an arbitrary subjective necessity, implanted in us, of connecting certain empirical representations according to the rule of causal

relation. I would not then be able to say that the effect is connected with the cause in the object, that is to say, necessarily, but only that I am so constituted that I cannot think this representation otherwise than as thus connected. This is what the skeptic most desires . . . nor would there be wanting people who would refuse to admit this subjective necessity, a necessity which can only be felt. (B 168)

Hume would scoff at the suggestion that his theory ranks with appeal to the harmony of the Creation. On the contrary, he rests the belief in a necessary connection of cause and effect in human nature, which need not be any more changeable or varied than any other part of nature, and which can be studied empirically.

Kant's more telling point is that Hume's empiricism leads him to dismiss a possible alternative. The two concur in denying that the belief in necessity can arise from experience or can be derived from reasoning about concepts. For Hume, however, any idea must be traced to a precedent impression and with no appropriate outer impressions, he has no recourse but inner impressions. Kant's alternative is the *"epigenesis of pure reason"* (B 167): our mental faculties themselves supply elements of a necessitarian concept of causation, which applies to events encountered in experience under specified conditions.

A hypothesis of divinely implanted conceptual elements would be no advance on one of a divinely implanted propensity to generate feelings of determination. To defend this alternative, Kant offers a novel normative argument that invokes some factual premises. Given that we are able to perform various cognitive tasks and given that elements required for those tasks cannot be derived from the senses, then we must posit faculties capable of supplying the prerequisites of cognition. When viewed in this light, the existence of such a faculty is neither extraordinary nor incomprehensible nor arbitrary. Since what is available for the senses in inadequate to explain the tasks we do, in fact, perform, any creature which is like us in basic cognitive constitution must have such a faculty.

Despite the many interpretive controversies, most commentators would agree with Lewis White Beck's broad picture of the argumentative strategy of the Second Analogy:

K: "Everything that happens, that is, begins to be, presupposes something upon which it follows by rule" . . .

P: Events can be distinguished from objective enduring states of affairs, even though our apprehension of each is serial . . .

H: Among events, we find empirically some pairs of similar ones which tend to be repeated, and we then make the inductive judgment: events like the first members of the pairs are causes of events like the second. . . .

H implies P and, by the arguments of the second analogy, P implies K. "That is Kant's answer to Hume."[35] Since Hume asserts H and Kant K, the only controversial member of the trio is P. What cognitive capacity is it that is presupposed by Hume and that requires us to employ the idea of rule-governed succession? Melnick takes it to be the ability to apprehend a succession;[36] for Beck, it is our capacity to recognise the difference between an event and a stationary object;[37] for Allison, it is our "knowledge of an order of successive states of an object;"[38] for Guyer, our ability to justify our judgments about events, and so succession in time.[39]

I have arranged these positions along a continuum, from the most minimal cognitive task to the fanciest. The fancier the task, the greater the danger of assuming more than Hume will or must grant. Guyer's claims for a justificatory reading of the second analogy seem vulnerable to this criticism. Kant's argument will be more devastating the less he assumes, so it is appropriate to start at the minimal end. Although I believe that he intends to argue that the mere perception of succession requires a necessitarian concept of causation,[40] I will not try to defend that controversial position here. For the purposes of this paper, it is sufficient to show how Kant's argument demonstrates that a very minimal task, one acknowledged by all, requires the sort of cognitive equipment that Hume will not permit to ground our notion of necessary connection. The minimal task I have in mind falls somewhere between seeing and judging. It is a matter of having a sufficient cognitive grip on an event, state A followed by state B, that permits either a propositional judgment, "B followed A" or merely the guidance of behavior. Assuming that thinking need not be propositional, it can be characterized as "thinking B followed A."

Despite the disagreement about the *explanandum*, I accept Guyer's account of how, exactly, the argument of the second analogy works. Using "A*" and "B*" to indicate perceptions and plain letters for the object of perceptions, Kant reasons as follows: "in a happening . . . B can be apprehended only after A; the perception A* cannot follow upon B* but only precede it" (A192/B237). But how could we know that B* has to follow A*? Nothing in the sequence of cognitive states can provide that information, since all cognitive states are successive. Hence we can only think that B followed A, and that B* had to follow A*, if something in the contents of A* and B* informs us that B had to follow A. And, what could that be except our recognition that A is a particular state of affairs and that states of affairs of this type are invariably followed by states of affairs of the type exemplified by B? That is, we can recognise that B* had to follow A* if and only if we have a rule stating that B's have to follow A's. Commentators have often regarded this argument as moving (invalidly) from the order of perceptions to the order of objects. As Guyer observes, however, Kant is surprisingly clear that we determine the order of perceptions by determining the order of objective succession, a point he repeats twice in three pages.

> In this case, therefore, we must derive the *subjective succession* of apprehension from the *objective succession* of appearances. Otherwise the order of apprehension is entirely undetermined, and does not distinguish one appearance [succession or coexistence] from another. Since the subjective succession by itself is altogether arbitrary, it does not prove anything as to the manner in which the manifold is connected in the object. The objective succession will therefore consist in that order of the manifold of appearance according to which, *in conformity with a rule*, the apprehension of that which happens follows upon the apprehension of that which precedes. Thus only can I be justified in asserting, not merely of my apprehension, but of the appearance itself [i.e. the objects], that a succession is to be met with in it. (A193/B238, Guyer's translation)

> It is therefore only in respect of rule according to which appearances [objects] in *their* succession, that is, *as they occur*, are determined by the preceding state that I make my subjective synthesis (of apprehension) objective, and it is only under this presupposition that the experience itself of something that happens is possible. (A195, B240, Guyer's translation, emphasis added)

The argument for an a priori[41] and necessary concept of "cause" rests on four essential premises:

1 We can think B followed A.

2 Time cannot be perceived.

3 All our cognitive states are successive.

4 The evidence of the senses can never justify a belief in necessity.

Kant presupposes Hume's argument for (4). (1), (2) and (3) can be nothing other than factual assumptions about our cognitive capacities.

Beck rejects (3): "This is certainly wrong . . . a consequence of his sensational atomism."[42] Again taking vision as the paradigm sense, Kant's position is scientifically correct, by the evidence of his day and our own. Today, the easiest way to show this is to appeal to saccadic eye movements. Current work reveals that our line of focus is constantly jumping from one place in the viewed scene to another, thus producing a succession of different cognitive states, even when viewing stasis. Oddly, if this process is interfered with experimentally, so that a piece of a scene is constantly projected to the same part of the retina, the image fades out to nothing.[43] Even in Kant's time, it was widely recognised that the eye was constantly in motion. Among other phenomena, constant motion was invoked to explain why individuals are seldom aware of defects in their retinas.[44]

Many readers have doubted the scope of (2). Seemingly, we can perceive succession and coexistence, even if not time itself. Arthur Melnick, for example, argues that we can be directly aware of succession, because two states of affairs could succeed each other in the "specious present."[45] It certainly seems as if we hear a sentence or a melody all at once, "in an instant." Even if we represent the sentence or tune in a momentary state, however, we do not take it in that way through our senses. The specious present is, after all, specious. If (2) is wrong, it takes more than simple introspection (a "source" Kant wisely and heartily disliked) to prove it.

I turn to an obvious objection to Kant's conclusion. Hume maintained that we say "cause" when we are repeatedly aware of the succession of particular types of events. Kant's argument is that we cannot think about successions unless we employ the notion of a causal rule. But how can we acquire the needed rules? Guyer's answer is that Kant follows Hume in believing that we acquire them inductively, by repeated experiences of succession. Hence, he concludes that, on pain of circularity, Kant's point must be justificatory and not genetic. He cannot be proposing that, absent causal rules, we could not even think that B succeeded A.[46]

I don't see why not. In his moral theory, Kant seems to be

involved in a similar "circle." We cannot have respect for the moral law without respecting humanity in our own and other persons; but we cannot have respect for persons without respecting the moral law. This does not commit him to thinking that we must have respect for persons before we have it, however. His point is that the two capacities come together. I take Kant's point about temporal ordering and causation to be the same. The capacity to think temporal succession and the capacity to think causally come together. He may be wrong on this point, but the error is not one of logic.

This problem arises because Kant is interested in genesis and there are two different kinds of genetic questions, one about origins and one about development. Kant's interest in the genesis of cognition reduces to one question about origins: does this cognitive task require elements that cannot be supplied by the senses? By contrast, developmental psychologists would want to know such things as: when do children become aware of time and causes? Is there a developmental pattern in temporal and causal thinking? Are any experiences essential to children being able to deal cognitively with time causation? Kant's only contribution to this subject is to argue that these topics should be handled together. He offers no hypotheses about the ontogenesis of either capacity, although he probably agrees with Hume that mature cognisers supplement and prune their stock of causal beliefs inductively.

Has Kant adequately "replied" to Hume? This issue is controversial, in part, because there are many reasonable standards of success. I'll look at just a couple of possible dimensions. The argument of the second analogy is radically incomplete. For example, Kant makes no effort to explain the force of "necessity" he invokes. If he is right, then some necessitarian concept of causation is necessary for cognition, but it is not obvious which. Presumably, it is not logical necessity nor his own more limited notion of necessity, true in any world we are capable of experiencing.[47] The obvious candidate is nomic necessity, but this is uninformative in the absence of an account of laws, which he does not even attempt until the dialectic and the third critique.

Kant's defense of a notion of "objective" causation is equally incomplete. As he explains at the outset, he aims to establish the objective validity of the categories in a special sense of that phrase: "The objective validity of the categories ... rests ... on the fact that ... only by means of them can any object whatsoever of experience be thought" (A 93/B126). In the present case, his conclusion is that events can only be thought if we employ a necessitarian concept of causation. It is tempting to think that this shows nothing at all about *objects* and that it is not so much a reply to Hume as an extension of his position. For Hume, our belief in the necessity of causes depended on a simple and inexplicable fact about us, how we react to experiences of constant conjunction. For Kant, it depends on a complex and non-arbitrary fact about us: given that we can think about events and given the evidence of our senses, our mental faculties themselves must supply an element of necessity in our concept of "cause." The problem is that, however sophisticated, we are still dealing with a fact about us.

Although this objection is almost inevitable, I believe that it rests on a misunderstanding. We cannot make up causal laws and impose them on the data. Our ability to use causal concepts depends on the particular contents of our perceptions. In the absence of constant conjunction, we could not use a necessitarian concept of causation. So if Kant is right, then our ability to think about events and temporal succession implies something about us and something about the world. The world we encounter must permit the use of this concept. It must be cognitively indistinguishable – in the very long run, when all the evidence is in – from a world in which all events have causes and causes necessitate their effects. The deeper problem about objectivity is that Kant leaves a crucial question unasked: how much homogeneity and how much diversity must be present in nature to meet our cognitive requirements? Again, this issue is only raised in the dialectic and the third critique – and never resolved to his satisfaction.[48]

Even waiving the issue of incompleteness, the argument of the second analogy fails as a proof of the cognitive necessity of using a necessitarian concept of causation. Since we cannot directly perceive succession, something in the contents of our perceptions must interact with something like a rule about temporal order to alert us to the presence of succession. Effects follow causes, so causal rules are obvious candidates for determining succession. However, Kant is in no position to argue for a universal negative generalization: There can be no others. Some promising alternatives have been suggested by recent work in widely different fields. Fodor, Bever, and Garrett demonstrate that our judgments about temporal order can be influenced by grammatical rules; at the opposite extreme, neurophysiology has discovered a hierarchical arrangement of cells that can serve as a motion, and so change-of-place, detector.[49]

Despite such serious faults, most Kant scholars regard the argument of the second analogy as a partial success. Further, there is quite widespread agreement that where it succeeds is in defending the general alternative empiricism is committed to ruling out, the possibility that our faculties themselves supply important elements in the contents of our cognition – the "epigenesis of pure reason."[50] Our ability to think about events and temporal succession was not taken to be problematic. The empiricist law of association could not be stated without using the concept of succession. Yet Kant shows that these basic cognitive capacities cannot be explained without appeal to mental mechanisms beyond sensory data and the law of association. Hume had recognised that our belief in causal necessity required additional mental equipment and offered the hypothesis of a feeling triggered by the experience of constant conjunction. He took this belief to be quite sophisticated, however, so the positing of a bit of additional machinery seemed no threat to the basic empiricist picture. Further, he could still provide an exact or philosophical definition of causation, in terms of constant conjunction, that appealed to nothing more than what we perceive through outer sense, precedence, and contiguity. Finally, although he recognised the centrality of causal reasoning to our cognitive and practical lives, he regarded the presence of the feeling standing behind it as accidental and inexplicable.

Kant's argument in the second analogy undermines the basic empiricist position by giving the lie to Hume's three hedges. It is not just sophisticated beliefs, but very basic capacities, that require contributions from our faculties. Second, since we cannot grasp either precedence of necessary connection just on the basis of sensory evidence, without contributions from our faculties, the point of Hume's philosophical definition is lost. Finally, Kant's argument reveals that this contribution from our faculties is not contingent. Any creatures that are like us in having these capacities and like us in terms of what they can take in through their senses must have faculties that contribute rules or something that functions like a rule. Hence, the empiricist account of cognition does not need minor supplementing, but drastic overhaul.

Hume did not consider his account of causation to be a failure or even to be in need of improvement. Still, I think it is widely agreed (at least among Kantians) that Kant's discussion of this topic succeeds in several ways that Hume's fails. It succeeds in the straightforward sense that it goes much more deeply into our ability to think causally. Kant reveals that the notions Hume takes to be unproblematic involve the same sorts of commitment to mental faculties as those he regards as needing special explanation. As just observed, it also succeeds where Hume "fails," in a decidedly Pickwickean sense of that term. Hume almost shows, albeit without intending to, that empiricism is incapable of explaining a central aspect of cognition, our ability to engage in causal reasoning. Kant succeeds in establishing the conclusion Hume never intended, but that he claims to have drawn from his predecessor's discussion of cause: epistemology must abandon the empiricist premise and undertake the task of carefully distinguishing the a priori contributions of our various faculties, and thereby determine the extent to which what we know is a function of our way of knowing. In short, empiricism must be replaced by transcendental philosophy.

The moral to be drawn from this exchange should by now be obvious. In these two respects in which Kant's argument succeeds – and is widely taken by Kant scholars to succeed – it does so because he questions basic empiricist assumptions about impressions and ideas, is willing to posit additional mental machinery, and is interested in the normative question of how even basic kinds of cognition are possible.

V CONCLUSION: COGNITIVISM VERSUS PSYCHOLOGISM

In these three crucial examples, Kant's replies to Hume succeed for exactly the same reason. He is able to show that Hume's own explanations presuppose cognitive capacities that demand more mental machinery then he, or empiricists generally, will allow. Our ability to have impressions and ideas that purport to represent requires a synthesis, and so a real connection, of mental states. Merely having stable perceptual images takes a productive imagination that reorganizes the data of sense in patterns differing from the spatio-temporal contiguity of sensory data. Thinking about events is possible only because we have something like rules to indicate temporal order.

Given the account so far, the final verdict is still open. Does Kant refute Hume or is he simply a better psychologist of cognition who extends what Hume began? The venerable, but opposing tendencies to read Kant as expanding Hume's psychologism or as decisively refuting it suggest that there must be some truth on each side. I conclude by arguing that Kant is a psychologist of cognition, but of the opposite kind to Hume.

Beginning with the positive, I will argue that Kant is a psychologist of cognition indirectly, by showing how very difficult it is to deny this claim. Paul Guyer has recently devoted his enviable learning and acumen to trying to show that, despite appearances, the central argument of the *Critique* is not psychological.[51] He concedes that the opening premise of the transcendental deduction looks psychological:

> The combination (conjunctio) of a manifold in general can never come to us through sense ... for it is an act of spontaneity of the power of representation, and, since one must call this understanding in contrast to sensibility, so is all combination, whether we become conscious of it or not, whether it be a combination of the manifold of intuition, or of several concepts ... an act of the understanding, which we will register to the general name synthesis.[52]

Nevertheless, he maintains that these statements actually express "conceptual truths."[53] Later he modulates his position.

> To be sure, Kant's argument ultimately depends on an assumption of what may have to be regarded as a matter of fact [and hence is not purely conceptual matter]: that the input of data for cognition are temporally successive, and thus that earlier items in a manifold can be reproduced only by being recognised to be represented by its current member. But to call this fundamental fact psychological, however contingent it may in the end be (if indeed we have any clear grasp of what is contingent and what not at this level), is to trivialize the concept of psychology.[54]

Finally, Guyer maintains that the argument is not psychological, even if its conclusion is.

> Thus Kant's deduction may even have a psychological conclusion [about the necessity of synthesis] without being a psychological argument. Somewhat more strongly, we might put the point thus: while the essential steps in Kant's arguments – that the manifold must be successively experienced and subsequently interpreted – may be matters of facts, these are facts of life rather than facts of psychology.[55]

It is tempting to apply the "duck test" recently popular in political circles: if it looks like a duck and walks like a duck and acts like a duck, then it is a duck. Guyer concedes that the premise, conclusion, and essential steps of the transcendental deduction are psychological. Against all that, he denies that the argument can properly be regarded as psychological on the grounds that the sort of factual premise Kant is assuming, that data are given over time, is also true of computers, which also require a "synthesizing of data."[56]

The force of Guyer's analogy with computers is not obvious. Kant stressed the fact that we take in data over time (e.g. A 99). Still, he seemed to think that this was a contingent fact about us. His contrast was with a divine intellect that has no need of senses and is, of course, timeless. As is clear from the previous sections, however, Kant makes many assumptions about our cognitive constitution beyond the successive intake of data. Contra the Wolffians, he assumes that cognitive states are not intrinsically representational in virtue of possessing a *vis representiva*.[57] He decisively rejects the classical theory that in perception we take in [whole] *simulacra* given off by objects.[58] And, of course, he denies that we can perceive time and objective succession just by the use of our senses. To avoid the epithet "psychological" Guyer is going to have to expand his list of the facts of life beyond all recognition.

Although Guyer's attempt to disguise the psychological character of the deduction only illustrates why it cannot be done, part of his point about computers is right. Kant intends his conclusion to apply beyond the class of *Homo sapiens*. His conclusions will be valid of all creatures that are like us in a number of psychological respects: they take in data over time, cannot perceive time or succession through the senses, and so forth. In that sense, his program differs from some psychological approaches to these topics. The crucial issue is why this is true. We have no reason to believe that he wished to produce a psychological theory that would extend to computers or Martians as well as to people.

Kant's conclusions have a broader scope, because his psychological efforts are importantly different from Hume's: He approaches the study of cognition from the opposite direction. Kuno Fischer got this point exactly right over one hundred years ago. Kant starts with the fact of cognition, that is, the cognitive tasks we actually perform. He carefully analyzes those tasks and then works backwards to the necessary faculties. As Fischer observed, he believed that

the character of a power or faculty can only be ascertained by its effects. Hence, the nature and action of the cognitive faculties can only be discovered by learning in what the fact of cognition and its possibility consists.[59]

Kant's conclusions generalize beyond human beings because he starts with cognitive tasks and some widely accepted facts about our cognitive powers. They generalize to precisely those creatures that are like us in these two respects.

By contrast, Hume starts with a psychological theory about human and animal cognition, taken partly from Locke and partly from Hutcheson. He tries to produce a science of human nature by applying that theory to different types of cognition. The aim is to sketch the actual causal forces that produce our beliefs. Where the theory he borrows is inadequate, he supplements it as best he can. Although Kant refers to many more cognitive faculties, he has no interest in the actual processes standing behind cognition. "Productive imagination," "form of intuition," "synthesis of apprehension" are not names of psychological processes that Kant hypothesizes from the comfort of his armchair. They are abstract functional descriptions of the kind of faculties that any creatures relevantly like us must have, which he posits on the basis of careful analyses of the cognitive tasks we perform. He has not merely changed the names of faculties from the familiar to the Baroque; he has changed the direction of research into cognition and the faculties that support it.

This difference in direction can be captured in the contemporary distinction between bottom-up and top-down approaches to cognition. Kant's cognitivism starts at the top, with the fact of cognition, Hume's psychologism at the bottom, with the science that he believed could explain cognition. Since Kant starts at the top and proceeds by considering what cognition requires, his approach is deeply normative and he is willing to posit additional mental processes, even though these can only be characterized functionally. The difference in direction thus accounts for the crucial differences observed in the three cases. It also accounts for the superiority of Kant's treatment of these topics. Since empiricism was an inadequate psychological theory, eighteenth-century students of cognition were well advised to be cognitivists rather than psychologists.

Today it is often said that cognition needs to be studied from both directions. The exchange between Hume and Kant offers a wonderful illustration of this point. Had Hume not tried to base his theory of human nature on the best science of his day, he would never have uncovered its weaknesses and (if Kant's self-reporting is accurate) inspired his German admirer to take a fundamentally different approach. On the other hand, it is very easy to see the theories of one's own time as inevitable and so to believe that a truly scientific approach to cognition must be bottom-up. Kant's "reply to Hume" provides a dramatic demonstration of the importance of testing the adequacy of purported theories of cognition by carefully examining the facts in need of explanation. Psychologism and cognitivism are opposed in the figures of Hume and Kant, but this justly celebrated episode in the history of philosophy demonstrates how each approach needs the discipline and instruction of the other.

NOTES

1 I take this to be part of the revolution in Hume scholarship inaugurated by Norman Kemp Smith's *The Philosophy of David Hume* (London: Macmillan, 1941, reprinted New York: Garland, 1983). Among others defending Hume's normative interests are Barry Stroud, *Hume* (Boston: Routledge & Kegan Paul, 1977); Anthony Flew, *Hume's Philosophy of Belief* (New York: Humanities Press, 1961); and Lewis White Beck, "A Prussian Hume and a Scottish Kant," reprinted in this volume.

2 Ram Adhar Mall, "Naturalismus and Kritizismus (Hume und Kant)," *Hume und Kant, Interpretation and Diskussion*, Herausgegeben von Wolfgang Farr (Freiburg/ München: Verlag Karl Alber, 1982).

3 Norman Kemp Smith, op. cit., especially Chapter 2; Robert Paul Wolff, "Hume's Theory of Mental Activity," V. C. Chappell, ed., *Hume* (New York: Doubleday, 1966) pp. 99–128. As will be obvious below, I interpret Wolff's results somewhat differently than he does.

4 See, for example, Alvin Goldman, *Epistemology and Cognition* (Cambridge, MA: Harvard University Press, 1986); Fred Dretske, *Knowledge and the Flow of Information* (Cambridge, MA: MIT Press, 1981); Gilbert Harman, *Thought* (Princeton: Princeton University Press, 1973); Hilary Kornblith, "Beyond Foundationalism and the Coherence Theory," *Journal of Philosophy*, 72 (1980): 597–612; Philip Kitcher, *The Nature of Mathematical Knowledge* (New York: Oxford University Press, 1983).

5 Goldman, op.cit.; Dretske, op. cit.; and Philip Kitcher, "The Naturalists Return", forthcoming in *Philosophical Review* 101 (1992).

6 Jürgen Bona Meyer, *Kant's Psychologie* (Berlin: Wilhelm Hertz, 1870).

7 Kuno Fischer, *Kant's Critick of the Pure Reason*, trans. John Pentland Mahaffy from *The History of Modern Philosophy* (London: Longmans, Green, reprinted New York: Garland 1976), p. 8.

8 P. F. Strawson, "Sensibility, Understanding, and the Doctrine of Synthesis: Comments on Henrich and Guyer," Eckart Förster, ed., *Kant's Transcendental Deductions* (Stanford, CA: Stanford University Press, 1989), p. 69. See also Dieter Henrich, "Kant's Notion of a Deduction and the Methodological Background of the First Critique," also in Förster, pp. 29–46.

9 Strawson's antipathy to psychological topics in the *Critique* is obvious throughout *The Bounds of Sense* (London: Methuen, 1966). For a telling remark of Henrich's see "The Proof-Structure of Kant's Transcendental Deduction," *Review of Metaphysics*, 22 (1969): 652.

10 Lewis White Beck, "Six Short Pieces of the Second Analogy," Beck, op. cit., p. 140.

11 Hans-Georg Hoppe, "Kants Antwort auf Hume," Farr, op. cit., p. 224.

12 Ibid., 227.

13 Robert Paul Wolff, op. cit.

14 Wolff stresses the fact that his reconstruction shows that Hume had, albeit implicitly, more psychological machinery than the law of association.

15 See "Kant on Self-Identity," *Philosophical Review*, 91 (1982): 41–72 and Chapter 4, "Replying to Hume, Heap", *Kant's Transcendental Psychology* (New York: Oxford University Press, 1990).

16 I will indicate by "T" and the page number in parentheses all references to David Hume, *A Treatise of Human Nature*, analytical index by L. A. Selby-Bigge, with text revised and notes by P. H. Nidditch, second edn. (Oxford: Clarendon Press, 1978).

17 The constant motion of the eye is referred to in William Porterfield's *A Treatise on the Eye and the Manner and Phenomena of Vision* (Edinburgh: Hamilton and Balfour, 1759), a standard text of the time.

18 Although it is somewhat clumsy, I translate "Vorstellung" as "cognitive state" or where appropriate, "content of a cognitive state," I avoid the more common "representation" because Kant does not believe that all *Vorstellungen* represent (A 320/B 376). All references to *Immanuel Kant Critique of Pure Reason*, translated by Norman Kemp Smith (New York: St Martin's Press) will be indicated in the usual way by citing the A or B page number in parentheses. Amended translations or my own are based on the Akademie Edition.

19 The references are given in note 16.

20 Again, see the reference in note 16.

21 As I argue in *Kant's Transcendental Psychology*, op. cit., p. 114, this is not quite right. We could also assign content to a state on the basis of the actions to which it leads. Nevertheless, this provides no defense of Hume's position, since distinct, isolated states would still lack content.

22 I discuss this restriction at greater length in Chapter 5 of *Kant's Transcendental Psychology*, op. cit., pp. 121–22.

23 For Kant, all cognitive states that belong to the same I think are pairwise connectable. I defend this strong notion of connectibility (ibid.).

24 For example, Stroud, op. cit., page 96, and John P. Wright, *The Skeptical Realism of David Hume* (Minneapolis: University of Minnesota Press, 1983), p. 38.

25 Kant owned a German translation of the *Inquiry*. See A. Warda, *Immanuel Kant Bücher* (Berlin: Verlag von Martin Breslaner, 1922), p. 50. I will indicate references to David Hume, *An Inquiry Concerning Human Understanding* (Indianapolis: Bobbs-Merrill, 1955) by I and the page number in parentheses.

26 See note 17.

27 Kant offers a number of useful examples of the construction of perceptual

images in the Pölitz lectures. See, for example, the passage cited in Vladimir Satura, "Kants Erkenntnispsychologie," *Kant-Studien*, 20 (1971): 114–15.

28 For a more extensive discussion of the relation between Kant's account of perception and judgment and the Law of Association, see *Kant's Transcendental Psychology*, op. cit., Chapter 3.

29 See above, p. n.

30 The *Refutation of Idealism* can be viewed as an attempt to provide a deductive argument in favor of the existence of "external" objects, but Kant does not regard that argument as the basis of our belief in them.

31 As Kant explains in the *Dialectic*, the regulative ideas of reason will lead us to dismiss claims that do not fit into a systematic account of nature (A 642/ B 670 ff).

32 The introductory chapter of Wright, op. cit., offers a useful discussion of this context.

33 See Wright's discussion of Hume's evolving views on this issue, ibid., p. 162 ff.

34 Ibid., pp. 149, 160–1.

35 Beck, "Six Short Pieces on the Second Analogy," op. cit., p. 135.

36 Arthur Melnick, *Kant's Analogies of Experience* (Chicago: University of Chicago Press, 1973), p. 80.

37 Beck, "Six Short Pieces on the Second Analogy," op. cit., 139.

38 Henry E. Allison, *Kant's Transcendental Idealism: An Interpretation and Defense* (New Haven: Yale University Press, 1983), p. 217.

39 Paul Guyer, *Kant and the Claims of Knowledge* (New York: Cambridge University Press, 1987), p. 258; see also p. 246. Earlier Guyer had suggested that what is to be proven in the second analogy is "all cases of empirically recognizable alterations in substances must *also* be successions of states of those substances according to rules" (p. 239). He adopts the stronger justificatory reading because of the problem I discuss six paragraphs hence.

40 I hold this view because in 26 of the B deduction Kant argues that the categories are required for perception itself. Further, one of the examples he gives in that passage is plainly an anticipation of the argument of the second analogy.

41 Kant's claim that a concept is "a priori" indicates that it contains elements that cannot be derived from the senses and that it is necessary for the possibility of cognitive experience. For a fuller discussion of the various senses of "a priori" in the *Critique*, see *Kant's Transcendental Psychology*, op. cit., pp. 15–19.

42 Beck, "Six Short Pieces on the Second Analogy," op. cit., p. 144.

43 For a standard textbook discussion, see Henry Gleitman, *Psychology* (New York: W. W. Norton, 1981), p. 195.

44 Porterfield, p. 221.

45 Melnick, op. cit., p. 84.

46 Guyer, op. cit., p. 258.

47 See the discussion of Kantian necessity in Philip Kitcher, "Kant and the Foundations of Mathematics," *Philosophical Review*, 84 (1975): 23–50.

48 See Burkhard Tuschling's discussion in "Apperception and Ether: On the Idea of a Transcendental Deduction of Matter," *Opus Postumum*, Förster, op. cit., pp. 193–216.

49 William Harper offers a clear explanation of this mechanism in "Kant's Empirical Realism and the Difference Between Subjective and Objective Succession," W. Harper and R. Meerbote, eds, *Kant on Causality, Freedom, and Objectivity* (Minneapolis: University of Minnesota Press, 1984), pp. 108–37. As is obvious in the text, I disagree with the moral Harper draws from his work. I discuss Fodor, Bever, and Garrett's work at greater length in *Kant's Transcendental Psychology*, op. cit.

50 Among those holding this position I include Norman Kemp Smith, *A Commentary to Kant's "Critique of Pure Reason"* (New York: Humanities Press, 1962), p. 370; Beck, "Six short Pieces on the Second Analogy", op. cit., p. 140; Allison, op. cit., p. 229; Melnick, op. cit., pp. 95–96; and Hoppe, op. cit., p. 224.

51 Paul Guyer, "Psychology and the Transcendental Deduction" in Förster, op. cit., pp. 47–68.

52 Ibid. Guyer cites this passage in his translation on page 57.

53 Ibid., p. 58.

54 Ibid., p. 65.

55 Ibid., p. 67.

56 Ibid., p. 65.

57 For a discussion of Christian Wolff's doctrine of the *vis representiva*, see Richard J. Blackwell, "Christian Wolff's Doctrine of the Sou," *Journal of the History of Ideas*, 22 (1961): 339–54, and Max Dessoir, *Geschichte der Neueren Deutschen Psychologie* (Amsterdam: E. J. Bonset, 1964), p. 69.

58 Kant explicitly rejects the possibility of *simulacra* in a passage in the *Prolegomena*, p. 51.

59 Citation given in note 8.

A NOTE ON THE SYNTHETICITY OF MATHEMATICAL PROPOSITIONS IN KANT'S *PROLEGOMENA*[1,2]

Daniel E. Anderson

Kant saw the claim that there are synthetical judgments "which are certain a priori, and which spring from pure understanding and reason" (*Prolegomena*, pp. 27–138) as fundamental to the critique of pure reason, which he saw as being in large measure an exploration of how such propositions are possible. The subsequent development of modern logics, and of non-Euclidean geometries, has frequently been taken as evidence against such a claim at least with regard to arithmetical or geometrical propositions. If this should prove to be so, then even the most sympathetic admirer of Kant would be compelled to admit that Kant's position was due for a careful – and thorough – rethinking. I shall not attempt here to defend Kant's claim in general. I shall attempt to defend it from the attack levelled against it by A. J. Ayer in *Language, Truth and Logic*.

I

"Kant," according to Ayer, "does not give one straightforward criterion for distinguishing between analytic and synthetic propositions; he gives two distinct criteria, which are by no means equivalent."[3] Ayer holds Kant's claim that "7 + 5 = 12" is a synthetic judgment to be grounded on the claim that "the concept of twelve is by no means already thought in merely thinking the union of seven and five;"[4] and that one of Kant's criteria, therefore, is "that the subjective intension of '7 + 5' does not comprise the subjective intension '12'."

Kant's second criterion, according to Ayer, is the one Kant actually states: that the predicate of an analytic proposition follows from the subject by the law of contradiction alone.

Therefore, according to Ayer, one of Kant's criteria is psychological, and the other logical. This allows Ayer to argue that the psychological criterion holds for such mathematical propositions as "7 + 5 = 12," but the logical criterion does not. He then says,

> From the rest of [Kant's] argument it is clear that it is this logical proposition, and not any psychological proposition, that Kant is really anxious to establish. His use of the psychological criterion leads him to think that he has established it, when he has not.[5]

At this point Ayer proceeds to present another, very different definition of syntheticity: "a proposition is analytic when its validity depends solely on the definitions of the symbols it contains, and synthetic *when its validity is determined by the facts of experience*."[6] In other words, "synthetic" is defined to mean "a posteriori", and the claim that there are no synthetic a priori propositions follows *analytically* from his definition of syntheticity. The logic of such a claim is impeccable. The question of whether or not synthetic a priori propositions are possible, however, cannot be resolved by a simple act of legislation.[7] Kant's claim might now be reformulated as a claim that propositions are possible that fit neither of these classifications, because they do not depend upon experience, and their predicates do not follow analytically from their subjects – and moreover, mathematical propositions are to be included among these.

The question of whether or not Kant actually did unwittingly adopt a psychological rather than a logical criterion is not easily resolved, but in the *Prolegomena* the weight seems actually to be on the other side.

In support of Ayer's interpretation it should be pointed out that Kant does say that

> the concept of twelve is by no means thought by merely thinking of the combination of seven and five; and analyze this possible sum as we may, we shall not discover twelve in the concept. We must go beyond these concepts, by calling to our aid some intuition which corresponds to one of the concepts ... and we must add successively the units of the five given

in intuition to the concept of seven. . . . Arithmetical judgments are therefore synthetical, and the more plainly according
as we take larger numbers; for in such cases it is clear that,
however closely we analyze our concepts without calling
intuition to our aid, we can never find the sum by such mere
dissection.[8]

This lends itself easily to the suggestion that the impossibility of
discovering "12" through the analysis of "7 + 5" is psychological
rather than logical – particularly since he seems to hold that the
argument for the syntheticity of such propositions rests on the need
for an intuition of some non-arithmetical entity such as "fingers"
or "points" in order to arrive at the sum.

The passage quoted above, however, is preceded by the claim
"that the concept of the sum of 7 + 5 contains merely their union
in a single number, without its being at all thought what the particular number is that unites them." In context with this, the assertion
that "we must go beyond these concepts, by calling to our aid some
intuition which corresponds to one of the concepts" (such as "fingers" or "points"), together with this further claim that "hence, our
concept is really amplified by the proposition 7 + 5 = 12, and we
add to the first concept a second concept not thought in it," is
clearly the statement of an empirical, rather than a psychological,
criterion.

This interpretation is further supported and explicated in the
Critique of Pure Reason. There, Kant draws a careful distinction
between "pure intuition" and "empirical intuition." Pure intuition
is "the pure form of sensible intuitions in general, in which all the
manifold of intuition is intuited in certain relations [and which] must
be found in the mind *a priori*,"[9] whereas empirical intuition is "that
intuition which is in relation to the object through sensation" [A20,
B35], and must [A47, B64] be *a posteriori*. Although (as he says at
A47, B64) a synthetic *a priori* proposition must be grounded upon
"an object *a priori* in intuition" (i.e. an object of pure intuition) he
later [A239, B298] states flatly that

the object cannot be given to a concept otherwise than in
intuition; for though a pure intuition can indeed precede the
object *a priori*, even this intuition can acquire its object, and
therefore objective validity, only through the empirical
intuition of which it is the mere form. Therefore all concepts,
and with them all principles, even such as are possible *a priori*,

relate to empirical intuitions, that is, to the data for a possible experience.

He then ties this claim directly to arithmetic [A240, B299]:

the concept of magnitude seeks its support and sensible meaning in number, and this in turn in the fingers, in the beads of the abacus, or in strokes and points which can be placed before the eyes.[10] The concept itself is always *a priori* in origin, and so likewise are the synthetic principles or formulas derived from such concepts; but their employment and their relations to their professed objects can in the end be sought nowhere but in experience, of whose possibility they contain the formal conditions.

Kant's position on the relation between empirical and pure intuitions, and how they stand with respect to synthetic a priori judgments, is explained most clearly, perhaps, in Section 2 of The system of the principles of pure understanding (A154, B193 to A158, B197). Two quotes from this section should be sufficient to clarify that position. At A156–7, B196 he says,

Experience depends . . . upon *a priori* principles of its form, that is, upon universal rules of unity in the synthesis of appearances. Their objective reality, as necessary conditions of experience, and indeed of its very possibility, can always be shown in experience. *Apart from this relation synthetic* a priori *principles are completely impossible.* For they have then no third something, that is, no object, in which the synthetic unity can exhibit the objective reality of its concepts. (My emphasis)

Then at A158, B197 he summarizes his conclusion:

Synthetic *a priori* judgments are . . . possible when we relate the formal conditions of *a priori* intuition . . . to a possible empirical knowledge in general. We then assert that the conditions of the *possibility of experience* in general are likewise conditions of the *possibility of the objects of experience*, and that for this reason they have objective validity in a synthetic *a priori* judgment. (His original emphasis)

Not only does this structure imply that Kant's criterion is empirical rather than psychological, it also implies that although synthetic propositions are possible a priori, their actuality rests on empirical intuition rather than pure intuition. In this sense, Ayer's assumption that Kant believed in the actuality of synthetic a priori propositions is open to serious challenge.[11]

II

Even if we were to grant Ayer his point regarding the psychological criterion, however, this would not justify his redefining syntheticity to exclude the possibility of synthetic *a priori* propositions. In order to do that, he would have to make some sort of case independent of his criticism of Kant for the conclusion that synthetic a priori propositions in fact are impossible.

Such an argument seems to be furnished by the fact that Whitehead and Russell, in *Principia Mathematica*, demonstrated that the propositions of cardinal arithmetic could be proved from the axioms of a logical system. The various axioms of the system could, of course, be conjoined into a single proposition, and the propositions of cardinal arithmetic (including "7 + 5 = 12") would follow from such a proposition by the law of contradiction alone. Since Kant defined analytical judgments as judgments in which the predicate "is already contained in the concept of the subject, of which it cannot be denied without contradiction,"[12] any proposition having the conjunct of the axioms as its subject, and some proposition of cardinal arithmetic as its predicate (say, "7 + 5 = 12") would seem to fit his definition of an analytical judgment. Thus, whether or not "12" follows analytically from the concept of "7 + 5," the proposition "7 + 5 = 12" would follow analytically from the conjunct of axioms, and Ayer's case would seem to be complete.

This case, however, fails to take account of the fact that Kant also says that "a synthetical proposition can indeed be established by the law of contradiction, but only by presupposing another synthetical proposition from which it follows, never by that law alone."[13] In terms of this, Ayer's case is seriously weakened.

The conjunct of the axioms — the proposition from which the propositions of cardinal arithmetic can be deduced by the law of contradiction — is itself arrived at by the process of conjunction. That process must in Kant's terms be taken as synthetic. Indeed, were it not synthetic then some of the axioms would necessarily follow by the law of contradiction from one of the others; i.e. the set of axioms would be redundant and all but one of them would therefore be eliminable. In order to make Ayer's case, therefore, it would be necessary to produce some single axiom – itself analytical in nature – from which all the propositions of cardinal arithmetic can be deduced. Thus, the fact that the propositions of cardinal arithmetic are deducible from the conjunct of the axioms in no way shows that such propositions meet Kant's criterion of analyticity. On the contrary, they seem to illustrate his claim that a synthetic proposition can follow by the law of contradiction from another synthetic proposition.

Ayer goes on to argue that even if Whitehead and Russell should be proved wrong,

> even if . . . it is not possible to reduce mathematical notions to purely logical notions, it will still remain true that the propositions of mathematics are analytic propositions, containing special terms, but they will be none the less analytic for that. For the criterion of an analytic proposition is that its validity should follow simply from the definitions of the terms contained in it, and this condition is fulfilled by the propositions of pure mathematics.[14]

The difficulty with this claim lies in the fact that Ayer is using his own definition of analyticity, and not Kant's. Ayer's definition – that the validity of the proposition "depends solely on the definitions of the symbols it contains"[15] – allows one to include among analytic propositions a complex proposition formed by the conjunction of two or more propositions which would in themselves be analytic according to Kant's criterion. But for Kant such a conjunction would necessarily be either redundant or synthetic.

In the light of this, Ayer's claim that "the axioms of a geometry are simple definitions, and . . . the theorems of a geometry are simply the logical consequences of these definitions"[16] in no way undermines Kant's position as Kant stated it. This would render all of geometry analytic according to Ayer's criterion of analyticity, but when reflected against Kant's criterion, the theorems of geometry would follow by the law of contradiction from the conjunct of the axioms; but the conjunct of the axioms would itself necessarily be synthetic. Thus Ayer's position would again merely illustrate Kant's claim that a synthetic proposition can follow by the law of contradiction from another synthetic proposition.

Considered in this light, Ayer's position seems to corroborate Kant's position rather than refute it.

NOTES

1 I am indebted to a student, Scott Livingston, whose research brought to my attention the passages in the *Prolegomena* which led to the development of the present thesis.

2 An earlier version of this paper was read before the Ohio Philosophical Association in April 1977.

3 A. J. Ayer, *Language, Truth and Logic* (Dover Publications, New York), p. 78.

4 Ibid., p. 7.

5 Ibid., p. 78.

6 Ibid. My emphasis.

7 Ayer's redefinition of analyticity – "[a proposition's] validity depends solely on the definitions of the symbols it contains" – is in fact not definitory, since he fails to explicate *how* validity "depends on" the definitions.

8 *Prolegomena*, p. 40.

9 A20, B34. All quotes are from the Norman Kemp Smith translation (Macmillan & Co., London and New York, 1958).

10 The passage in the *Prolegomena* where Kant refers to "fingers" and "points" has an exact parallel in the *Critique* at B15. His use of these terms here is therefore not coincidental.

11 Worth noting in this connection is the fact that for Kant the term "a priori" is always adverbial, never adjectival.

12 *Prolegomena*, p. 39.

13 Ibid.

14 *Language, Truth and Logic*, p. 82.

15 Ibid., p. 78.

16 Ibid., p. 82.

WAHRNEHMUNGSURTEILE AND ERFAHRUNGSURTEILE RECONSIDERED

Theodore E. Uehling Jr.

Sections 18, 19, and 20 of the *Prolegomena* deal almost exclusively with the division of empirical judgments into judgments of perception (*Wahrnehmungsurteile*) and judgments of experience (*Erfahrungsurteile*). This distinction has long been considered one of the most problematic in the entire *Prolegomena* and has been singled out for special treatment by many commentators, especially those dealing with the relationship between the first ("A") and second ("B") editions of the *First Critique*. The distinction, for example, can be made to bear upon the reading of both the "A" and "B" transcendental deductions. Critical treatments of it have undergone some evolution; the tendency earlier in this century was to consider it as somewhat of an anomaly, the result, perhaps, of a moment of blindness on Kant's part. Hence, Kemp Smith, H. J. Paton, and A. C. Ewing all tend to dismiss the distinction with varying degrees of vehemence, although Ewing finds acceptable some of the implications of the distinction. More recent commentators, such as J. Bennett, G. Bird, and T. K. Swing, while differing substantially in their treatments of the two types of judgment, do consider them worthy of considerable and careful attention. Bird, in particular, attaches importance to the *Prolegomena* distinction, both in his analyses of Kant's epistemology and in the context of his evaluation of some of P. Strawson's argumentation in the *Bounds of Sense*.[1] G. Prauss deals with Kant's problematic distinction in his recent *Erscheinung bei Kant*, as does L. W. Beck in his even more recent *Hatte denn der Philosoph von Königsberg keine Träume?*.[2] The purpose of this paper is, first, to re-examine Kant's distinction and, second, to consider the critical considerations of Kant's distinction.

I

Empirical judgments (those whose possibility rests upon sense perception or empirical intuition, although not necessarily exclusively) are not all judgments of experience. In order, Kant claims, for an empirical judgment to be a judgment of experience, a priori concepts of the understanding must be "superadded" (*hinzukommen*) to that which is given in empirical intuition (18₁65: IV 297).³ If an a priori concept of the understanding is not required for the actuality of the empirical judgment, then it is a judgment of perception. Hence, empirical judgments are subdivided into judgments of experience and judgments of perception. The former are objectively valid (they "agree" with the object) whereas the latter are only subjectively valid, and involve only a "logical connexion of perception in a thinking subject" (18₂65 : IV 298). The objective validity of judgments of experience is made possible by the pure concepts of the understanding and it is their "superaddition" which distinguishes judgments of experience from those of perception, since both contain data given in empirical intuition.

This is basically Kant's argumentation through the second paragraph of section 18; it seems straightforward and, on the face of it, unproblematic (although, as we shall see, its simplicity is extraordinarily deceptive). One is likely first to cringe upon reading the first sentence of the next paragraph (18₃65: IV 298):

> All our judgments are at first merely judgments of perception; they hold good only for us (that is, for our subject), and we do not till afterward give them a new reference (to an object) and desire that they should always hold good for us and in the same way for everybody else.

The initial difficulty with this is threefold. First, the "at first" (*zuerst*) may suggest that Kant is trying to explain how experience comes to be or to give the generic history of the development of human experience. If this were the case, then Kant's account would directly conflict with the first paragraph of section 21*a* (21 a₁70: IV 304):

> In order to comprise the whole matter in one idea, it is first necessary to remind the reader that we are discussing, not the origin of experience, but that which lies in experience. The former pertains to empirical psychology and would even then never be adequately explained without the latter, which

belongs to the critique of knowledge, and particularly of the understanding.

Now Kant's analyses in the *First Critique* and *Prolegomena* are, in the main, consistent with his view that he is not concerned with examining the "origin of experience." Rather, Kant's analyses are of the distinguishable but inseparable elements of experience; he shows what is contained in experience, to wit, a set of distinguishable elements which are inseparable with regard to time order. Unfortunately, his "at first" suggests a kind of separation which would be relevant only in a generic history of human experience.[4]

Second, the addition of "all" to "at first" may suggest either that no judgment is independent of some sort of "basic" judgment of perception or that all judgments of perception will undergo a transformation into judgments of experience. In the first case, certainly pure aesthetic judgments are quite independent of judgments of perception. In a pure aesthetic judgment there is an element of sensation involved, namely, the sensation of the harmony of the two cognitive faculties, imagination and understanding,[5] but this sense of "sensation" is radically different from sensation involved in a judgment of perception (sensations such as "warmth", "bitter", "sweet", etc.) In the second case Kant, as we shall see, explicitly argues that judgments of perception fall into two classes; those which *can* become judgments of perception and those which *cannot*.

Third, if *all* our judgments are at first judgments of perception but if *some* of them cannot become judgments of experience (i.e. if a concept of the understanding cannot, legitimately, be "superadded"), then there seems to be a serious conflict with the "B" transcendental deduction where Kant maintains that "all synthesis . . . even that which renders perception possible, is subject to the categories."[6] This, in fact, points to one of the major difficulties with the *Prolegomena* distinction between perception uncategorized and experience, and it will be dealt with in what follows.

The remainder of the first sentence of 18_3 reinforces the feeling that Kant is doing what he claims he ought not to do, i.e. giving a generic history of human experience. The notion that we first form subjectively valid judgments and then "afterwards" (*nur hinten*) refer those judgments to an object because we "desire" or "want" (*wollen*) them to be objectively valid seems eminently psychologistic. What Kant does accomplish, however, is to connect objective validity with necessary universality. A judgment of experience is objectively valid because it "agrees with the object" and since "all judgments concerning the same object must likewise agree among themselves," it must be necessarily universal, i.e. objective validity entails necessary universality. In the remainder of 18_3, Kant stresses that the entailment works in the opposite direction as well, i.e. necessary universality entails objective validity. This much, at least, is consistent with the *First Critique*.

Thus, at the beginning of 19_1 ($19_1 66$: IV 298), Kant states that objective validity and necessary universality are equivalent, and characterize judgments of experience. A judgment of experience is objectively valid precisely because the "given perceptions" (*der gegebenen Wahrnehmungen*) are universally and necessarily connected. The objective validity cannot rest upon the given perceptions themselves but rather upon that which connects universally and necessarily, i.e. the pure concepts of the understanding.

19_2 ($19_2 47$: IV 299) with its important note contains a set of illustrations which indicates, along with 20_3, the division of judgments of perception into two classes. This division has been generally overlooked[7] but I think that it is important for making some sense out of sections 18, 19, and 20. The examples which Kant gives at the beginning of 19_2, ("the room is warm," "sugar [is] sweet," "wormwood [is] bitter") are judgments of perception which cannot become judgments of experience even if a concept of the understanding were superadded, "because they refer merely to feeling, which everyone knows to be merely subjective and which of course can never be attributed to the object." Hence, Kant rather clearly seems to be asserting that there can be "awareness" apart from the understanding and its acts of synthesizing according to the categories. An appearance of some sort has been given without conforming to the pure concepts of the understanding but, of course, this appearance cannot be the basis of a "knowing consciousness," since there is only a subjectively valid connection among the elements of the appearance. All judgments of experience, however, stand under conditions (the categories) which make them universally valid and, hence, objectively valid. The judgment, "air is elastic," while at first (*zunächst*) only a judgment of perception, can become a judgment of experience, since it, unlike the first three examples, can stand under the categories. As Kant puts it in 20_3 ($20_3 68$: IV 301): "Air is elastic", becomes universally valid and a judgment of experience only because certain judgments precede it which subsume the intuition of air under the concept of cause and effect." In his note to 20_3, Kant gives us a second example of a judgment of perception which can become a judgment of experience: "When the sun shines on the stone, it grows warm." When the category of causality is added to the given perceptions involved in the judgment of perception, then the judgment becomes objective and has the form "The sun warms the stone" (presumably, the sun causes the feeling of warmth in the stone).

The division of judgments of perception into two categories, besides implying an explicit distinction between feeling and cognition and hence implying that there can be consciousness or awareness of some sort apart from the categories, indicates as well that Kant in the *Prolegomena* thought that judgments of perception were independently actual. That is to say, they are more than merely the product of an analysis of judgments of experience into their inseparable "parts" or "ingredients." It seems that they are, in fact, quite separable from judgments of experience and, presumably, we can form a large number of such subjectively valid judgments which can never become more than merely subjectively valid. Hence, Kant clearly seems to hold that not all perception or awareness is cognitive experience, and this again seems inconsistent with the "B" deduction position that all synthesis, including that which makes perception possible, is subject to the categories. In judgments of perception which cannot become judgments of experience, there is an empirical synthesis of perceptions in the perceiving subject which is *not* subject to the categories. Yet, against this, Kemp Smith, for example, writes that "the central argument of the *Analytic* is directed to prove . . . [the thesis] that save through the combination of intuition and conception no consciousness whatsoever is possible."[8]

20_1 ($20_1$67: IV 300) seems to repeat the grounds for the distinction between judgments of perception and judgments of experience which we have already considered. However, in the first sentence it should be noted that Kant emphasizes the "analysis" of experience (*Erfahrung überhaupt zergliedern müssen*) in order to see what is contained within it, namely, elements contributed by sense and elements contributed by the understanding. His language, in other words, is far more consistent with $21a_1$ than the language of the first sentence of 18_3. Even more importantly, when, in the second and third sentences of 20_1, Kant identifies the two elements of experience as perception and *judging*, judging is described as belonging "only to the understanding." Hence, when Kant tells us that this judging "may be twofold," yielding either judgments of perception or judgments of experience, it thus appears as if judgments of perception are not independent of the understanding, since no judgment is possible without an activity of the understanding. We are told repeatedly in the *First Critique* that the understanding judges by means of its concepts or categories; hence, it now seems that no judgment, not even a judgment of perception which *cannot* become a judgment of experience, is independent of the activity of the understanding, although Kant seemingly still wants to maintain that that kind of judgment is independent of subsumption of its perceptual element under the categories.

$20_2(20_267$: IV 300) does not help clarify the issues which arose in 20_1. We are again told that a pure concept of the understanding is necessary in order for perception to become experience. The example involving the subsumption of the intuition "air" under the concept of cause is less clear than the examples given in 19_2 and 20_3, a point which Kant explicitly recognises in 20_3 and its note. The examples in 20_3 have already been commented upon; the remaining sentences of 20_3 are repetitious.

The first sentence of 20_4 (20_468–9: IV 301–2) adds nothing to Kant's argumentation. Following that, however, we discover that not only empirical judgments (as judgments of experience) are a product of subsumption under pure concepts of the understanding but that the judgments of pure mathematics equally require subsumption. Kant uses his example of a synthetic a priori judgment in geometry from Part I of the *Prolegomena*: "A straight line is the shortest distance between two points." This judgment, he tells us,

> presupposes that the line is subsumed under the concept of quantity, which certainly is no mere intuition, but has its seat in the understanding alone and serves to determine the intuition (of the line) with regard to the judgments which may be made about it, in respect to their quantity.

II

The exposition of and preliminary commentary upon Kant's distinction between judgments of experience and judgments for perception has served to indicate that it involves a number of difficulties and seemingly apparent inconsistencies. These difficulties and inconsistencies have hardly gone unnoticed. Many of Kant's commentators have leapt upon his distinction with considerable glee. Kemp Smith calls the distinction "entirely worthless and can only serve to mislead the reader. It cuts at the very root of Kant's Critical teaching."[9] He points out further that

> to accept this distinction is to throw the entire argument [of the transcendental deduction] into confusion. This Kant seems to have recognised in the interval between the *Prolegomena* and the second edition of the *Critique*. For in the section before us [the "B" transcendental deduction] there is no trace of it.[10] . . . The distinction drawn in the *Prolegomena* is only, indeed, a more definite formulation of the distinction which runs through the first edition of the *Critique* between the indeterminate and determinate object of consciousness. The more definite formulation of it seems, however, to have had the happy effect of enabling Kant to realise the illigitimacy of any such distinction.[11]

Given the obvious difficulties and inconsistencies which we have already seen, one is tempted to sympathize with Kemp Smith's scowling rejection of the distinction. But then again perhaps he is too hasty.

Ewing, in his *Short Commentary*, treats the *Prolegomena* distinction as being loosely parallel to the doctrine of the *Critique of Aesthetic Judgment* that a synthesis of imagination can be independent of a synthesis of the understanding. That is, in both the *Prolegomena* and *Critique of Aesthetic Judgment* some kind of awareness or consciousness seems possible without the categories, and this, of course, conflicts with the opening sentences of the "B" deduction. Ewing confesses that he cannot "effect a reconciliation between the *Critique of Pure Reason* and the *Critique of Judgment* and *Prolegomena* in this matter" but concludes that "it seems . . . that Kant holds that apart from the categories we should still have consciousness in the sense of feeling but not in the sense of cognition."[12] Hence, Ewing rejects Kemp Smith's contention that the *Prolegomena* distinction was thoroughly a mistake, yet he is by no means prepared to endorse the *Prolegomena* argumentation as it stands. Ewing does, by the way, commit a rather glaring error. On page 92 he gives as examples of judgments of perception "the room is warm or sugar is sweet" and follows that by stating that "[they] can be made into 'judgments of experience' by being brought under the categories." This obviously ignores Kant's division of judgments of perception into two distinct classes, which I pointed to in the first section of this paper.

Paton argues that there can be no knowledge apart from the categories but wishes to leave open the question "whether intuitions can exist in human consciousness without being referred to an object." He contends that "it would be a mistake to say on *a priori* grounds that they cannot be found."[13] But despite that, Paton is not willing to accept the *Prolegomena* distinction: "Kant's distinction of 'judgements of perception' and 'judgements of experience' in the *Prolegomena* . . . suggests strongly that he believed intuitions could be present in consciousness without being referred to objects by means of the categories; but this may be dismissed as an afterthought and not a very happy one."[14] Parton does not tell us why he believes the distinction to be an afterthought and why it is unhappy; he certainly does not allow the distinction to serve as evidence for the view that Kant held that consciousness of something is possible apart from the categories. With regard to this last point, Paton simply does not find sufficient or conclusive evidence for either side and hence maintains that he does not know what Kant's view was. Thus, among our three earlier commentators, Paton's position is somewhat a middle ground; none of the three finds the *Prolegomena* distinction acceptable but Ewing is the most willing and Kemp Smith the least willing to accept one doctrine that the distinction seems to imply, i.e. that apart from the categories there can be consciousness or awareness of some sort, although this would not be called "knowing consciousness."

Bennett's treatment of the distinction[15] takes a few rather interesting turns. He views the distinction between judgments of perception and judgments of experience as allied to the distinction between judgments which do not employ the concept of an object and judgments which do employ the concept of an object. Bennett also notices that at B 140–2 (III: 113–14) the distinction seems to recur although the terminology of the *Prolegomena* is not present. In particular, he notices that in the *Critique* at B 142 Kant cites an objective judgment ("It, the body, is heavy") as well as citing its subjective counterpart (a "relation of the same representations that would have only subjective validity"): "If I support a body, I feel an impression of weight." Bennett contends that this parallels the method of the *Prolegomena* of citing both the subjective and objective "versions" of judgments. He comments further that the "subjective" example given in the *Critique* is really quite objective since it "employs the concept of a body and so says something about the objective realm;" hence, Bennett is willing only to concede that the objective examples are "more" objective than subjective ("less" objective) counterparts. Bennett correctly discerns that at B 140–2, Kant does limit "judgment" to "judgments of experience;" he then concludes that "this restriction of the meaning of 'judgment' is arbitrary and illegitimate: Kant gives no reason for denying what he clearly admits in the *Prolegomena*, namely, that there can be judgments of perception as well as of experience." Hence, Bennett would presumably want to retain some distinction between perception and experience, or the less objective and the more objective. Unfortunately, although he tells us "that we can see roughly what distinction Kant wants to draw," he does not share with us even this rough insight and thus we do not know what weight to attach to the admission in the *Prolegomena* that perception and experience differ. One suspects that upon analysis they do differ. The question still remains, however, whether a perception which cannot also be called in Kant's terminology "an experience" can occur. On the face of it, there seems to be no good reason to deny, especially outside the Kantian analyses, that we have perceptions and that we connect those perceptions in ways that are only subjectively valid. And hence I find considerable difficulty in accepting an argument such as Kemp Smith's that

> Kant's final Critical teaching . . . [is that] only through concepts is apprehension of an object possible, and only in and through such apprehension do concepts come to consciousness. . . . The co-operation of concept and intuition is necessary for consciousness in any and every form, even the simplest and most indefinite.[16]

In an earlier work on Kant,[17] I argued that the distinction between judgments of perception and judgments of experience along with the division of judgments of perception into two classes implied that Kant drew an explicit distinction between feeling and cognition. I was particularly anxious to maintain the viability of the *Prolegomena* distinction because I saw a relatively close relationship between judgments of perception and empirical aesthetic judgments on the ground that through both kinds of judgment we can judge certain sensations to be pleasant or unpleasant, i.e. that human beings stand in relation to things in non-cognitive ways. With regard to Kant's assertion at the beginning of the "B" deduction that "all synthesis, therefore, even that which renders perception possible, is subject to the categories," I argued that no irreconcilable difficulties would arise if one kept in mind the two classes of judgments of perception.

Judgments of perception proper, those which can never become judgments of experience and, hence, can never become objectively valid, such as "the room is warm," involve no category directed synthesis of given perceptions. On the other hand, judgments of perception which are valid of objects are obviously not judgments of perception at all, but judgments of experience. What is misleading is Kant's use of the term "become," for the use of this term suggests that Kant is giving a generic history, whereas he rather consistently argues (with the exception of passages in sections 18 and 19, to which I have already referred) that he is not. Kant really ought not talk about one kind of judgment "becoming" another kind of judgment. Hence, I concluded that

> not all perception or awareness is cognitive experience, and that which is not is that in which the matter given to sense is not synthesized and therefore not attributed to objects or nature as appearance but merely to the capacity of feeling in the human being . . . [Kant's] statement that all our judgments are at first merely judgments of perception is . . . an unfortunate way of stating what his analysis shows, for it suggests . . . that he is doing empirical psychology and setting out the elements in experience in their generic order. What the analysis does show is that there are two different kinds of judgment about perception, and not that one kind precedes in time the other.[18]

Some reviewers argued that I was far too insistent in arguing for no categorization at the "level" of judgments of perception which cannot become judgments of experience, since Kant's examples seem to indicate that categorization is required there as well, as we have seen Bennett point out. On much the same point, L. W. Beck, in correspondence to me,[19] wrote:

> I see . . . that you anticipate one of the main points in my paper ["*Hatte denn der Philosoph von Königsberg keine Träume*"], to wit, the analogy between the distinction between judgments of sensation [perception] and judgments of experience and that between empirical and pure aesthetic judgments. There are some terminological differences since I use "empirical aesthetic judgment" in a slightly different sense and compare *Wahrnehmungsurteile* to *Urteile des sinnlichen Angenehmen*; and I am anxious to maintain a certain level of categorial synthesis

even on the level of *Wahrnehmungsurteile*. But I shall acknowledge your priority with respect to one of my main points.

While it might seem appropriate to reply to Beck at this point,
especially regarding the "certain level of categorial synthesis," I will
consider first some of the views of Graham Bird regarding
Wahrnehmungsurteile – Erfahrungsurteile, and then attempt some general
conclusions regarding the distinction.

Bird deals extensively with the *Prolegomena* distinction and other
parallel distinctions in the *Critique*,[20] and what he says seems to me
to merit serious consideration. In general, Bird views the *Prolegomena*
distinction as an empirical illustration of a transcendental distinction
and, as empirical, quite inadequate as an illustration of a transcendental account of the categories. According to Bird, Kant draws a
distinction between empirical and transcendental questions. With
regard, for example, to objects of perception, one might ask "What
do you see?" Such a question is a decidedly empirical one and
invites equally empirical answers, such as "I see a rainbow" or "I
see the rain."[21] However, the question "What do you see?" may be
taken in a transcendental sense. Bird comments: "In this way such
a question would be designed to ask not what is perceived on some
particular occasion, but rather *what kind or type of thing is perceived
when we perceive anything whatever.*"[22] A transcendental answer to the
question understood in this transcendental sense might be, perhaps,
"I perceive appearances rather than things as they are in themselves."
Bird is quite right in contending that it would sound absurd to give
a transcendental answer to the question empirically understood and
inadequate to give empirical answers to the question in its transcendental sense. Consider Kant's examples involving the relation
between the sun shining on the stone and the perception of warmth.
"When the sun shines on the stone, it grows warm" is, for Kant, a
mere judgment of perception, whereas "The sun warms the stone"
involves the addition to the perception of the concept of cause
"which necessarily connects with the concept of sunshine that of
heat" and, hence, this judgment is necessary and universally valid (a
judgment of experience). Empirically, according to Bird, a judgment
of perception expresses no categorial claim whereas transcendentally,
the relation expressed in the preceding judgments cannot be
expressed without making a categorial claim. Hence, judgments of
perception are not candidates for general acceptance whereas judgments involving categorial claims, such as claims about causal con-

nections, are such candidates. Bird wishes us to take special note of Kant's language in talking about judgments of perception and experience, particularly when Kant states that he "desires" or "intends" (18₃65: IV 298) that a judgment of experience should be universally valid. Bird writes that "Kant speaks rather of the intention that a claim should be generally accepted than its actual acceptance. . . . The distinction between subjective and objective judgments lies partly in our intentions in asserting them"[23] (i.e. what we intend them to be candidates for).

We do, then, according to Bird, formulate judgments through which we assert more than subjective connections (these judgments have a "superior status") and he believes that Kant's problem is in large measure "accounting for this superiority." He asserts that "this problem could perhaps be solved by showing that the superior judgments are more closely related than the others to the categories."[24] We know, of course, that this is exactly what Kant attempts to do when he appeals to the category of causality in his two examples of judgments of experience, and hence attempts to justify their objectivity as over and against the mere subjectivity of judgments of perception. Bird contends that Kant's illustrations do not really substantiate his incisive division of empirical judgments since "even empirically subjective judgments are transcendentally objective." Bird writes further:

> To say of something that it is transcendentally objective is to say that it can be conceived independently of any particular experience, but not independently of every experience. Even personal experiences are, therefore, transcendentally objective, since such things as pains are conceived independently of any particular pain experience. It is for this reason that a claim about my pain can be true for others, or for myself at another time, even though it is not true of them. But particular claims about personal experiences are empirically subjective, for they are not true independently of any particular experience; if they are true at all, they are true of a particular experience. Categorial claims, however, expressing for example a causal connection are not, in this way, dependent for their truth on any particular experience, and so are empirically, as well as transcendentally, objective. The empirical distinctions between objective and subjective judgments reflect the relative distinctions between claims true of public and claims true of private

objects, or between impersonal and personal claims. These distinctions are exemplified in our experience and so are empirical; but all these judgments are objective transcendentally.[25]

Hence Bird, like Beck, disallows the possibility of what I have called judgments of perception proper, i.e. judgments which have no reference whatsoever to anything other than a particular individual's claim about a particular set of sense perceptions, Bird on the grounds that all judgments are transcendentally objective and Beck on the grounds that some categorization is required even on the level of judgments of perception such as "I perceive that this room is warm" (which is not intended as a candidate for general acceptance). Bird's analysis strikes me as acute; obviously, we form subjective empirical judgments, such as Kant's judgments of perception proper, but they are subjective only in the form of the relation of a particular perceiver to a particular set of sense perceptions. Such a judgment is, of course, not necessarily true of other individuals; that I perceive that this room is warm does not imply that this room feels warm to all who are now in a position to perceive the temperature of the room. But frequently, assuming a common way to "measure" and talk about sensations, my judgment that the room is warm is in fact true for others; that is, others could truly assert the same judgment. And, in fact, when I assert that the room is warm, I may intend that others assert this as well and that we share (or become aware of) a common connection of perceptions. While this will not make these judgments necessarily objective in Kant's sense, it will tend to destroy Kant's division of judgments of perception into two rather distinct classes. What indeed we may have in judgments of perception which do not involve an a priori concept is a spectrum of judgments ranging from those which are eminently singular and even idiosyncratic to those which are clearly true for most other individuals of a given set and which I intend to be true of most of those other individuals. And, if Bird's analyses are correct, all of them will be *transcendentally* objective anyway.

In sum, I have become convinced that there is no one reading of the *Prolegomena* distinction which would have the merit of making the doctrines of the *Prolegomena*, *First Critique*, and *Third Critique* perfectly consistent. To attempt to generate one reading primarily in order to save Kant from charges of inconsistency would, I think, be a mistake, and reflect that kind of exercise which was undertaken by Kant's supporters during the heyday of the "patchwork" theory. Insofar as possible, the Kantian theses should be allowed their head in each of the works, respectively, and if this is done it is probably inevitable that the Kantian analyses will lead to prima facie inconsistencies (such as that between the "B" deduction and the *Prolegomena* distinction as such). But I now suspect that the confrontation with inconsistencies (and obscurities) is one of the prices which the contemporary student of Kant must be prepared to pay.

NOTES

1 With regard to the latter, see his *Recent Interpretations of Kant's Transcendental Deduction, Akten des 4. Internationalen Kant-Kongresses*, Teil I, ed. G. Funke and J. Kopper (Berlin and New York: Walter de Gruyter, 1974), pp. 1–14.

2 *Akten des 4. Internationalen Kant-Kongresses*, Teil III, ed. G. Funke (Berlin, 1975), pp. 26–34.

3 The numbers in parentheses should be read as follows: The first number with subscript is the section number, the subscript indicating the paragraph number within that section, and the following number is the page number in this edition; the page number in Volume IV of the *Akademie* edition is given after the colon. References to other of Kant's writings include the customary *Akademie* numbers.

4 For a further discussion of this point, see my *Notion of Form in Kant's Critique of Aesthetic Judgment* (The Hague and Paris: Mouton, 1971), pp. 49–51. See also H. J. Paton, *Kant's Metaphysic of Experience* (London: Allen & Unwin, 1951), I, pp. 575–77, and A. C. Ewing, *A Short Commentary on Kant's Critique of Pure Reason*, 2nd edn. (London: Methuen & Co. Ltd., 1961), pp. 93–5.

5 See Kant's *Critique of Judgment*, trans. James C. Meredith (London: Oxford University Press, 1952), especially pp. 58–60; V 217–19.

6 *Critique of Pure Reason*, trans. N. Kemp Smith (London: Macmillan & Co. Ltd., 1958), p. 171, B 161; III 125.

7 T. K. Swing has explicitly noticed it. See his *Kant's Transcendental Logic* (New Haven: Yale University Press, 1969), p. 141.

8 *A Commentary to Kant's Critique of Pure Reason*, 2nd edn. (New York: Humanities Press, 1962), p. 168.

9 Ibid., p. 288.

10 Kemp Smith is wrong on this point. The distinction is reflected at B 140–2; III 113–14, as Graham Bird notices in *Recent Interpretations*, p. 14, and as Jonathan Bennett points out in his *Kant's Analytic* (Cambridge: Cambridge University Press, 1966), p. 132.

11 *Commentary*, p. 289.

12 *Short Commentary*, p. 93.

13 *Kant's Metaphysic*, I, 331.

14 Ibid., n. 1.

15 *Kant's Analytic*, pp. 132–4.

16 *Commentary*, p. 168.

17 *Notion of Form*, pp. 45–55.
18 Ibid., pp. 54–5.
19 6 April 1973. Quotation used with the permission of Professor L. W. Beck.
20 In his *Kant's Theory of Knowledge* (London: Routledge & Kegan Paul, 1962), especially pp. 140–8.
21 I have modified slightly the formulation which Bird gives in *Kant's Theory*, pp. 40–2.
22 *Kant's Theory*, p. 41. My emphasis.
23 Ibid., p. 143.
24 Ibid.
25 Ibid., p. 145.

KANT, ANALOGY, AND
NATURAL THEOLOGY

Jerry H. Gill

Two years after publishing his first *Critique*, Kant offered the philosophical world his *Prolegomena to Any Future Metaphysics* as something of a popularized version of the argument contained in the former work. While there are variations in the *Prolegomena* from both editions of *The Critique of Pure Reason*, it basically follows the same development of thought and presents the same conclusions. The *way* these conclusions are presented, however, both in concept and vocabulary, is occasionally quite distinct. This is especially true with respect to the "conclusions" of the *Prolegomena*, wherein his treatment of the limitations which must be placed on metaphysics in general and natural theology in particular are set forth.

What is of special interest here is the specific way Kant discusses the distinction between "the bounds" and "the limits" of pure reason as they pertain to what can be known and said about God, and his introduction of the notion of *analogy* as a means of understanding the "positive" aspect of his overall negative conclusions concerning natural theology. I am particularly interested in his remarks on these topics to the degree that they might provide a way of overcoming the strong dichotomies established by Kant himself between the phenomenal and noumenal worlds. In this manner perhaps the skepticism and/or existentialism, as well as the limited humanism, which are traditionally said to follow from Kant's philosophy, can be seen as mere interpretational alternatives.

I

Kant begins his conclusions to the *Prolegomena* by suggesting that just as it would be absurd to hope for knowledge of things in themselves beyond the categories of the understanding, so it would be a "greater absurdity" to fail to acknowledge the existence of such realities, "for this would be to wish to have the principles of the possibility of experience considered universal conditions of things in themselves" resulting in these principles becoming "transcendent" (p. 110). It would seem, incidentally, that this is a passage which Fichte, Hegel, Schopenhauer, and even Emerson would have done well to ponder at some length.

Next, Kant admits that although the human mind cannot *know*, content-wise, beyond all possible experience, we cannot abstain entirely from seeking to do so, since "experience never satisfies reason fully." Here he acknowledges what some have called the "metaphysical urge," the desire to find some substantive, rather then merely formal, reality amidst the fog banks that lie beyond the shoreline of what in the first *Critique* Kant termed "the island of truth," bounded by the categories of the understanding. There, Kant seems intent on playing a kind of philosophical "catcher in the rye," saving would-be metaphysicians from certain suicide by drowning. Here, he seems more open to entertaining the possibility that such excursions may not be fatal after all.

This possibility seems to hinge, at least in part, on the distinction made in the *Prolegomena* (pp. 111–12) between "the bounds of reason" and "the limits of reason," a distinction which Kant does not, to my knowledge, make in the first critique. Bounds, according to Kant, "always presuppose a space existing outside a certain definite place and inclosing it," much like a fence or the walls of a room. Bounds are impositions which confine the range of our activity from *without*, they crowd us in. Limits, on the other hand, "are mere negations which affect a quantity so far as it is not absolutely complete, perhaps as a tether or an horizon might restrict our range of activity or vision from *within* our standpoint, so to speak.

Now, human reason experiences the restrictions provided by the categories of the understanding as *limits* when it is working in the areas of formal and empirical science, but as *bounds* with respect to the things in themselves. In the former case, there is no incompleteness in principle or quality but only in quantity regarding what can be known, while in the latter case this is not true; thus in the latter case the very incompleteness suggests something *beyond* itself. As Kant says: "Metaphysics leads us towards bounds in the dialectical attempts at pure reason, not undertaken arbitrarily . . . but stimulated thereto by the nature of reason itself." It is nature itself that has endowed us with the predisposition to seek "not only the bounds of the use of pure reason, but also the way to determine them" (p. 112).

In Kant's view then, it is the transcendental ideas (of God, freedom, and immortality), which we can neither keep from thinking nor ever give content to, that lead us, not only to the acknowledgement of the reality of the bounds of reason, but to their *location* and *nature* as well. The very existence of such ideas leads us to "the spot" where experience, structured by the categories of the understanding as the phenomenal world, "touches the void (that of which we can know nothing, namely noumena)" (p. 112). Kant's use of embodied kinesthetic and tactile metaphors at this juncture is especially interesting in its own right and we shall have opportunity to return to it before finishing up.

The main point here is that whereas limits are experienced exclusively as negations, *bounds* carry as well a *positive* significance. The point at which what we know, phenomenal reality, "connects" with what we do not know, noumenal reality, is the point at which we are rationally forced to *think* the transcendental ideas even though we can never rationally *know* them, content-wise. These ideas necessitate positing the existence of the noumena, of things in themselves, beyond our experiences within the phenomenal world because they "actually have reference to something distinct from them ... as appearances always presuppose an object in itself and therefore suggest its existence whether we can know of it or not" (p. 113).

At this point Kant introduces a distinction between deism, à la Hume, on the one hand, and two kinds of theism on the other. It is clear that he wants to go further than Hume by making room for some form of natural theology, even though it is generally thought that apart from the ethical structure of practical reason Kant saw no place whatsoever for a rational approach to religion. Kant accepts Hume's critique of all attempts to project human characteristics onto the divine nature on the basis of "*dogmatic* anthropomorphism" as simply futile exercises in transcendent metaphysics (p. 114). However, he goes on to maintain that a *transcendental* metaphysics, one which engages in "*symbolical* anthropomorphism" is not only viable but is necessitated by the nature of reason itself (p. 115).

Dogmatic anthropomorphism is avoided by refraining from attributing the phenomena of human nature and experience directly to the noumenal divine reality. But if "we attribute them to the relation of this being to the world and allow ourselves a *symbolical* anthropomorphism" we focus, according to Kant, on "language only and not the object itself" (p. 115). It is this focus on *rationality* and *language* which I want to examine more closely presently, but first a few words on the difference between this move and that made by Kant in his critiques of pure and practical reason.

Traditionally, Kant is interpreted, and not without good reason, as eliminating religion from the realm of *pure* reason and confining it to the realm of *practical* reason alone. As he says near the end of the first *Critique*, "I have set aside reason in order to make room for faith." It is this basic dichotomy, grounded in the absolute separation between the phenomena and the noumena, that has given rise to the split which has dominated contemporary philosophy until very recently, namely that between analytic and existentialist thought. Currently, however, there is a growing number of thinkers on both sides of this split engaged in the exploration of ways to overcome it. Those who interpret Wittgenstein as a phenomenologist,[1] together with those who interpret phenomenology linguistically,[2] are especially suggestive in this regard.

What is needed, it would seem, is a deeper understanding of the symbolic relation between thought and action on the one hand, as well as between language and reality on the other. Now here, in the *Prolegomena*, we find Kant himself speaking in ways that suggest these very notions, albeit somewhat cryptically. It is time to take a closer look.

The basis of Kant's "chastened" theism lies in the distinction between dogmatic and symbolic anthropomorphism; the latter only attributes characteristics of human experience to the *relation* of God to the world, not to God's nature as such, and thus is concerned with language rather than noumenal reality. At this point (pp. 115–16), Kant enters into a fairly detailed discussion of analogical predication, one which is extremely reminiscent of Aquinas' treatment of the same subject. To speak of God as "Supreme Understanding and Will" in relation to the world is not to convey knowledge of divinity as it is in *itself*, but only as it is known *to us*, just as to speak of a shipbuilder or a commander as wise and powerful, respectively, says nothing about them *as such* but only in relation to their ship or their regiment.

> Such a cognition is one of analogy and does not signify (as is commonly understood) an imperfect similarity of two things, but a perfect similarity of relations between two quite dissimilar things. By means of this analogy, however, there remains a

244

concept of the Supreme Being sufficiently determined *for us*, though we have left out everything that could determine it absolutely or *in itself*; for we determine it as regards the world and hence as regards ourselves, and more do we not require. (pp. 115–16)

This shift from the idea of analogy of attribution to that of analogy of *relationality* is quite parallel to Aquinas' shift to the "analogy of proportionality." In fact, in a footnote on the above quoted paragraph, Kant actually speaks in a manner that could be mistaken as coming directly from Aquinas' own pen. Not only does he stress the "as with this, so with that, each as it is appropriate to its own nature" pattern, but he even focuses on the relationship of *causation* as the crucial similarity.

For instance, as the promotion of the welfare of children (= a) is to the love of parents (= b), so the welfare of the human species (= c) is to that unknown character in God (= X), which we call love; not as if it had the least similarity to any human inclination, but because we can suppose its relation to the world to be similar to that which things of the world bear one another. But the concept of relation in this case is a mere category, namely, the concept of cause, which has nothing to do with similarity. (pp. 115–16)

On this basis Kant moves beyond the limited deism allowed by Hume to a theism which still avoids attributing human characteristics to divinity. For his brand of theism only speaks of God on the basis of analogies drawn from the categories of the understanding in a *formal* rather than a material fashion. Rationality, for instance, is attributed to God, not directly and *per se*, but as the *ground* of rationality as it is experienced in the world. Thus we speak of the world *as if* its existence and nature are the result of the wisdom of a supreme being by analogically transferring the *ground* of causal relationships from this world to its source. Kant calls this chastened or critical theism "the true mean between dogmatism, which Hume combats, and skepticism, which he would substitute for it" (p. 117).

Kant continues to develop the spatial and kinesthetic *metaphor* of a boundary, which differs markedly from the static and passive imagery of the first *Critique*, in order to underscore his contention that the brand of theism he is promoting signifies a *positive* cognitive dimension as well as a negative one. He stresses the point that a boundary "belongs to that which lies within as well as to the space that lies without" itself and thus yields "an actual positive cognition" when reason "acquires by enlarging itself to this boundary" (p. 118). The bounds of reason constitute a *relation* between the phenomenal reality of experience and the noumenal reality beyond our experience.

It is in this way that Kant lays the foundation for a viable natural theology. Using the positive, relational cognition derived from the boundary between the noumena and the phenomena, natural theology can, indeed must, posit a supreme being as the "*cause*" of the world of sense "in order to guide the use of reason within it according to principles of the greatest possible (theoretical as well as practical) unity . . . though only of course by analogy" (p. 118). As I indicated earlier, it will prove helpful to return to Kant's use of the metaphorical and analogical modes before we are finished. For at the very least this constitutes the unique contribution of the *Prolegomena vis-à-vis* natural theology, while at the most it may well provide a fulcrum for initiating, a fresh approach to this time-worn topic.

By way of wrapping up his considerations of this general topic, Kant begins by summarizing the positive results of natural theology in terminology which would lead anyone familiar with contemporary theology to think it has come from the pen of Paul Tillich. He reaffirms the limited character of our reasoning about God and then says:

> But this limitation does not prevent reason from leading us to the objective boundary of experience, namely, to the relation to something which is not itself an object of experience but is the ground of all experience. Reason does not, however, teach us anything concerning the thing in itself; it only instructs us as regards its own complete and highest use in the field of possible experience. (p 119)

Kant allows himself to speculate, not metaphysically but "anthropologically," as to the purpose of our being endowed with the disposition to transcend the phenomenal world. He concludes that the transcendental ideas serve to free us from limited human experience not for contemplative and speculative ends, "but in order that practical principles may be assumed as at least possible; for practical principles, unless they find scope for their necessary expectation and hope, could not expand to the universality which reason unavoidably requires from a moral point of view" (p. 120). A bit further on he suggests that the idea of a supreme being, in particular, as intelligent cause destroys materialism, naturalism, and fatalism, thus affording "scope for the moral Ideas beyond the field of speculation" (p. 120).

Here we see Kant providing the transition between his first and second *Critiques*, between pure reason and practical reason. The standard interpretation at this juncture, and surely the *Critiques* themselves (as well as *The Foundations of the Metaphysics of Morals* and *Religion Within the Bounds of Reason Alone*) give ample basis for this interpretation, is familiar enough. Pure reason provides no ground whatsoever for metaphysics and theology, while practical reason requires, in some sense, the "postulating" of the reality of God, freedom, and immortality. Yet, here in the *Prolegomena* we find Kant exploring metaphors and speaking of analogies in a manner that might suggest a more integral connection between the pure and the practical dimensions of experience and rationality. In the second section of this paper I wish to return to some of these highly interesting and hopefully fruitful possibilities.

II

Let us begin with Kant's rather extensive and straightforward use of metaphor and analogy by way of developing the positive aspect of his approach to natural theology. Although he, as well as nearly all those who consider themselves "modern," generally speaks condescendingly of "mere metaphor" and "only analogy," in this section of the *Prolegomena* Kant never really apologizes for relying on such informal and imprecise means of presenting and arguing for his conclusion. In my opinion this represents a strength rather than a weakness in his posture. For I am convinced, partly as a result of noting it in such great thinkers as Kant himself, that when we reach the deepest level of thought it is the metaphoric mode that best enables us to deal with the issues at hand. This is not an unfortunate limitation, but is rather appropriate to and necessitated by the complexity and comprehensiveness of deepest truth.

Kant's fundamental distinction between bounds and limits, together with his subsequent development of it in terms of the former providing a positive cognition of the reality of the noumenal realm and divine existence, is of special interest. This is so because it represents a rather sudden shift from the predominance of passive and static images that characterizes his previous accounts of such matters, especially in the first *Critique*. The categories of the understanding, which constitute the bounds of reason, are nearly always treated in terms which imply limited or no activity on the part of the knower. In spite of the fact that the hallmark of Kantian philosophy is its emphasis on the active part the mind plays in shaping experienced reality, it remains true that Kant's treatment of the structure and structuring of the mind is itself characterized by such images as eyeglasses, filter systems, and passive sense perception.

Thus Kant's image of boundaries which are *approached* through space and whose surface is *contacted* by the embodied knower is a rather remarkable and, I must add, welcome departure from his usual visual perspective. For far too long the history of Western thought, at least since Plato, has been dominated by the root metaphor of knowledge being a kind of passive visual experience of the real. Kant has strongly contributed to this tradition, and thus his employment of more *kinesthetic* and *tactile* images is an important development, indeed. The major difficulty is that he did not explore this possibility far enough, nor in the right direction. The same potential arises when, in speaking about analogical speech about God, he mentions the cruciality of *relationship*, but once again he lets it drop.

What is needed precisely at this juncture, in my view, is an extension of this active, embodiment motif so as to construe our relationship with reality as *interactional* rather than *observational*. Following Kant's "hints," I would propose thinking of the knower and the known as inextricably connected, as two dancers holding hands and moving in the dark. As one dancer, the knower is unable to extricate him or herself from the dance in order to confront the other dancer, reality, directly as a "thing in itself." Nor is the knower able simply to create any type of dance he or she wishes, for reality has an agenda of its own, as well. Nevertheless, through *interactive* cooperation, conflict, and resolution, the two together create the world *as we know it*, and thus the knower comes "to know" reality.[3]

The same issue arises when Kant speaks of our reasoning analogically from the world to its cause as we do from a watch or ship to its maker. He focuses here on the *relationship* between the artifact and the creator, and in passing mentions that relationship between a "regiment and its commander." What is surprising, however, is that Kant never notices that while the relationship in the former, more traditional cases is a one-way, causal, and thus passive one from the point of view of that which is made, in the latter case this is not true. A commander does not *cause* or create a regiment in a one-way fashion; rather, the relationship between them is an *interactive*, personal one that far exceeds the limitations of mere causal connections. Kant would have been well advised to pursue this example more thoroughly.

The significance of all this for our purposes here is indeed considerable. Clearly, the results of one's approach to natural theology are going to be different depending on the sort of root metaphor one begins with. Kant's overall commitment to a *visual metaphor* leads him to an interpretation of the bounds of reason whose inherent passivity and staticity renders the cognitive gulf between the human and the divine essentially unbridgeable. Had he followed up on his more interactive motif, employing movement and touch, he might have been able to develop an interpretation of the bounds of reason which enables our knowledge of reality, including God, to be more relational and positive. The *epistemic distance* inherent in the visual metaphor of cognition is essentially avoided in a more kinesthetic and tactile metaphor. Error, here, is seen more as a false or surprise move, as the unhappy result of a dialectical process of cognition which involves interpretive and observational activity as symbolically interrelated.

If we begin by assuming a gap between the knower and the known, between ourselves and reality, and then set about to devise ways of overcoming this gap, Kant's approach is about as helpful as one can find. What, it must be asked, is the rationale for such an initial assumption? It is, of course, necessary to avoid anthropomorphism in anything like the literal sense when speaking of God. However, does the choice between literalism and silence exhaust the possibilities? Given the Judeo-Christian belief in the image of God in human nature, as well as the created structure of the world, it would seem more likely and profitable to begin by assuming an interactive relationship between ourselves and God.

Speaking strictly in a philosophical sense, given the fact that our basic way of being in and understanding the world is by means of interacting with it *corporately* and *corporially*, it would seem most productive to begin by defining reality and our knowledge of it in terms of increasingly complex and comprehensive dimensions of "experienced reality," rather than by stratifying it into a this-worldly realm and a transcendent realm from the start. Then the problem of our knowledge of "things in themselves" simply would never arise, since it would be seen from the outset to be a pseudo-problem. For, if noumenal reality is *defined* as essentially independent of our minds,

249

then our knowledge of it is out of the question from the beginning. The whole issue reduces to a matter of how we are to conceive of the relationship between the knower and the known.

On the face of it, it would seem that the knower and that which is known must be in some form of interactive relationship to each other. The very nature of the knowing process, from the way infants seek meaning and knowledge through movement and oral-tactile grasping, to Heisenburg's principle of indeterminacy which calls attention to the symbiotic character of knowledge and reality at the subatomic level, necessitates a non-passive, non-static understanding of the relation between the knower and the known. What we *know* is constituted by the interaction between what there *is* to be known and our *efforts* to know it. Why should it be thought to be otherwise?

Kant had it right when he insisted on the active nature of the human mind, but he failed to see that when the issue is approached from this direction the concept of "things in themselves" has no function whatsoever. There is nothing left unexplained or unknown; what we can know we know through interaction, and what we cannot know we have no need or way to talk about. This is neither a limitation nor a lack, it is simply the nature of human cognition. We are led into thinking that we are somehow falling short of true knowledge by first positing "things in themselves" and then lamenting that we cannot know them. We overlook the fact that our very act of positing such a notion is itself a function of human cognition; the concept of "unknowable knowledge" is meaningless at best and counter-productive at worst. To put it differently, the very distinction Kant makes between how things are "in themselves" and how they are known "by us" is itself made *within* the structures and functions of human cognitive activity. So, in an important sense, even "things in themselves" only have meaning in relation to our knowledge of them.

My own suggestion is that this whole problem of knowledge of "things in themselves," both in Kant and in a large portion of Western epistemology, derives from what Wittgenstein termed "a one-sided diet." By focussing on our perceptual knowledge of *physical* objects as the paradigm case of cognition, we are led to the mistaken idea that the known is and remains whatever it is, independent of any interaction with us, the knowers. The truth of the matter is, that quite apart from the fact that such an account of physical reality and knowledge is highly questionable, the vast majority of our knowledge is of much more complex, intangible, and relational dimensions. Language, history, persons, aesthetic and moral values, politics, and religion are all clearly *relational* realities about which it makes no sense whatsoever to speak of what is known as being and remaining what it is apart from the interaction of the knower. Persons, to take the most relevant example are not who and what they are independently of their interaction with one another. A person *is* a friendly person (or a "slow learner," or a "nigger") largely *because and as* they are related to as such. Moreover, we *become* persons by entering into relationship with other persons, and vice versa.

Had Kant and others taken such relational realities as their model, it might never have occurred to them to speak of the "thing in itself" independently of its interactive relationship with those cognitive agents whose *participation* in them constitute both their nature and the knowledge of them. This is especially true of the knowledge of God. By far the dominant tradition in Western philosophy and theology alike has defined God more in terms of abstract, static forms, unmoved movers, mathematical concepts, etc. than in terms of persons, processes, and relationships. This is, incidentally, a very unbiblical, unHebraic Greek tendency that has taken over Western thought. The point here is that Kant was caught up in this tradition and thus failed to see both the pitfalls to which it leads and the possibilities provided by a *relational* understanding of both reality and knowledge.

To come at this whole issue from a different, yet equally viable angle, much of the difficulty arises from Kant's rigid dichotomy between the two functions or types of reasoning, *pure* and *practical*. His whole philosophic posture is predicted on keeping these two dimensions of human existence quite separate, pure or theoretic reason involving *cognition* and practical, moral reason involving *volition*. As I mentioned earlier on, it is this dichtomy which has led to the fact/value split that so thoroughly permeates the modern mind and is especially well focused in the antagonism between analytic and existentialist thought. The former is based broadly on Kant's first *Critique* and the latter on his second *Critique*, but they both accept the initial separation between pure and practical reason.

Kant himself, here in the Conclusion of the *Prolegomena*, makes some moves which could perhaps form the basis for a reproachment between these two equally essential dimensions of human life, but he does not follow through with them. He specifically addresses this possibility when he suggests that the purpose of our "metaphysical urge" is to guide the use of reason within the phenomenal world "according to principles of the greatest possible (theoretical as well as practical) unity" (p. 118). He goes on to conclude that only by means of the transcendental ideas (of God, freedom, and immortality) are the principles of practical reason able to provide the universality necessary for a rational basis of *moral activity* (pp. 120–21). However, Kant is never really able to coordinate this connection or *unity* between the two types of reason because he began by defining them as essentially separate. Here again, we might well ask why it was necessary to set things up this way at the outset.

In addition to the obvious fact that in our everyday experience these two dimensions of life are not separable, there are several philosophical reasons for objecting to this epistemological dualism. As many thinkers have made abundantly clear in recent decades,[4] obtaining knowledge about the world is not a simple matter of examining "the facts" without reference to various prior *commitments*, both theoretical and valuational. The facts we get are in large measure a function of the questions we ask, as the issue of whether light is "really" particles or waves clearly indicates. Moreover, as Michael Polanyi has demonstrated,[5] even our preference for truth as well as our efforts to discover and communicate knowledge, is at bottom a *commitment* to the possibility of making veridical judgments and to our capacities to know reality. Such commitments are not *first* established rationally and *then* valued; if anything it would seem that the priority is the other way around. At the very least it seems misguided, if not pernicious, to pretend that the so-called "objective" and "subjective" aspects of human experience can, let alone should, be separated.

In conclusion, I wish to return briefly to Kant's suggestion that a "symbolical anthropomorphism" avoids the difficulties of traditional theistic talk of God because it "concerns language only and not the object itself" (p. 115). Here again we see the pivotal dualism that has plagued Kant throughout his monumental philosophy, even in those places, such as the Conclusion to his *Prolegomena*, where he seems to be struggling against it. The faulty understanding of metaphoric and analogical expression, to say nothing of the overstated contrast between language and reality, undermines any serious effort to propose a positive cognition at the base of natural theology. Had he not begun by assuming the necessity of such dualisms, Kant might have been able to develop further his highly suggestive insights concerning the metaphoric and analogical character of theological thought and language. Indeed, these very notions themselves provided a foothold for a fresh approach to such matters, but Kant was unable to disentangle himself from his prior commitments.

NOTES

1 Cf. Nicholas Gier, *Wittgenstein and Phenomenology* (Buffalo, NY: Buffalo University Press, 1981).
2 Cf. especially Maurice Merleau-Ponty, *Signs* (Evanston: Northwestern University Press, 1981) and Paul Picoeur, *The Rule of Metaphor* (Chicago: Chicago University Press, 1978).
3 This particular image was suggested by Merleau-Ponty's remarks about our being connected to reality by threads which we can slacken but never drop nor follow through to the "other side." See the Preface to his *Phenomenology of Perception* (New York: Humanities Press, 1961).
4 I have in mind the works of N. R. Hanson, P. Feyerabend, T. Kuhn, P. Winch, and I. Barbour.
5 See his *Personal Knowledge* (Chicago: Chicago University Press, 1953) and *Knowing and Being* (Chicago: Chicago University Press, 1968).

SELECTED BIBLIOGRAPHY

Alexander, H. G. Necessary Truth. *Mind*, 66, 507–21, October 1957.

Alexander, Peter. The Presidential Address: Incongruent Counterparts And Absolute Space. *Proceedings of the Aristotelian Society*, 85, 1–21, 1984–85.

Allinson, Robert E. The Second Apology Revisited: Did Kant Refute Hume? *Journal of the West Virginia Philosophical Society*, 21–3, Spring 1976.

Allison, Henry E. *Kant's Transcendental Idealism*. New Haven, Yale University Press, 1983.

Allison, Henry E. *The Kant-Eberhard Controversy*. Baltimore, Johns Hopkins University Press, 1973.

Allison, Henry E. Transcendental Affinity – Kant's Answer To Hume. In *Proceedings Of The 3rd International Kant Congress*, Lewis White Beck (ed.), 203–10. Dordrecht, Reidel, 1972.

Aquila, Richard E. *Representational Mind: A Study Of Kant's Theory Of Knowledge*. Bloomington, Indiana University Press, 1983.

Atkinson, R. F. Hume on Mathematics. *Philosophical Quarterly*, 10, 1960.

Aune, Bruce. *Knowledge Of The External World*. New York, Routledge, 1991.

Bagchi, K. Kant's Transcendental Problem As A Linguistic Problem. *Philosophy*, 46, 341–5, October 1971.

Baier, Annette. *Moral Prejudices*. Harvard University Press, Cambridge, 1994.

Baier, Annette. Moralism And Cruelty: Reflections On Hume And Kant. *Ethics*, 103(3), 436–57, April 1993.

Balaban, Oded and Avshalom, Asnat. The Ontological Argument Reconsidered. *Journal of Philosophical Research*, 15, 279–310, 1990.

Baldner, K. Causality and Things in Themselves. *Synthese*, 77, 353–73, 1988.

Ball, Stephen W. Hegel On Proving The Existence Of God. *International Journal of the Philosophy of Religion*, 10, 73–100, 1979.

Barber, Kenneth F. and Gracia, Jorge J. E. (eds) *Individuation And Identity In Early Modern Philosophy*, Suny Pr, Albany, 1994.

Beanblossom, Ronald E. Kant's Quarrel With Reid: The Role Of Metaphysics. *History of Philosophy Quarterly*, 5, 53–62, January 1988.

Beck, L. W. Kant On The Uniformity Of Nature. *Synthese*, 47, 449–64, June 1981.

Beck, L. W. *Essays on Kant and Hume*. New Haven, Yale University Press, 1978, pp. 80–100.

Beck, L. W. Once More Unto The Breach: Kant's Answer To Hume, Again. *Ratio*, 9, 33–7, June 1967.

Beck, L. W. Is There a Non-sequitur in Kant's Proof of the Causal Principle? *Kant-Studien*, 67, 385–9, 1976.

Beck, L. W. Rejoinder To Professors Murphy And Williams. *Ratio*, 11, 82–7, June 1969.

Beck, L. W. Uber Die Regelmassigkeit Der Natur Bei Kant. *Dialectica*, 35, 43–56, 1981.

Bencivenga, Ermanno. Knowledge As A Relation And Knowledge As An Experience In The Critique of Pure Reason. *Canadian Journal of Philosophy*, 15, 593–615, December 1985.

Bennett, Jonathan. *Kant's Analytic.* Cambridge, Cambridge University Press, 1966.

Bernardete, Jose. "The Deduction of Causality." In *The Philosophy of Immanuel Kant*, Richard Kennington (ed.), Washington DC, Catholic University of America Press.

Berry, Christopher J. *Hume, Hegel And Human Nature.* Boston, Nijhoff, 1982.

Blachowicz, James A. Metaphysics And Material Necessity. *New Scholas*, 49, 16–31, Winter 1975.

Brenner, William H. *Elements Of Modern Philosophy: Descartes Through Kant.* Englewood Cliffs, Prentice-Hall, 1989.

Brett, Nathan. Hume's Debt To Kant. *Hume Studies*, 9, 59–73, April 1983.

Brown, Norman J. A Kind of Necessary Truth. *Philosophy*, 50, 37–54, January 1975.

Buchdahl, Gerd. Causality, Causal Laws And Scientific Theory In The Philosophy Of Kant. *British Journal of Philosophical Science*, 16, 187–208, November 1965.

Buchdahl, Gerd. *Kant And The Dynamics Of Reason.* Oxford, Blackwell, 1992.

Burke, J. David Hume's Influence on Kant and its Limits. In A. Goetze and G. Pflaum, *Vergleichen und Verdndern.* Munich, 1969.

Burnyeat, Myles (ed.) *The Skeptical Tradition.* Berkeley, University of California Press, 1983.

Capaldi, Nicholas. The Copernican Revolution In Hume And Kant. In *Proceedings Of The 3rd International Kant Congress*, Lewis White Beck (ed.), 234–40. Dordrecht, Reidel, 1972.

Chipman, Lauchlan. Things In Themselves. *Philosophy and Phenomenological Research*, 33, 489–502, June 1973.

Coleman, Dorothy P. Hume's "Dialectic." *Hume Studies*, 10, 139–55, November 1984.

Collins, James. Kant's "Logic" As A Critical Aid. *The Review of Metaphysics*, 30, 440–61, March 1977.

Cooke, Vincent M. Kant And Substance. *Proceedings of the American Catholic Philosophical Association*, 61, 143–50, 1987.

Cottingham, John. The Cartesian Legacy. *The Aristotelian Society*, Supplementary vol. (66), 1–21, 1992.

Cover, J. A. (ed.) *Central Themes in Early Modern Philosophy.* Indianapolis, Hackett, 1990.

Cramer, Konrad. Non-Pure Synthetic a priori Judgments. In *Proceedings of the 3rd International Kant Congress*, Lewis White Beck (ed.), 245–54, Dordrecht, Reidel, 1972.

Daniel, S. C. The Nature And Function Of Imagination In Hume And Kant. *Indian Philosophy Quarterly*, 15, 85–97, January 1988.

Delaney, C. Kant's Challenge: The Second Analogy As A Response To Hume. *Dialogue* (Pst), 32(2–3), 51–6, April 1990.

Deleuze, Gilles. *Kant's Critical Philosophy.* (Paris, Presses Universitaires de France, 1963; New York, The Athlone Press, 1984).

Desjardins, Gregory. Terms Of 'De Officiis' In Hume And Kant. *Journal of Historical Ideas*, 28, 237–42, April to June 1967.

Driscoll, John. Unity, Succession, And Personal Identity In Hume. *Studies in Philosophy and the History of Philosophy*, 6, 121–34, 1973.

Dryer, D. P. *Kant's Solution for Verification in Metaphysics.* Toronto, University of Toronto Press, 1966.

Engel, S. Morris. Kant's Copernican Analogy: A Re-examination. *Kant-Studien*, 54, 243–51, 1963.

Ewing, A. C. *Kant's Treatment of Causality.* London: Kegan Paul, Trench, Trubner & Co., 1924.

Faber, M. D. "Objectivity And Human Perception: Revisions And Crossroads." In *Psychoanalysis And Philosophy*. Alberta, University of Alberta Press, 1985.

Feigle, H. "What Hume Might Have Said to Kant. . . ." In M. A. Bunge, *The Critical Approach to Science and Philosophy.* New York, the Free Press of Glencoe, 1964.

Fenner, David E. W. Hume, Kant, And The Subjectivity Of Causality. *Explorations of Knowledge*, 10(1), 25–32, 1993.

Ferre, Frederick. In Praise Of Anthropomorphism. *International Journal of the Philosophy of Religion*, 16, 203–12, 1984.

Flew, Antony G. N. The Cultural Roots Of Analytical Philosophy. *Journal of Chinese Philosophy*, 6, 1–14, March 1979.

Friedman, Michael. Kant On Space, The Understanding, And The Law Of Gravitation: *Prolegomena* Section 38. *Monist*, 72, 236–84, April 1989.

Gagnon, Maurice. L'epistemologie genetique de Piaget et le probleme de la causalité. *Dialogue* (Canada), 14, 119–41, March 1975.

Garceau, B. Les travaux de jeunesse de Hegel et l'interpretation de sa philosophie de la religion. *Philosophiques*, 1, 21–49, April 1974.

Glouberman, M. Causation, Cognition, And Historical Typology. *Dialectica*, 34, 211–28, 1980.

Glouberman, Mark. Transcendental Idealism And The End Of Philosophy. *Metaphilosophy*, 24(1–2), 97–112, January to April 1993.

Goose, K. Hat Kant Hume's Treatise gelesen? *Kant-Studien*, 62, 355–60, 1971.

Gotterbarn, D. Hume, Kant and Analyticity. *Kant-Studien*, 65, 274–83.

Gracyk, Theodore A. Kant's Shifting Debt To British Aesthetics. *British Journal of Aesthetics*, 26, 204–17, Summer 1986.

Gram, M. S. (ed.) *Kant: Disputed Questions.* Chicago, Quadrangle Books, 1967.

Gram, M. S. *Kant, Ontology, and the A Priori.* Evanston, Ill., Northwestern University Press, 1968.

Gram, M. S. The Crisis of Syntheticity: The Kant-Eberhard Controversy. *Kant-Studien*, 7, 155–80, 1980.

Grene, Marjorie. *The Knower And The Known.* New York, Basic Books, 1966.

Guyer, Paul. *Kant and the Claims of Knowledge.* Cambridge, Cambridge University Press, 1987.

Guyer, Paul. "Psychology And The Transcendental Deduction." In *Kant's Transcendental Deductions*, Forster, Eckart (ed.). Stanford, Stanford University Press.

Hanfling, Oswald. Hume's Idea Of Necessary Connexion. *Philosophy*, 54, 501–14, October 1979.

Harper, William A. (ed.) *Kant On Causality, Freedom, And Objectivity.* Minneapolis, University of Minnesota Press, 1984.

Harper, William A. "Kant's Empirical Realism." In *Kant On Causality, Freedom, And Objectivity*, Harper, William A. (ed.), Minneapolis, University of Minnesota Press, 1984.

Hartnack, Justus. The Language Of Causality. *Dialogos*, 11, 7–21, November 1977.

Hartnack, Justus. Del Empirismo Radical Al Idealismo Absoluto I: De Hume A Kant. *Teorema*, 8, 143–58, 1978.

Hatfield, Gary. *The Natural And The Normative: Theories Of Spatial Perception From Kant to Helmholtz.* Cambridge, MIT Press, 1991.

Henrici, Peter. Anthropologische Prolegomena Zur Metaphysik: "Prolegomenes anthropologiques A La Metaphysique." *Bijdragen*, 3, 254–62, 1989.

Hintikka, Jaakko. "Kant on the Mathematical Method." In *Kant Studies Today*, L. W. Beck (ed.), LaSalle, II: Open Court, 1969.

Hintikka, Jaakko. Kantian Intuitions. *Inquiry*, 15, 341–45, Autumn 1972.

Howison, G. H. Hume and Kant. *Journal of Speculative Philosophy*, 19, 85–9, 1885.

Hundert, E. J. *The Enlightenment's "Fable."* New York, Cambridge University Press, 1994.

Hutchings, Patrick. Why Natural Theology, Still, Yet? *Sophia* (Australia), 3–7, July 1991.

Jacquette, Dale. Kant's Second Antinomy And Hume's Theory Of Extensionless Indivisibles, *Kant-Studien*, 84(1), 38–50, 1993.

Johnson, Paul F. Transcendental Arguments And Their Significance For Recent Epistemology. *Dialogue* (Pst), 26, 33–39, April 1984.

Kemp Smith, Norman. Kant's Relation to Hume and to Leibnitz. *Philosophical Review*, 24, 1915.

Kemp Smith, Norman. *A Commentary to Kant's Critique of Pure Reason.* New York, Humanities Press, 1918.

Kenny, Anthony. "Descartes To Kant." In *The Oxford History Of Western Philosophy*, Kenny, Anthony (ed.), New York, Oxford University Press, 1994.

Kitcher, Patricia S. Kant's Paralogisms. *Philosophical Review*, 91, 515–47, October 1982.

Kitcher, Patricia S. Changing The Name Of The Game: Kant's Cognitivism Versus Hume's Psychologism. *Philosophical Topics*, 19(1), 201–36, Spring 1991.

Korner, Stephan. *Kant.* London, Penguin Books, 1955.

Kowalczyk, S. The Idea of God in Kant's Works. *Studies in Philosophical Christianity*, 22, 41–69, 1986 (in Polish).

Kuehn, Manfred. The Early Reception Of Reid, Oswald And Beattie In Germany: 1768–1800. *Journal of the History of Philosophy*, 21, 479–96, October 1983.

Kuehn, Manfred. "Kant's Transcendental Deduction: A Limited Defense Of Hume." In *New Essays On Kant*, Den Ouden, Bernard (ed.), pp. 47–72. New York, Lang, 1987.

Kuehn, Manfred. *Scottish Common Sense in Germany: 1768–1800.* Montreal/Kingston, McGill-Queen's University Press, 1987.

Kuehn, Manfred. "Kant's Critique of Hume's Theory of Faith." in *Hume and Hume's Connexions*, ed. M. A. Stewart and J. P. Wright. Edinburgh University Press, 1994, pp. 239–255.

Kulenkampff, Jens. The Objectivity Of Taste: Hume And Kant. *Nous*, 24(1), 93–110, March 1990.

Kumar Das, Paritosh. Philosophy As The Science Of Man: David Hume. *Indian Philosophy Quarterly* (Supp 16), 1–10, January 1989.

Laing, B. M. Kant And Natural Science. *Philosophy*, 19, 216–32, November 1944.

Langsam, Harold. Kant, Hume, And Our Ordinary Concept Of Causation. *Philosophy and Phenomenology Research*, 54(3), 625–47, September 1994.

Lauener, H. *Hume und Kant*. Bern, Francke Verlag, 1969.

Leavitt, Frank J. Kant's Schematism And His Philosophy Of Geometry. *Studies in the History of Philosophy and Science*, 22(4), 647–59, December 1991.

Levin, Jerome D. *Theories Of The Self*. Washington, DC, Taylor Francis, 1992.

Livingston, Donald W. Hayek As Humean. *Critical Review*, 5(2), 159–77, Spring 1991.

Lloyd, Genevieve. *The Man Of Reason: "Male" And "Female" In Western Philosophy*. Minneapolis, University of Minnesota Press, 1984.

Lovejoy, A. O. "On Kant's Reply to Hume." In *Kant: Disputed Questions*, M. S. Gram (ed.). Chicago: Quadrangle Books, 1967.

Lovejoy, A. O. Kant's Antithesis of Dogmatism and Criticism. *Mind*, 1906, reprinted in Lovejoy 1967.

Lowe, Walter. *Theology And Difference: The Wound Of Reason*. Bloomington, Indiana University Press, 1993.

Macbeath, Murray. "Kant." In *Philosophers Of The Enlightenment*, Peter Gilmour (ed.). Edinburgh, Edinburgh University Press, 1989.

Mackinnon, D. M. Kant's Philosophy Of Religion. *Philosophy*, 50, 131–44, April 1975.

McRae, Robert. Kant's Conception Of The Unity Of The Sciences. *Philosophy and Phenomenological Research*, 18, 1–17, September 1957.

Malherbe, M. L'empirique et le transcendantal dans les philosophies de Hume et de Kant. *Rev Métaph Morale*, 83, 447–81, October to December 1978.

Malter, Rudolf. L'analyse comme procédé de la métaphysique: L'opposition à la méthodologie Wolffienne dans la "presschrift" de Kant en 1763 (1764). *Archives de Philosophie* 42, 575–91, October to December 1979.

Maurer, Armand. Reflections On Metaphysics And Experience. *Proceedings of the American Catholic Philosophical Association* 61, 26–34, 1987.

Melchert, Norman. Kantian Freedom Naturalized. *History Philosophy Quarterly*, 67–75, January 1990.

Melnick, A. *Kant's Analogies of Experience*. Chicago, University of Chicago Press, 1973.

Michaelson, G. E. *The Historical Dimensions Of A Rational Faith*. Washington DC, University Press of America, 1979.

Miethe, T. L. The Cosmological Argument. *New Scholasticism*, 52, 285–305, 1978.

Miller, Thomas G. Goffman, Positivism And The Self. *Philosophy of the Social Sciences*, 16, 177–95, June 1986.

Molina, Fernando. A Reconstruction Of C. I. Lewis' Lectures On Kant. *Philosophy Research Archives*, 7, No 1469, 1981.

Moors, M. Kant's Transcendentaal Idealisme Van Fenomenen. *Tijdschr Filosof*, 50, 82–130, March 1988.

Morgan, Vance. Kant And Dogmatic Idealism: A Defense Of Kant's Refutation Of Berkeley. *Southwest Journal of Philosophy*, 31(2), 217–37, Summer 1993.

Murphy, Jeffrie G. Kant's Second Analogy As An Answer To Hume. *Ratio*, 11, 75–8, June 1969.

Murphy, Richard T. Husserl's Relation To British Empiricism. *Southwest Journal of Philosophy*, 11, 89–106, Autumn 1980.

Nagel, Gordon. "Substance and Causality." In *Kant On Causality, Freedom, And Objectivity*, William A. Harper (ed.), pp. 108–47. Minneapolis, University of Minnesota Press, 1984.

Noel, Justin. Space, Time And The Sublime In Hume's "Treatise." *British Journal of Aesthetics*, 34(3), 218–25, July 1994.

Nuovo, Victor. Rethinking Paley. *Synthese*, 91(1–2), 29–51, April to May 1992.

Nuyen, A. T. Sense, Reason And Causality In Hume And Kant. *Kant-Studien*, 81(1), 57–68, 1990.

Nuyen, A. T. The Fragility Of The Self: From Bundle Theory To Deconstruction. *Journal of Speculative Philosophy*, 6(2), 111–22, 1992.

Palmquist, Stephen. Triangulating God. *Faith and Philosophy*, 11(2), 302–10, April 1994.

Palmquist, Stephen. Faith As Kant's Key To The Justification Of Transcendental Reflection. *Heythrop Journal*, 25, 442–55, October 1984.

Palmquist, Stephen. "The Kingdom Of God Is At Hand!" (Did "Kant" Really Say "That"?) *History of Philosophy Quarterly*, 11(4), 421–37, October 1994.

Paton, H. J. *Kant's Metaphysic of Experience*. London, G. Allen & Unwin, 1936.

Patten, S. C. Hume's Bundles, Self-Consciousness And Kant. *Hume Studies*, 2, 59–75, November 1976.

Peters, Curtis H. *Kant's Philosophy Of Hope*. New York, Lang, 1993.

Peterson, John. Kant's Dilemma Of Knowledge And Truth. *Thomist*, 48, 241–8, March 1984.

Pitcher, Patricia. Reasoning in a Subtle World. *Southern Journal of Philosophy*, 30 (supp), 1987–95, 1991.

Reinach, Adolf. Kant's Interpretation Of Hume's Problem. *Southwest Journal of Philosophy*, 7, 161–88, Summer 1976.

Rescher, Nicholas. *Kant's Theory of Knowledge and Reality: A Group of Essays*. Washington, University Press of America, 1983.

Richmond, James. *Faith And Philosophy*. London, Hodder & Stoughton, 1966.

Robinson, Helier J. The Category Of Imperceptibles. *Idealistic Studies*, 6, 239–53, September 1976.

Rod, Wolfgang. Humes Skeptizismus Als Entwurf Eines Neuen Philosophischen Paradigmas. *Grazer Philosophische Studien*, 44, 211–32, 1993.

Rohatyn, Dennis A. Kant's "Disproof" Of God. *Sophia*, 13, 30–1, July 1974.

Sauve, Denis. Kant et le "probleme de Hume." *Dialogue* (Canada), 19, 590–611, December 1980.

Schalow, Frank. The Problem Of Religious Discourse For Critical Philosophy. *Dialogue* (Pst), 25, 1–6, October 1982.

SELECTED BIBLIOGRAPHY

Schipper, E. W. Kant's Answer To Hume's Problem. *Kant-Studien*, 53, 68–74, 1962.

Schultz, F. M. Education And The Quest For Apodictic Clarity: Reflections On Kant's Prolegomena. *Proceeding of Philosophy and Education*, 41, 127–36, 1985.

Schumacher, John. A Prolegomena To Any Future Inquiry: The Paradigm Of Undivided Wholeness. *International Philosophy Quarterly*, 21, 439–60, December 1981.

Seth, Andrew. *Scottish Philosophy: A Comparison of the Scottish and German Answers to Hume*, 1890. Reprinted by Burt Franklin, New York, 1971.

Shear, Jonathan. The Experience Of Pure Consciousness: A New Perspective For Theories Of Self. *Metaphilosophy*, 14, 53–62, January 1983.

Shwayder, D. S. Hume Was Right, Almost; And Where He Wasn't, Kant Was. *Midwest Studies of Philosophy*, 9, 135–50, 1984.

Smith, Wrynn. Kant and the General Law of Causality. *Philosophical Studies*, 32, 113–28, August 1977.

Steiner, Mark. Kant's Misrepresentations Of Hume's Philosophy Of Mathematics In The "Prolegomena". *Hume Studies*, 13, 400–17, November 1987.

Stenius, Erik. Kant And The Apriority Of Mathematics. *Dialectica*, 35, 147–66, 1981.

Stirling, James Hutchison. *What Is Thought*. New York, Garland, 1984.

Stroble, Paul E. Without Running Riot: Kant, Analogical Language, And Theological Discourse. *Sophia* (Australia), 32(3), 57–72, November 1993.

Swindler, James K. *Weaving: An Analysis Of The Constitution Of Objects*. Rowman & Littlefield, Savage, 1991.

Tagore, Saranindra N. Husserl's Conception Of Hume's Problem: Toward A Transcendental Hermeneutic Of Hume's "Treatise." *Man World*, 27(3), 257–69, July 1994.

Thouard, Denis. Une philosophie de la grammaire d'après Kant: La "sprachlehre" d'a fbernhardi. *Archives de Philosophie*, 55(3), 409–35, Summer 1992.

Torrance, Thomas F. *Transformation & Convergence In The Frame Of Knowledge*. Grand Rapids, Eerdmans, 1984.

Torretti, Roberto. La Geometria En El Pensamiento De Kant. *Anales de Seminario Metafisca*, 9, 9–60, 1974.

Van Cleve, James. "Another Volley At Kant's Reply To Hume." In *Kant On Causality, Freedom, And Objectivity*, William A. Harper (ed.), pp. 42–57. Minneapolis, University of Minnesota Press, 1984.

Walsh, William Henry. *Kant's Criticism Of Metaphysics*. Edinburgh, Edinburgh University Press, 1975.

Ward, Andrew. On Kant's Second Analogy And His Reply To Hume. *Kant-Studien*, 77, 409–22, 1986.

Warnock, Mary. *Imagination*. Berkeley, University of California Press, 1976.

Watson, John. Kant's Reply to Hume. *Journal of Speculative Philosophy*, 10, 113–34, 1887.

Williams, M. E. Kant's Reply To Hume. *Kant-Studien*, 56, 71–8, 1965.

Wolff, Robert P. Kant's Debt To Hume Via Beattie. *Journal of Historical Ideas*, 21, 117–23, January to March 1960.

Wolff, Robert P. *Kant's Theory of Mental Activity*. Harvard, 1963.

Wood, Allen W. Kant's Dialectic. *Canadian Journal of Philosophy*, 5, 595–614, December 1975.

Wood, Allen W. "Rational Theology, Moral Faith, And Religion." in *The Cambridge Companion to Kant*, Paul Guyer (ed.). New York, Cambridge University Press, 1992.

Wright, John P. Hume's Rejection Of The Theory Of Ideas. *History of Philosophy Quarterly*, 149–62, April 1991.

Young, J. Michael. Kant's Notion Of Objectivity. *Kant-Studien*, 70, 131–48, 1979.

Young, J. Michael. Kant's View Of Imagination. *Kant-Studien*, 79, 140–64, 1988.

Zemach, Eddy M. Strawson's Transcendental Deduction. *Philosophy Quarterly*, 25, 114–25, April 1975.

INDEX